Bahá'í Children's Classes
and Retreats: Theme #4

# Bahá'u'lláh:
# The Glory of God

Dr. Randie S. Gottlieb

Published by
*UnityWorks* LLC

# Bahá'u'lláh: The Glory of God
## Teacher's Guide with Lesson Plans for Ages 8-12

ISBN 978-0-9828979-4-2

© 2004 UnityWorks LLC. First edition 2004 (spiral bound).
Second edition, 2009. Second printing, 2010. Third printing, 2012.

All rights reserved. No part of this book may be reproduced or transmitted in any form or by any means without prior written permission from the publisher.

UnityWorks hereby grants permission for one children's class teacher or Bahá'í school to copy student handouts as needed. Handouts are also available for downloading from: www.UnityWorksStore.com.

The small fee charged for our materials helps to cover printing costs, the development of new products, and the maintenance of our website to make these resources more widely available. If you find these items useful, please let others know about them. Thank you!

**Available from: www.UnityWorksStore.com**

Quotations from the Bahá'í writings reprinted with permission of
the National Spiritual Assembly of the Bahá'ís of the United States
and the Bahá'í Publishing Trust of Wilmette, IL.

Special thanks to my husband, Steven E. Gottlieb, M.D.
for his support and editorial assistance.

Appreciation to Jordan Gottlieb for assistance
with the cover design and pre-press work,
and to Roger Olsen for musical transcription.

Cover illustration, Kamal Siegel

Clip art images taken or adapted from:
The Big Box of Art from www.Hemera.com

All websites and references listed
are correct at the time of publication.

Published by UnityWorks, LLC
www.UnityWorksStore.com
Yakima, Washington, USA

*Dedicated to the Walker Family*
*Sue, Dave, Ben and Seth*

For their friendship and assistance with our
children's classes and retreats over the years

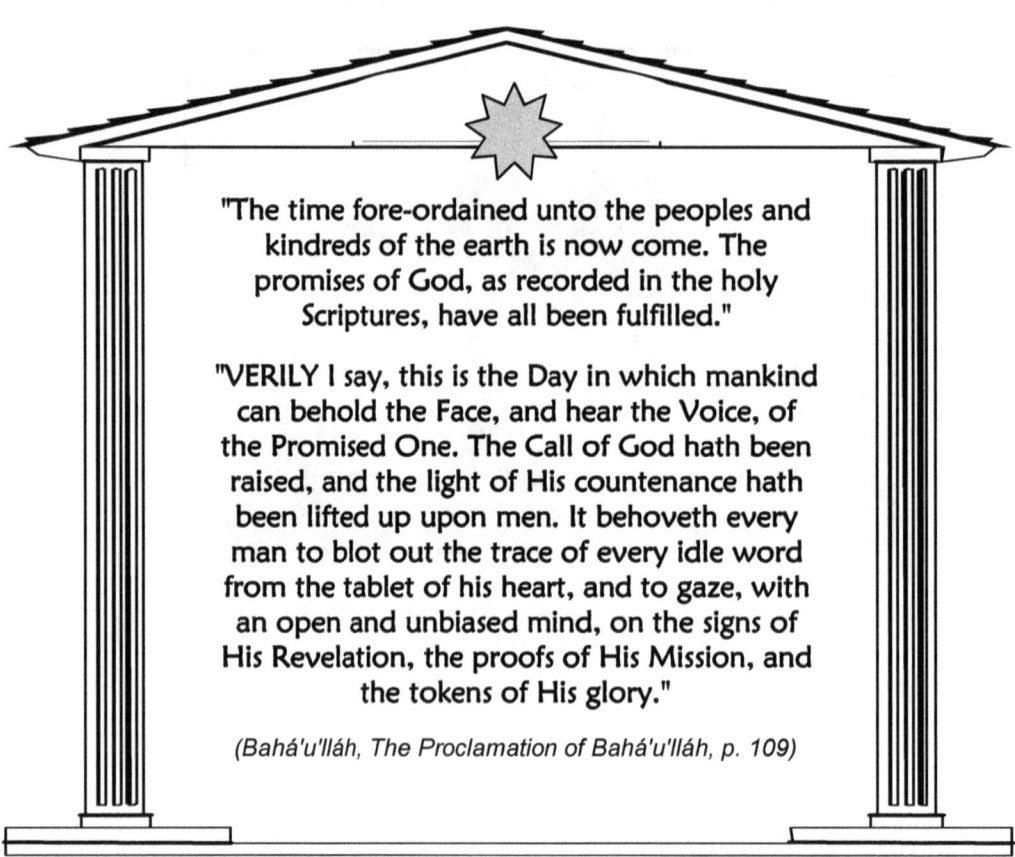

"The time fore-ordained unto the peoples and kindreds of the earth is now come. The promises of God, as recorded in the holy Scriptures, have all been fulfilled."

"VERILY I say, this is the Day in which mankind can behold the Face, and hear the Voice, of the Promised One. The Call of God hath been raised, and the light of His countenance hath been lifted up upon men. It behoveth every man to blot out the trace of every idle word from the tablet of his heart, and to gaze, with an open and unbiased mind, on the signs of His Revelation, the proofs of His Mission, and the tokens of His glory."

*(Bahá'u'lláh, The Proclamation of Bahá'u'lláh, p. 109)*

Bahá'u'lláh: The Glory of God

# TABLE OF CONTENTS

Introduction ................................................................. 1
Overview ..................................................................... 2
To the Organizers ........................................................ 4
    Teachers .................................................................. 4
    Special Role of Youth ............................................... 4
    Schedule ................................................................. 5
    Handouts ................................................................. 5
    Sample Retreat Flyer with Registration Form ............ 6
    Sample Retreat Schedules ...................................... 7
To the Teacher ........................................................... 10
Opening Activities and Orientation Program ................ 13

**LESSONS**
    1. Birth of Bahá'u'lláh, Early Life and Station ........... 21
    2. Declaration of Bahá'u'lláh .................................... 35
    3. Exiles and Imprisonment ..................................... 77
    4. Clouds of Glory ................................................... 91

Children's Performance .............................................. 109
Handouts .................................................................... 125
    Song Sheet ............................................................. 127
    Quotations .............................................................. 129
    Stories from the Life of Bahá'u'lláh .......................... 131
Music .......................................................................... 149
Closing Activities and Follow-up ................................. 167
References for Teachers ............................................. 171
Bibliography ................................................................ 203
Works by the Same Author ......................................... 205
List of Activities by Chapter ........................................ 209
Index of Activities by Category ................................... 211

# Bahá'u'lláh: The Glory of God

# INTRODUCTION

Bahá'u'lláh has prescribed unto all people, "that which will lead to the exaltation of the Word of God amongst His servants, and likewise, to the advancement of the world of being." "To this end," He states, "the greatest means is education of the child." [1]

"My highest wish and desire," proclaims 'Abdu'l-Bahá, "is that ye who are my children may be educated according to the teachings of Bahá'u'lláh...that ye may each become a lighted candle in the world of humanity." [2]

He adds that we should "let them make the greatest progress in the shortest span of time." [3]

The Universal House of Justice has likewise called upon us to involve Bahá'í children in "programmes of activity that will engage their interests [and] mold their capacities for teaching and service." [4]

The International Teaching Centre has affirmed that "these young people should then be seen as a door to entry by troops and as a fruitful source of teachers...not simply as children for whom activity must be arranged...but as a living creation of God necessary at this very moment for the purposes of God..." [5]

The purpose of these classes, then, is to systematically familiarize children with the fundamental truths of the Bahá'í Revelation, and to increase their desire and capacity to teach and serve. Additional goals are to strengthen bonds of friendship, and to provide an enjoyable Bahá'í activity which children will enthusiastically look forward to and invite their friends. In the words of one participant:

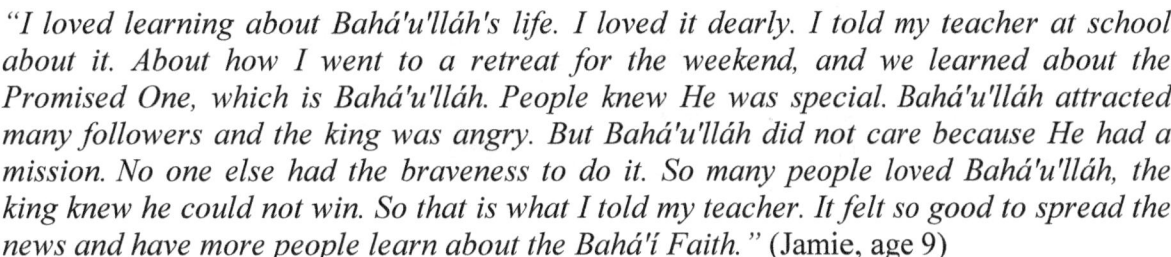

*"I loved learning about Bahá'u'lláh's life. I loved it dearly. I told my teacher at school about it. About how I went to a retreat for the weekend, and we learned about the Promised One, which is Bahá'u'lláh. People knew He was special. Bahá'u'lláh attracted many followers and the king was angry. But Bahá'u'lláh did not care because He had a mission. No one else had the braveness to do it. So many people loved Bahá'u'lláh, the king knew he could not win. So that is what I told my teacher. It felt so good to spread the news and have more people learn about the Bahá'í Faith."* (Jamie, age 9)

---

**References**

1. Bahá'í Education: A Compilation, p. 4
2. Selections from the Writings of 'Abdu'l-Bahá, p. 141
3. Bahá'í Education: A Compilation, p. 71
4. Ridván 2000 Message
5. To the Boards of Counselors, 5 Dec. 1988

**Bahá'u'lláh: The Glory of God**

# OVERVIEW

## TEACHER'S GUIDES FOR CHILDREN'S CLASSES

It is hoped that this easy-to-use teacher's guide, the fourth in a series for the Bahá'í education of children, will be a useful resource for Bahá'í summer and winter schools, Holy Day programs and weekend retreats. It might also be included in a parent's toolkit for home schooling, or form part of the religious curriculum for a full-time Baha'i-inspired academic school—such as the one our family established in Puerto Rico where many of these lessons were developed.

Anticipating future needs, with a few minor modifications, some of the theme books might also be appropriate for upper elementary public school classrooms. "The Manifestation of God," for example, would be well-suited for a class on comparative religion, and "The Power of Unity," could offer a valuable contribution to a unit on diversity and the oneness of humankind.

Each book is filled with fun, hands-on, kid-tested learning activities designed for ages 8-12. These activities were developed and tested in the field, in response to the needs of teachers and children, and have been used successfully in multiple settings over many years.

The lessons incorporate a variety of instructional strategies as recommended in the Bahá'í Writings on education, such as learning through play, questioning, memorization, consultation, reflection, stories, speeches, music, arts and crafts, science, independent investigation, lectures, group discussion, plays and recreational activities.

When used as part of an intensive program, such as a summer school or weekend retreat, the teacher will need to select activities to fit within the time allotted. If the lessons are part of an ongoing program such as a daily or weekly academic class, one or more activities can be selected for each session, until the entire course has been completed. Utilized in this way, there is sufficient material in each book for several months of weekly classes.

The lessons are user-friendly and ready-to-go with very little outside preparation needed by the teacher. Essentially everything is included, with the exception of craft supplies and common household items. Each book has a sample retreat schedule, detailed lesson plans, instructions and patterns for making classroom materials, copy-ready student handouts, song sheets, music, and plans for a children's performance. When optional materials are recommended (e.g., photographs or videos), the sources are given.

Each teacher's guide focuses on a distinct theme, with all of the lessons, songs, crafts and other learning activities integrated around that theme. The series includes:

**(1) GOD AND THE UNIVERSE**
- The Kingdoms of Creation
- God, the Creator
- Prayer, Our Connection with God
- What Is a Human Being?

**(2) THE MANIFESTATION**
- Station of the Manifestation
- Introduction to the Prophets
- Progressive Revelation
- One Common Faith

**(3) THE BÁB: GATE TO BAHÁ'U'LLÁH**
- His Birth and Early Life
- Declaration of the Báb
- Martyrdom of the Báb
- The Primal Point

**(4) BAHÁ'U'LLÁH: THE GLORY OF GOD**
- His Birth, Early Life and Station
- Declaration of Bahá'u'lláh
- Exiles and Imprisonment
- Clouds of Glory

**(5) THE POWER OF UNITY**
- The Power of Unity
- Unity in Diversity
- The Colors We Are
- Overcoming Prejudice

Additional theme books are being prepared on 'Abdu'l-Bahá, Bahá'í Principles, Bahá'í Laws and Institutions, Consultation for Kids, and The Bahá'í Community.

## CHILDREN'S RETREAT PLANNING GUIDE

These theme books can be used in conjunction with the *Bahá'í Children's Retreat Planning Guide,* which is available from **www.UnityWorksStore.com**. It covers the following topics:

- ❑ Scheduling
- ❑ Sponsorship
- ❑ Participants
- ❑ Teachers
- ❑ Other volunteers
- ❑ Facility
- ❑ Publicity
- ❑ Finances
- ❑ Pre-registration
- ❑ Materials
- ❑ Site preparation
- ❑ Sample schedule
- ❑ On-site registration
- ❑ Orientation
- ❑ Outdoor activities
- ❑ Children's performance
- ❑ Closing activities
- ❑ Food, forms, signs

Bahá'u'lláh: The Glory of God

# TO THE ORGANIZERS

## Teachers

This teacher's guide includes four lessons on Bahá'u'lláh. One individual could teach all four lessons; the classes can be team-taught; or a different person might be asked to lead each class.

## Special Role of Youth

Capable youth and junior youth can be invited to assist with the classes and activities. We have found that many former participants are eager to return to the children's retreats as volunteers. Inspired by this experience, a high percentage of them have gone on to complete junior youth animator training, and several have arisen to organize children's classes or junior youth groups in their home communities.

The participation of youth volunteers at the retreat is also a great help for the adults and a joy for the younger children, while offering the youth an opportunity to apply their institute training and to acquire new skills. The youth are given guided experience and hands-on teaching practice. They return home with new confidence, encouraged and motivated to support local children's classes. In addition, a wonderful community atmosphere is created with all age groups working together to educate the children.

In the words of one youth:

> *"The retreats have been an integral part of my growing up experience, and I'm so grateful for the opportunity to come and help out now as a youth. It's really special to see my brothers and cousins and their friends, and know that they'll grow up with the same wonderful friendships and learning experiences and shared memories that my generation of youth gained.*
>
> *"I learned a lot about myself and discovered how to help kids learn and grow, and ways to make their experience happy. Although I went through all the same lessons myself, it's still great to hear and see the lessons again. Us kids have so much fun every time and I am always looking forward to the next retreat."* (Brynne Haug, age 16)

**Youth volunteers: Kierra, Yuri, Alonso, Layli, Alex, Brynne, Carew**

## Schedule

If planning a weekend retreat, the lessons can be scheduled over a two-day or a three-day period. Sample schedules for both are included below. The two-day schedule offers participants a choice of some of the crafts and activities. The three-day schedule includes more of the crafts and classroom activities, additional time for memorization practice, an evening talent show, and a group consultation on how to share with others the concepts learned at the retreat. For an ongoing class, all of the activities can be included.

## Handouts

Some handouts are included with the lessons, while others have been grouped near the end of this book for convenience in photocopying. They can also be downloaded from: **www.UnityWorksStore.com** (click on Children's Classes > Bahá'u'lláh > student handouts). The handouts can be copied one at a time as needed for a particular class, or all at once as part of the handout packet for a summer school or weekend retreat.

The **Schedule, Songs** and **Quotations** should be photocopied for all participants and included in their folders during registration. If each item is copied on paper of a different color, it will be easier for the children to find. The songs and quotations should each be copied on two sides of the page to save paper and for ease of use.

The seventeen-page packet titled "Stories from the Life of Bahá'u'lláh" (from the title sheet through the quiz) should be copied back-to-back on plain white paper, stapled together and included in the student folders.

Each instructor should be given **To the Teacher** (pages 10-12), a copy of the appropriate lesson plan, and **References for Teachers** (found at the end of this book), along with the handouts mentioned above. Teachers should also make copies of any additional handouts needed for their specific lessons.

The coordinator of the children's performance will need copies of the entire **Children's Performance** section (pages 109-124), in addition to the schedule, song sheet, page of quotations, and the packet of "Stories From the Life of Bahá'u'lláh."

The song leader will need **To the Music Coordinator** and copies of each song, found in the section on music (pages 149-166).

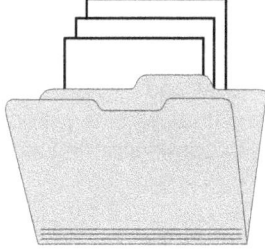

Bahá'u'lláh: The Glory of God

— Sample Flyer —

# BAHÁ'Í CHILDREN'S RETREAT

THEME: Bahá'u'lláh, The Glory of God — Sponsored by the Bahá'ís of Our Town

## KIDS: AGES 8 –12

*Join us for a fun weekend of Bahá'í classes with prayers, singing, arts & crafts, archery, games, storytelling, hiking, great food & more!*

**October 15-17**
Noorani Home, 1919 Unity Lane
Our Town, WA 98765 - (919) 765-4321

**COST:** $35 per child or $30 if paid before Sept. 15. Additional children from same family, $20 each. Scholarships available. Make checks payable to: Bahá'ís of Our Town. Space is limited, apply now!

*Participants should bring: sleeping bag, pillow, towel, toothbrush and paste, comb, any medicines with clear instructions, bathing suit, sturdy shoes, pajamas and change of clothes. Please do NOT bring: electronic games, radios, CDs, iPods, etc.*

*Starts Friday at 5:30 p.m. with registration and dinner. Ends at 2:00 p.m. on Monday*

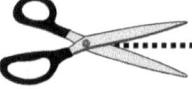 ·······································································································

## BAHÁ'Í CHILDREN'S RETREAT

*Mail this form to: Lua Smith, 1863 Ridván Lane, Our Town, WA 98765*
*Email: lsmith@gmail.com - Tel: (919) 123-4567*

Name of child (print): _____  Age: ____ Sex: ____

Address: _____ Phone: _____

Email: _____ Fee enclosed: $ _____ Partial scholarship requested: $_____

Emergency contact: _____ Phone: _____

Medical or dietary information: _____

The child named above has my permission to attend the Bahá'í Children's Retreat on Oct. 15-17, 2010, at the Noorani home in Our Town. I understand that s/he is participating at her/his own risk. If necessary, I hereby give the event organizers permission to administer first aid and obtain emergency medical treatment.

_____   _____   _____
Parent or Guardian (print name)   Signature   Date

Bahá'u'lláh: The Glory of God

— Sample 2-Day Weekend Schedule —

# Bahá'í Children's Retreat

Noorani home, Our Town, October 15-17, 2010

## *"Bahá'u'lláh: The Glory of God"*

**FRIDAY**

| | |
|---|---|
| 5:30 pm | Registration, decorate folders |
| 6:00 | Dinner |
| 7:30 | Prayers, introductions, singing |
| **8:00** | **Orientation program** |
| 9:00 | Volunteer briefing |
| 9:30 | Group song, prayers and bedtime |
| 10:00 | Lights out |

**SATURDAY**

| | |
|---|---|
| 7:30 am | Morning prayers |
| 8:00 | Breakfast |
| 8:30 | Singing |
| **8:45** | **Class #1: His Birth, Early Life & Station** (90 min.) |
| 10:15 | Break |
| **10:45** | **Class #2: Declaration of Bahá'u'lláh** (90 min.) |
| 12:15 pm | Lunch and quiet time |
| **1:30** | **Class #3: Exiles and Imprisonment** (75 min.) |
| **2:45** | **Walk to Baghdad** (45 min.) |
| 3:30 | Snack and outdoor activities |
| 4:30 | Rehearsal for children's performance |
| 6:00 | Dinner |
| 7:00 | Prepare refreshments, rehearse songs |
| **8:00** | **Children's performance** |
| 9:15 | Refreshments and campfire |
| 10:00 | Group song, prayers and bedtime |
| 10:15 | Lights out |

**SUNDAY**

| | |
|---|---|
| 8:00 am | Morning prayers |
| 8:30 | Breakfast |
| 9:00 | Singing |
| **9:15** | **Class #4: Clouds of Glory** (1 hr. 45 min.) |
| 11:00 | Outdoor activities |
| 12:00 pm | Lunch |
| 12:30 | Clean-up |
| 1:00 | Closing activities, evaluation, graduation |
| 1:30 | Group photo |
| 1:45 | Dessert |
| 2:00 | Check lost-and-found; farewells |

Bahá'u'lláh: The Glory of God

— Sample 3-Day Weekend Schedule —

# Bahá'í Children's Retreat

Noorani home, Our Town, October 15-18, 2010

## "Bahá'u'lláh: The Glory of God"

**FRIDAY**

| | |
|---|---|
| 5:30 pm | Registration, decorate folders |
| 6:00 | Dinner |
| 7:30 | Prayers, introductions, singing, orientation |
| **8:00** | **Orientation program** |
| 9:00 | Volunteer briefing |
| 9:30 | Group song, prayers and bedtime |
| 10:00 | Lights out |

**SATURDAY**

| | |
|---|---|
| 7:30 am | Morning prayers |
| 8:00 | Breakfast |
| 8:30 | Singing |
| **8:45** | **Class #1: His Birth, Early Life & Station** (90 min.) |
| 10:15 | Break |
| **10:45** | **Class #2: Declaration of Bahá'u'lláh** (90 min.) |
| 12:15 pm | Lunch and quiet time |
| 1:30 | Craft activities |
| 3:00 | Snack and outdoor activities |
| 4:30 | Memorization practice (alone, pairs or groups) |
| 5:15 | Group singing practice or free time |
| 6:00 | Dinner |
| 7:30 | Singing and share memorized quotes |
| 8:15 | Evening snack |
| 8:30 | Evening program (Bahá'í video, talent show, etc.) |
| 9:30 | Group song, prayers and bedtime |
| 10:00 | Lights out |

**SUNDAY**

| | |
|---|---|
| 8:00 am | Morning prayers |
| 8:30 | Breakfast |
| 9:00 | Singing |
| **9:15** | **Class #3: Exiles and Imprisonment** (75 min.) |
| **10:30** | **Walk to Baghdad** (45 min.) |
| 11:15 | Outdoor activities |
| 12:00 pm | Lunch and quiet time |
| **1:30** | **Class #4: Clouds of Glory** (1 hr. 45 min.) |
| 3:15 | Snack and outdoor activities |
| 4:15 | Rehearsal for children's performance |
| 6:00 | Dinner |

Bahá'u'lláh: The Glory of God

— Sample 3-Day Weekend Schedule, continued —

**SUNDAY**
- 7:00 pm — Prepare refreshments, rehearse songs
- **8:00** — **Children's performance**
- 9:15 — Refreshments and campfire
- 10:00 — Group song, prayers and bedtime
- 10:15 — Lights out

**MONDAY**
- 8:30 am — Morning prayers
- 9:00 — Breakfast
- 9:30 — Singing
- **9:45** — **Group consultation on how to share what we learned**
- 10:30 — Outdoor activities
- 12:00 pm — Lunch
- 12:30 — Clean-up
- 1:00 — Closing activities, evaluation, graduation
- 1:30 — Group photo
- 1:45 — Dessert
- 2:00 — Check lost-and-found; farewells

*"Thanks for a wonderful children's retreat. I really enjoyed it. I loved all the crafts and how they related with Bahá'u'lláh. The food was delicious as well."* (Raul)

**Youth volunteer, Brynne Haug, studying the life of Bahá'u'lláh with Grayson and Raul.**

Bahá'u'lláh: The Glory of God

# TO THE TEACHER

> *"Among the greatest of all services that can possibly be rendered by man to Almighty God is the education and training of children."*
> 'Abdu'l-Bahá, Selections from the Writings of 'Abdu'l-Bahá, p. 133

## Teacher's Guide

The teacher's guide on the following pages contains detailed lesson plans with fun, hands-on, kid-tested learning activities. It includes copy-ready student handouts and simple patterns for making instructional materials. The lessons are user-friendly and ready-to-go with little outside preparation needed by the teacher. They are organized in a sequential, step-by-step format, with each activity building on the previous one. Each lesson can also stand alone. The activities can be used for Bahá'í summer and winter schools, Holy Day programs, cluster gatherings and weekend retreats. They can also form part of the religious curriculum for an academic school.

This teacher's guide begins with an overview of the *Children's Classes and Retreats* series, sample schedules, an orientation program and lesson plans. The lessons are followed by plans for a children's performance, student handouts, a section on music (with song sheets, musical scores and instructions for group singing), and closing activities with suggestions for follow-up. A comprehensive list of the activities in each lesson, and a separate index of activities by category (music, crafts, stories, etc.), can be found at the end of the book. A compilation of selected passages on the theme of each lesson is included as a reference for teachers. A bibliography completes the manual.

## Four Lessons

Each teacher's guide includes four lessons on the chosen theme. The lessons are designed to present basic Bahá'í teachings to children ages 8-12. The suggested time for each activity is in parentheses after the heading. However, if students need additional time to practice a skill, or if the class is engaged in a fruitful discussion and wishes to continue, the time can be extended, and another part of the lesson can be omitted or saved for a future class session. Be flexible.

When the lessons are used as part of an intensive program, such as a summer school or weekend retreat, you will need to select activities to fit within the time allotted. If the lessons are part of an ongoing program such as a daily or weekly academic class, one or more activities can be selected each time, until the entire course has been completed. Utilized in this way, there is sufficient material in the book for several months of weekly classes.

An ongoing class can begin with a welcome for new students, followed by singing, prayers, a review of the previous lesson (including student presentations), and the selected activities. At the beginning of each class, consider scheduling "circle time," to give children an opportunity to share news of interest to the group or to consult on pressing concerns. End the class with a review of the lesson, recitation of any memory quotes, more singing, and refreshments.

## Preparing to Teach

In order to present these lessons effectively, you will need to read the lesson plan and become familiar with the objectives and the concepts to be taught. For a deeper understanding of each topic, you can also study the *References for Teachers* found at the end of the manual. Your presentation should be practiced until it feels smooth and comfortable.

Explanatory notes to the teacher are not meant to be read as a script, but are intended only as a guide. Key phrases and highlights from these notes can be written on the board before or during the lesson.

All instructional materials should be made or obtained well in advance. Handouts should be photocopied for students and volunteers, and either included in their folders when they arrive, or distributed during each class as needed.

## Class Discussions

During class discussions, all students should be encouraged to participate, not just the ones who speak first or loudest. A child who is silent can be asked, "Maria, what do you think about this?" Have students raise their hands rather than shouting out the answer. A simple comment like, "I'm happy to see so many of you raising your hands quietly," will reinforce this rule.

If a student's answer is incorrect, rather than saying, "No, that's wrong," it is better to respond with, "Good try. You're on the right track," or "That's an interesting thought!" Then ask another question or give a small hint that will help the child succeed. Be patient and enthusiastic. Encouragement is generally more motivating than criticism. Do not allow the children to laugh at or tease each other.

With a larger group, you may find it useful to ring a bell or develop a hand signal to bring the children back to order after a discussion or other class activity. Raising your hand while standing quietly in front of the class can be very effective. As soon as one person notices the teacher, that person should stop talking and raise his/her hand. As others notice, they should join in. Teach children the signal, and practice it a few times before starting the discussion.

## Volunteers

Youth and adult volunteers can be asked to assist you with learning activities and classroom management. Volunteers can be put in charge of discussion groups. They can help with craft projects, lead the singing, teach one of the classes, work one-on-one with students who need extra assistance, and remove a disruptive child if necessary. Discipline is easier to maintain if volunteers are spaced throughout the room during the lesson.

Bahá'u'lláh: The Glory of God

## Children's Performance*

This guidebook includes instructions for a children's performance that will give children an opportunity to demonstrate and reinforce what they have learned. Friends, families, neighbors and co-workers can be invited to the show. The fact that children will be performing in front of a live audience serves as excellent motivation for them to learn the material presented in class. The presentation may include prayers, singing, stories, recitation of Bahá'í passages, demonstrations to illustrate various concepts, an exhibition of arts and crafts, a puppet theater, a short play and a quiz show.

The children's performance also provides an opportunity for home visits to parents before and after the show, to invite them and to talk in more depth about some of the themes presented.

A detailed agenda and plans for the performance are included in this manual. The children will need time to rehearse. If the program is part of a larger summer school or weekend retreat, the planning committee may schedule rehearsal time and appoint someone to coordinate the program. During class sessions, the teacher should make note of those children who seem to grasp the material well, and who could present it in front of an audience.

> *"It is the hope of 'Abdu'l-Bahá that those youthful souls ...will be tended by one who traineth them to love."*
> 'Abdu'l-Bahá, Selections from the Writings of 'Abdu'l-Bahá, p. 134

* Note: While our student presentations have typically been scheduled for the evening, they could be held at any time. In the two-day weekend retreat format, Saturday evening is often the most convenient time for inviting neighbors and friends. This means that activities from the fourth class on Sunday morning will not be included in the presentation. If the performance follows a three-day retreat schedule or a weekly format, these activities can easily be added to the final program.

Bahá'u'lláh: The Glory of God

# OPENING ACTIVITIES

If these lessons are being used as part of an intensive program, such as a summer school or weekend retreat, it is usually a good idea to provide some self-directed activities for children during the registration period, while they are waiting for others to arrive. After checking in, they can be shown to a table to decorate their folders or to work on other projects (see theme book #1 on *God and the Universe* for ideas). If desired, a separate table with the appropriate materials can be set up for each station. The instructions should be posted and volunteers can be asked to assist the children. These activities can also be incorporated into an ongoing weekly class.

## Orientation Program

The orientation program on the first day is designed to make everyone feel welcome and to help them get to know each other. Explain to the group that we will be learning about **Bahá'u'lláh** and we will focus on four important topics:

(1) His birth, early life and station.
(2) His declaration as a Messenger of God.
(3) His exiles and imprisonment in order to bring us the Word of God.
(4) His message to the kings of the earth, and why they failed to recognize Him.

**A sample orientation program is outlined below:**

1. Welcome
2. Opening music
3. Selected prayers
4. Reading of the letter from the sponsoring institution
5. Introductions [A]
6. Orientation [B]
7. Review of the schedule
8. Ice-breakers and warm-up activities (see below)
9. Group singing (see song sheet in handout section)

A. <u>Introductions</u>: Each person can be asked to introduce him or herself, sharing their name, town, and one interesting personal fact. As a variation, people can be asked to act out a hobby or favorite activity, without using any words, and the group can guess what it is.

B. <u>Orientation</u>: This should cover information about classes, supervision, the role of volunteers, any house rules, food, safety, recreation and relating to others. See the *Bahá'í Children's Retreats Planning Guide* for details.

After the orientation and review of the schedule, you can organize one or more warm-up activities (see next page) which will serve as ice-breakers and help to introduce the theme. The orientation program can be followed by a snack and a short video (e.g., segments from a recent Bahá'í Newsreel), which can be played for the children during the briefing for volunteers.

Bahá'u'lláh: The Glory of God

# Warm-up Activities

**1. Unity Bingo** (20 min.)

This is a fun mixer which can be tailored to the participants. The sample Bingo sheet on the following page is available online (www.UnityWorksStore.com > Children's Classes > student handouts) as part of the download packet for this teacher's guide. It can be customized with your own set of questions.

You will need Bingo sheets, pencils or pens, and small prizes for all. A youth can be put in charge of checking completed Bingo pages and handing out the prizes.

**Instruct the participants to:**

- Walk around the room and obtain one signature per square.
- Each square should be signed by a different person, unless there are fewer than twenty people, in which case some will need to sign twice.
- You can put your own name in one of the squares.
- Fill in all the squares to get a prize.
- Everyone wins!

Cicily completes her Bingo sheet

Bahá'u'lláh: The Glory of God

Sample Bingo Sheet          Name: _____

# Unity Bingo

Walk around the room and obtain one signature per square.
Each square should be signed by a different person, unless there are fewer
than twenty people, in which case some will need to sign twice. You can put your
own name in one of the squares. Fill in all the squares to get a prize. Everyone wins!

**Find someone who . . .**

| Who is attending their first Bahá'í children's retreat | Who drove more than 2 hours to get here | Who has a brother or sister attending this retreat | Who has been a Bahá'í for more than 10 years |
|---|---|---|---|
| Who has been on a Bahá'í teaching trip | Who has taught a Bahá'í children's class | Who has been on Pilgrimage | Who can name five or more Prophets of God |
| Who plays a musical instrument | Who speaks Spanish | Who can say a Tongan prayer | Who is under 10 years old |
| Who lives in Washington | Who lives in Oregon | Who lives on the Yakama Nation Reservation | Whose first or last name starts with "G" |
| Who likes to sing | Who likes to dance | Who likes to read | Who plays soccer |

Bahá'í Children's Classes and Retreats: Theme 4, p. 15

## 2. What Am I? (10 min.)

The chart on the following page contains twenty words that appear in *Stories from the Life of Bahá'u'lláh*. Before the activity, photocopy the chart (enlarging if possible) and post on the wall. For a large group, you may need to make several copies to post around the room, or one much larger chart written legibly by hand.

| birds | garden | messenger | puppet |
|---|---|---|---|
| box | gold | mirror | roses |
| chains | heart | mountain | snow |
| crown | king | prison | sun |
| fish | light | prisoner | tent |

Then write each item separately on a sticky label, or make another photocopy of the chart and cut into separate squares. If there are more than twenty people, make two labels for some items so that each person will have one. Keep the labels out of sight until the game begins.

At the start of the activity, explain that each person will have a word taped to his or her back, but they won't be able to see what it is. The words come from stories about Bahá'u'lláh that they will soon be reading in class. (Show them the chart that has been posted on the wall.)

They will be working in pairs, asking each other "yes" or "no" questions in order to figure out who or what they are. They should refer to the chart to help focus their questions. They may not ask directly, "Am I a bird?" or other word listed on the chart. A sample dialog is shown below. After one person's object is discovered, it will be the other person's turn.

Am I bigger than an airplane?

| Child #1 | Child #2 |
|---|---|
| Am I a person? | No. |
| Am I an animal? | No. |
| Am I bigger than an airplane? | Yes. |
| Am I made out of rock? | No. |
| Am I found in the sky? | Yes. |
| I'm the sun, right? | Yes, you're the sun! |

After explaining the activity, have the participants pair up, preferably with someone they don't know, and introduce themselves. While introductions are underway, walk around the room and tape a label on each person's back. (Use sticky labels, or attach the cards with masking tape.) Youth and adults can play as well. If the group is a large one, assistants can help speed up the labeling process. Those who finish early can be given additional labels.

Bahá'u'lláh: The Glory of God

Photocopy and enlarge this chart for posting on the wall. Make another copy of the chart and cut into separate squares, or make hand-written sticky labels for each participant.

| \multicolumn{4}{c}{Terms from **"Stories from the Life of Bahá'u'lláh"**} | | | |
|---|---|---|---|
| birds | fish | messenger | puppet |
| box | garden | mirror | roses |
| chains | gold | mountain | snow |
| clouds | heart | prison | sun |
| crown | king | prisoner | tent |

### 3. Just for Fun (10 min.)

Prepare a set of cards with jokes and riddles appropriate for children (see samples below). Print all of the questions on one color of cardstock (e.g., blue), and all of the answers on another color (e.g., yellow). Select the same number of jokes as there are participants. For example, if there are ten players, you will need ten questions and their answers. Then cut into individual cards.

Mix up and distribute the blue cards so everyone has one. Do the same with the yellow cards. Then have one person with a blue card stand and read their question, using a strong clear voice. Whoever has the matching yellow card should stand and share the answer. Don't read the joke number unless no one gets the punch line. Younger children may need assistance. Continue around the room until all the questions and answers have been shared.

| | Joke or Riddle (blue ↓) | | Punch Line or Answer (yellow ↓) |
|---|---|---|---|
| 1 | What is a frog's favorite music? | 1 | Hip hop! |
| 2 | Why did the boy give his house some jogging shoes? | 2 | He wanted to see a home run! |
| 3 | How do you repair a broken duck? | 3 | Duck-tape! |
| 4 | Why did the math book cry? | 4 | It had so many problems! |
| 5 | What is a dragon's favorite game? | 5 | Swallow the leader! |
| 6 | What's smarter than a talking cat? | 6 | A spelling bee! |
| 7 | Which animal went into the tiger's cage and came out alive? | 7 | The tiger! |

Bahá'u'lláh: The Glory of God

| | **Joke or Riddle** (blue ↓) | | **Punch Line or Answer** (yellow ↓) |
|---|---|---|---|
| 8 | What did the Baby Corn say to the Mommy Corn? | 8 | Where's the Pop Corn? |
| 9 | What did one plate say to the other? | 9 | Dinner's on me! |
| 10 | What is a baby's motto? | 10 | If at first you don't succeed, cry, cry again! |
| 11 | What's the difference between a teacher and a train? | 11 | A teacher says "spit out that gum" and a train says "choo choo choo"! |
| 12 | Doctor, doctor, I keep thinking I'm invisible. | 12 | Who said that? |
| 13 | Doctor, doctor, I keep thinking I'm a comedian. | 13 | You must be joking! |
| 14 | What time is it when an elephant sits on a fence? | 14 | Time to fix the fence! |
| 15 | How do you spell cat backwards? | 15 | C-A-T  B-A-C-K-W-A-R-D-S! |
| 16 | What time is it when a clock strikes thirteen? | 16 | Time to fix the clock! |
| 17 | What do sea monsters eat? | 17 | Fish and ships! |
| 18 | What do lazy dogs do for fun? | 18 | Chase parked cars! |
| 19 | Which month has 28 days? | 19 | All of them! |

Bahá'í Children's Classes and Retreats: Theme 4, p. 19

Bahá'u'lláh: The Glory of God

| | Joke or Riddle (blue ↓) | | Punch Line or Answer (yellow ↓) |
|---|---|---|---|
| 20 | What do you get when you cross a parrot with a tiger? | 20 | I don't know, but when it talks, you'd better listen! |
| 21 | What word is always pronounced wrong? | 21 | Wrong! |
| 22 | What gets wetter the more it dries? | 22 | A towel! |
| 23 | What gets bigger the more you take away from it? | 23 | A hole! |
| 24 | What building has the most stories? | 24 | The library! |
| 25 | Why is 6 afraid of 7? | 25 | Because 7 - 8 - 9. |
| 26 | What can you break just by saying its name? | 26 | Silence. |
| 27 | What invention lets you walk through walls? | 27 | A door! |
| 28 | What do Winnie the Pooh and Alexander the Great have in common? | 28 | They both have the same middle name! |
| 29 | What are two things you can't eat for lunch? | 29 | Breakfast and dinner! |
| 30 | Which word in the dictionary is always spelled incorrectly? | 30 | Incorrectly! |

## LESSON #1

# His Birth, Early Life and Station

Bahá'u'lláh: The Glory of God – Lesson #1

# His Birth, Early Life and Station

**Objectives:** Students will be able to describe:
- Significant events from Bahá'u'lláh's early life.
- His imprisonment in the Síyáh-Chál.
- His station as the Messenger of God for this Day.

*Before class, prepare all instructional materials on the list at the end of this lesson. Post any maps and pictures of Iran. Set out a dictionary and put large world map on wall. Orient volunteer assistants. Distribute folders and pens or pencils to each participant.*

### 1. SONG: "Shine Your Light" (5 min.)

Have students take out their song sheets and sing along. Ask the music coordinator for assistance if needed.

### 2. INTRODUCTION TO BAHÁ'U'LLÁH (5 min.)

Ask students to take out their story packets and turn to the second page, titled "Introduction to Bahá'u'lláh." Read the introduction to them, adding the questions and comments noted on the teacher's version included with this lesson.

### 3. PICTURES (5 min.)

Show students pictures of Iran, so they can see what it looked like at the time of Bahá'u'lláh.

### 4. STORIES FROM THE LIFE OF BAHÁ'U'LLÁH (45-60 min.)

Explain to the students that they will be working in small groups to learn about the life of Bahá'u'lláh. There are eight numbered stories in their packets, starting with #1: *The Baby Who Never Cried*. Each group will read a different story, then share what they have learned with the entire class.

#### Organizing the Activity

A. First determine how many groups, and thus how many stories, you will need. Groups should have at least two and preferably three people. If there are 21 children, for example, you might form seven groups with three children per group. The groups do not need to be exactly even. Some may have five children and some only two, but 3-4 is ideal, as it gives everyone a chance to speak and allows for a variety of opinions.

A class with 20 children, for example, might be divided as follows:

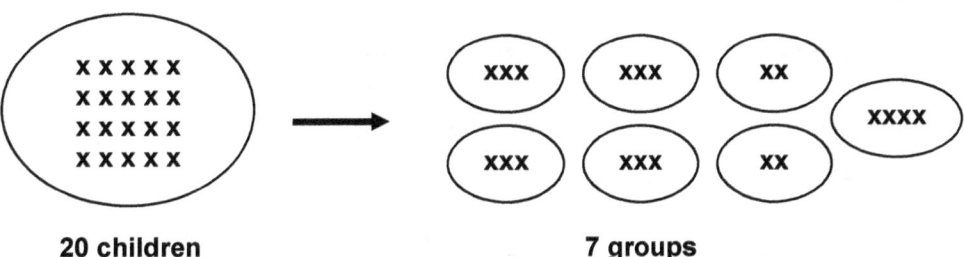

**20 children** → **7 groups**

With fewer children, you will have fewer groups. As a variation, if this lesson is part of a weekly class, you might select two or three stories each time, or have the entire class read the same story together, choosing a different one each week.

B. Next determine which stories to use and assign each story to a youth or adult volunteer. Give each volunteer a copy of the instruction sheet (included at the end of this lesson).

1. The Baby Who Never Cried
2. A Dream of Many Fish
3. The Puppet Show
4. Father of the Poor
5. The Black Pit
6. Banished to Baghdad
7. The Hermit in the Mountains
8. The Writing Lesson

C. Then have the volunteers stand in three different corners of the room depending on the reading level of their assigned story.

- Easier (story # 1, 2, 8)
- Medium (story # 3, 4, 5)
- Harder (story # 6, 7)

"Younger children go with Sue or Leon. Those who like to read difficult books, go with Yuri or Farzam. Spanish speakers should go with Carmen."

D. Ask students to choose a story based on their age or reading level. Have them stand with the volunteer in charge of that story. If children need help deciding, use their grade level as a guide. If some students are more comfortable in a different language (e.g., Spanish), you can group them by language if a suitable volunteer is available.

Bahá'u'lláh: The Glory of God – Lesson #1

E. Groups can move to another room or outside if desired. Allow them about 15 minutes to work, and walk around to observe their progress.

F. Call the groups back together and ask each one to report, starting with story #1. Students should stand up and speak in a strong, clear voice. This is good practice for the children's performance. Help them stick to the time limit so there will be time for the remaining activities.

## 5. PEER QUESTIONS (10-15 min.)

| Who | Where |
|---|---|
| What | Why |
| When | How |

Say the following words and write them in large print on the board:

Ask students to take out the notebook paper from their folders and write 2-3 questions about the story they just read. The questions should begin with one of the words on the board. For example: "**Where** was Bahá'u'lláh born?" and "**Why** did His teachers send Him home from school?"

Proceed around the room, calling on each student to ask one of their questions. Then call on another student to answer it. Have the children raise their hands. Continue with a second round of questions if there is time, and praise students for their efforts.

*Collect all folders and pencils.*

## 6. BLACK PIT EXPERIENCE (20-30 min.)

The purpose of this activity is to help the children imagine what it might have been like in the Síyáh-Chál (see story #5). Prepare a dark, cramped space to conduct the activity, for example, a cold basement hallway with all the lights turned off. If a suitable room is not available, an area can be created under a sheet or tent. Aim for as much realism as possible.

You will need:

- Pictures of large rats (see end of lesson) placed strategically along the walls
- A sturdy canvas bag or backpack filled with 25 pounds of weight
- A bathroom scale to confirm the weight of the bag
- Several 2x4 wooden boards or a wooden ladder to simulate stocks
- A length of thick metal chain or a metal ladder to symbolize the chain
- A heavy barbell or other item weighing about 50 pounds

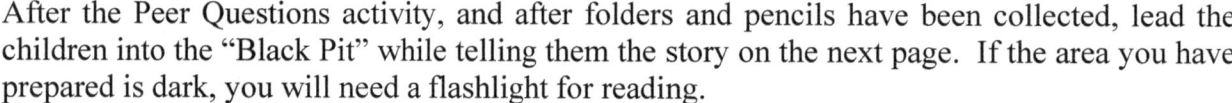

After the Peer Questions activity, and after folders and pencils have been collected, lead the children into the "Black Pit" while telling them the story on the next page. If the area you have prepared is dark, you will need a flashlight for reading.

*After the lesson, dismiss the children for a break before Class #2.*

Bahá'u'lláh: The Glory of God – Lesson #1

# THE BLACK PIT EXPERIENCE

*Read or tell this story to the children for activity #6.*

- Do you remember the story of the Black Pit? Let's pretend we're going there.

**Lead children slowly and quietly down the stairs and have them sit on the floor in the dark. Arrange them in two rows facing each other, with alternating outstretched legs.**

- Have you ever been in a dark cave or a crowded place that smelled like garbage?
- Try to remember what it was like.
- What if there were no bathrooms and you had to stay there for many months?
- What if there were rats all around and no lights?
- Close your eyes and try to imagine it.

- Although Bahá'u'lláh was a good man and innocent of any crime, He was arrested and taken, barefoot and in chains, to a dark underground prison.
- This dungeon was called the Síyáh-Chál.
- Can you say Síyáh-Chál? Again.
- Does anyone know what that means? *(Black Pit)*
- Bahá'u'lláh and His friends were forced to stay in the Síyáh-Chál for four months.
- The prison was cold and wet and dirty and swarming with rats.
**(Shine flashlight on walls to show rats.)**

- Bahá'u'lláh was surrounded by 150 thieves and murderers.
- It was crowded and Bahá'u'lláh and His fellow prisoners were chained together.
- Most of the men had no clothes and not even a mat to sleep on.
- There were no toilets either, so the prison was filthy and the smell was horrible.
- Bahá'u'lláh's feet were in stocks and there was a chain around His neck that weighed over 100 pounds.
- Now open your eyes. Can you guess how much this bag weighs?
**(Pass bag down each row and let children feel its weight.)**

- The chain around Bahá'u'lláh's neck weighed 100 pounds—four times as much as this bag.
- That barbell weighs 50 pounds. You can try lifting it after the story.
- Let's put these chains over our shoulders to remind us of Bahá'u'lláh's chains. **(Add chains.)**
- The prisoners' feet were also in stocks. **(Place boards across the children's ankles.)**

- How long was Bahá'u'lláh in the Síyáh-Chál? *(4 months)*
- That's where he saw the Maid of Heaven.
**(Shine flashlight on ceiling to symbolize the event.)**

- How much did the chains around His neck weigh? *(51 kilos or over 100 lbs.)*
- Those chains left permanent scars on His neck and shoulders, but He didn't complain.
- Instead, every night, to comfort the others, he led them in a special prayer:

**ALL SING:** "God Is Sufficient" (5 min.)

*Note: If the children want to try lifting the 50-pound weight, show them how to lift carefully, bending their knees. Have a volunteer spotter to assist.*

Bahá'u'lláh: The Glory of God – Lesson #1

Bahá'u'lláh: The Glory of God – Lesson #1

Bahá'u'lláh: The Glory of God – Lesson #1

**Teacher's version for activity #2**

# Introduction to Bahá'u'lláh

God is invisible. Because we can't see Him, He sends us Messengers to tell us about Him and to teach us how to live. Bahá'u'lláh is the Messenger of God for this Day.

*Remember when we talked about the Messengers?*
*Can you name some of them?* (Krishna, Buddha, Moses, Jesus…) **Good!**
*Which Prophet came right before Bahá'u'lláh? That's right – the Báb.*

These Messengers are like perfect mirrors reflecting God's light to mankind. Bahá'u'lláh is reflecting God's light for today. When we look at Him, it's like looking at God. When we love and obey Him, it's the same as loving and obeying God.

*Can you say His name?* (Bahá'u'lláh) **Good!** *Once again?* (Bahá'u'lláh) **Excellent!**

Bahá'u'lláh was also a person like us in many ways. He had a mother and father, brothers and sisters. He ate and slept. Sometimes He was hungry and sometimes He was sad.

Bahá'u'lláh was born in Persia (Iran) about 200 years ago *(show map)*. Even as a baby, His parents knew there was something special about Him. Did you know that His family was very rich? His father had a high position in the court of the king. When Bahá'u'lláh grew up, He married and had children. For a time, the family was very happy together.

But every Prophet of God has enemies who don't like the new teachings He brings. Bahá'u'lláh had enemies too. They put Him in prison, stole all of His belongings and even tried to kill Him. But His enemies were unable to stop the spread of His teachings, and today the Faith of Bahá'u'lláh has spread all around the world.

*We're going to read some stories about Bahá'u'lláh's life, but first, let's look at some pictures of the land where He was born.*

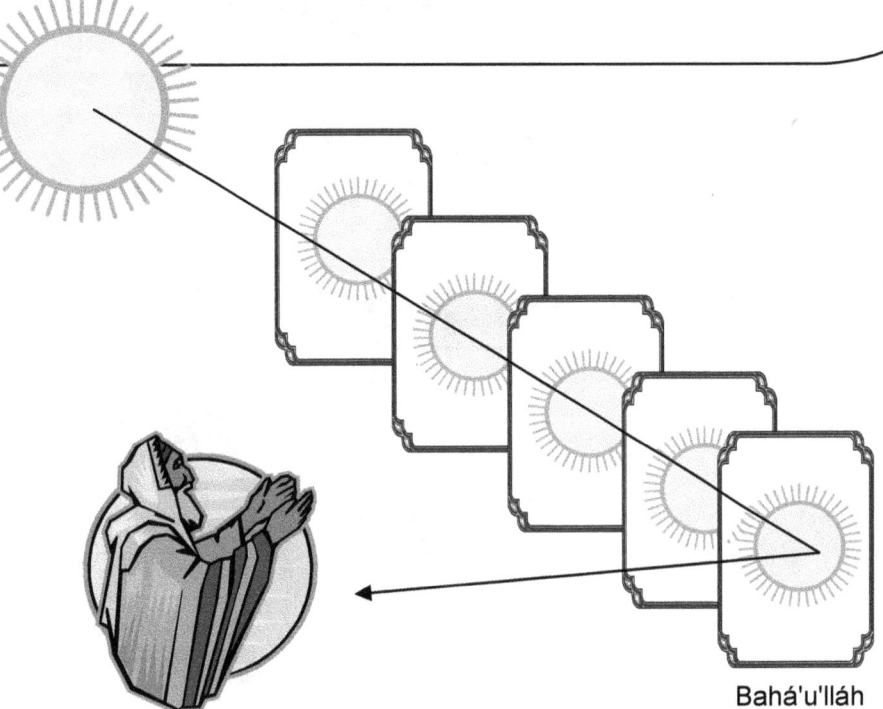

Bahá'u'lláh

Bahá'í Children's Classes and Retreats: Theme 4, p. 27

Bahá'u'lláh: The Glory of God – Lesson #1

*Old city gate.*

Illustration by John Hollins (see note, p. 33)

Bahá'u'lláh: The Glory of God – Lesson #1

"This writing is not from a dervish," said the teacher, "but a royal person from the court of the king."

Illustration by John Hollins
(see note, p. 33)

Bahá'í Children's Classes and Retreats: Theme 4, p. 29

Bahá'u'lláh: The Glory of God – Lesson #1

*Many important people from Baghdad came to visit Bahá'u'lláh.*

Illustration by John Hollins (see note, p. 33)

Bahá'u'lláh: The Glory of God – Lesson #1

*Illustration by John Hollins (see note, p. 33)*

*The gardeners picked hundreds of roses and piled them in the middle of Bahá'u'lláh's tent. When His friends came in for tea, the pile of roses was so high they couldn't see over it.*

Bahá'u'lláh: The Glory of God – Lesson #1

**Instructions for group leaders for activity #4**

# Stories from the Life of Bahá'u'lláh

Gather your small group and find a quiet place. You will have about 15 minutes to work. Have the children read the story out loud. They can take turns reading the paragraphs.

The comprehension questions at the end of the story are designed to help the children understand and remember what they read. Ask the questions and give hints and encouragement if needed, but don't answer for them. Do not allow the children to laugh at or tease each other. Take notes below.

Prepare the group to share their story with the class using their own words. They will have three minutes to report. Each child should have a part. Older or more capable students might have a larger role. For example, one student might recount the main points of the story, calling on other students to fill in certain details. Some groups may wish to add music, puppets or sound effects to their presentation.

Bahá'u'lláh: The Glory of God – Lesson #1

# MATERIALS NEEDED

- ❑ White board, easel, markers, eraser
- ❑ Folder, notebook paper, pen or pencil for each student
- ❑ Dictionary
- ❑ Large map of the world
- ❑ Song sheets for each student [A]
- ❑ Stories from the Life of Bahá'u'lláh (story packet) [A]
- ❑ Introduction to Bahá'u'lláh (teacher's version)
- ❑ Pictures of Iran and Iraq showing what they may have looked like at the time of Bahá'u'lláh [B]
- ❑ Instructions for Group Leaders for Activity #4 (one copy for each volunteer)
- ❑ Pictures of rats; tape or pushpins for attaching rats to walls [C]
- ❑ Sturdy canvas bag or backpack filled with about 25 pounds (11 kilos) of weight
- ❑ Bathroom scale
- ❑ Enough 2x4 boards to cover all the children's ankles [D]
- ❑ Length of thick chain or a metal ladder to symbolize chains
- ❑ Item weighing about 50 pounds (23 kilos), e.g., water container, barbell, bag of salt pellets
- ❑ References for teachers (included at the end of this manual)

---

A. Included in the Handouts section of this manual. The stories, along with full-page color illustrations to accompany the stories, are available in the download packet for this teacher's guide: **www.UnityWorksStore.com** > Children's Classes > Bahá'u'lláh > student handouts. The illustrations can be posted on the wall during classes as an aid for visual learners and to help bring the stories to life.

B. Four drawings illustrating places and events in the life of Bahá'u'lláh are included with this lesson and can be posted on the walls during the retreat. The pictures are also available in the download packet for ease of photocopying.

Note: These beautiful illustrations were done by John Hollins and appeared in the children's book, *Stories of Bahá'u'lláh as Told by Pokka,* by Betty Reed. The book (ISBN 0 900125 37 3) was published in England by the UK Bahá'í Publishing Trust around 1972.

The book shows no date or copyright information, and despite an extensive search, no record of Mr. Hollins could be found. It was therefore decided to include these drawings with proper credit to the artist, with the hope that he would be pleased to know that a new generation of children would enjoy his work. Any additional information about the artist would be appreciated.

Bahá'u'lláh: The Glory of God – Lesson #1

In addition, many Bahá'í bookstores distribute pictures and postcards of Bahá'í holy places. For black-and-white photos see Balyuzi's book, *Bahá'u'lláh: The King of Glory*. For color photos, check old National Geographic magazines, as well as the following websites:

- www.dejkam.com/iran
- www.travelphotoarchive.com
- www.worldisround.com/articles/17252
- www.trekearth.com/gallery/Middle_East/Iran
- www.destinationiran.com/Iran_Photo_Gallery.htm
- www.pbase.com/k_amj/throughout_iran&page=all
- http://ngm.nationalgeographic.com/2008/08/iran-archaeology/iran-photography

Computer images can be viewed online or arranged into a slide show. Pictures can also be printed out and posted around the room. Plastic page protectors (available at office supply stores) will help preserve the prints.

C. Copy the page of rats (included here) five times on cardstock, and cut along dotted lines to make ten rats. A small red gummed circle (the kind used to reinforce notebook paper holes) can be stuck over each eye for a more sinister looking creature.

D. The boards represent stocks, an old form of punishment, where a person's feet were placed between holes in a board and locked in place (see http://en.wikipedia.org/wiki/Stocks).

\* \* \* \* \*

## LESSON #2

# The Declaration of Bahá'u'lláh

Bahá'u'lláh: The Glory of God – Lesson #2

# The Declaration of Bahá'u'lláh

**Objectives:** Students will be able to:
- Describe the circumstances of Bahá'u'lláh's declaration in the Garden of Ridván.
- Explain His station as the Promised One of all religions.

---

*Before class, prepare all instructional materials on the list at the end of this lesson.*
*Write memory quote neatly on the board with one phrase on each line.*
*Prepare craft activity and orient volunteer assistants.*
*Set up felt board and treasure chest. Distribute student folders.*

---

1. **SONG: "Bahá'u'lláh"** (5 min.)

Have students take out their song sheets and sing along. Ask the music coordinator for assistance if needed.

2. **FELT LESSON: "The Promised One"** (15-20 min.)

Present the felt lesson titled "The Promised One" (see patterns and instructions at the end of this lesson). Then ask three children if they would like to try presenting it without your help in front of the class. They may also wish to volunteer for the children's performance.

3. **MEMORY QUOTE** (5-10 min.)

Have students take out their page of quotations and locate quote #7: *"Verily, I say..."* It should already be written on the board. Help students to memorize the words:

   A. <u>Understanding</u>: Read the quote aloud slowly, then ask students:

- Who said these words? *(Bahá'u'lláh)*
- What does "verily" mean? *(Truly)*
- Who is Bahá'u'lláh talking about and what does He mean?

Verily I say, this is the Day in which mankind can behold the Face, and hear the Voice, of the Promised One.

Bahá'u'lláh

*(Bahá'u'lláh is saying that He is the Promised One. This was not a vision, a dream, or some future event. People could actually see Him and hear Him.)*

   B. <u>Repetition</u>: Read the quote again slowly and have students repeat after each phrase. Read it again, faster. Then read two phrases at a time as students repeat. (As a memory aid, you can point to your eye when saying the word "behold," and cup your hand behind your ear when saying "hear.")

Bahá'í Children's Classes and Retreats: Theme 4, p. 36

Bahá'u'lláh: The Glory of God – Lesson #2

C. **Backwards Buildup:** Read the last phrase and have students repeat it until it is memorized. Then add the previous phrase and read through to the end. Continue in this manner until you have reached the beginning. By that time, most children should have the entire passage memorized.

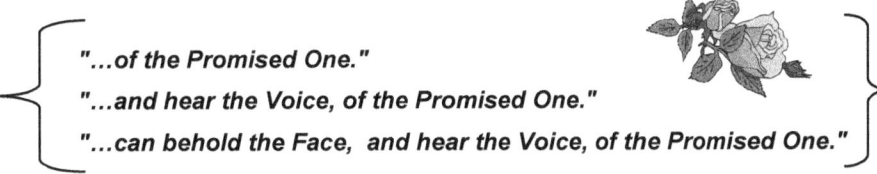

> "...of the Promised One."
> "...and hear the Voice, of the Promised One."
> "...can behold the Face, and hear the Voice, of the Promised One."

D. **Disappearing Act:** Then, using an eraser, swipe a diagonal path through the entire passage. This will leave a blank space on each line. Ask for student volunteers to read the passage again. Let everyone take a turn. Then make another eraser swipe and ask for another round of volunteers. Continue until the passage has completely disappeared.

E. **Recitation:** Ask for student volunteers to close their eyes and recite the quote from memory. Call on the most capable ones first so they can serve as models.

> *Tell students they can work with a friend to memorize other quotes for the performance. Encourage them to memorize additional passages after returning home.*

## 4. DECLARATION STORY (15-20 min.)

A. Have children take out their story packets and turn to "The Declaration of Bahá'u'lláh" just after story #8. Remind them that when Bahá'u'lláh first received His mission in the Síyáh-Chál, he saw a beautiful Maid of Heaven. She pointed to Him and called Him "God's Treasure," but it wasn't time to tell people yet.

*Show the children a small treasure box filled with "jewels." Open the lid so the children can see, and allow some of the jewels to spill out. Then close it again. Explain that the treasure is still there, but it was hidden until Bahá'u'lláh declared. That's when He told people He was a Messenger of God.*

Ask: "Why do you think Bahá'u'lláh was called God's Treasure? Was it for His earthly riches?"

*(For His life and teachings. The Word of God is worth more than all the riches in the world.)*

B. Call on youth volunteers or capable students to read each paragraph aloud. Then have the reader make up one or two questions about that paragraph and call on other children to answer. Have the children raise their hands.

After the paragraph which ends, "Now it was time to tell His friends the good news" (illustrated by stars), open the treasure chest and hold up the jewels.

Bahá'u'lláh: The Glory of God – Lesson #2

## 5. SONG: "Can't You See the New Day" (5 min.)

> *Collect student folders.*

## 6. CRAFT ACTIVITY CENTERS (45-90 min.)

These activities (see instructions on following pages) are designed to reinforce the material presented during class For a weekend retreat, there may only be time for one or two craft activities. For an ongoing class, you might try a different craft each time. When students have completed a project, they should clean up their work area and assist others who may need help.

The "Dream of Many Fish" mobile has multiple steps and long instructions, but is not as complicated as it looks and is well worth the effort. The simpler version (using pipe cleaners and a standing base) should take less than an hour. The more challenging version (using a hanger and string) may take 90 minutes or more.

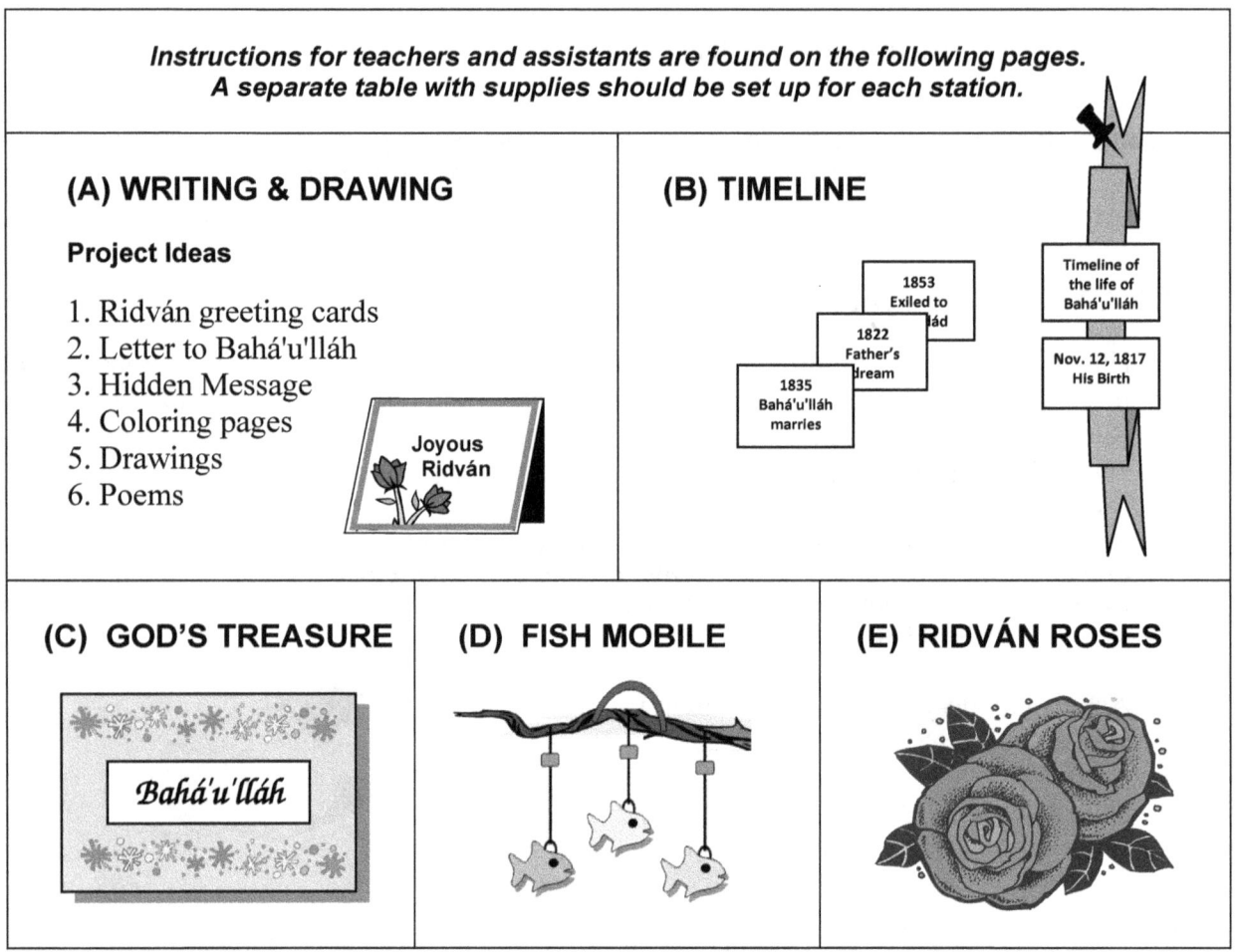

*Instructions for teachers and assistants are found on the following pages.
A separate table with supplies should be set up for each station.*

**(A) WRITING & DRAWING**

**Project Ideas**

1. Ridván greeting cards
2. Letter to Bahá'u'lláh
3. Hidden Message
4. Coloring pages
5. Drawings
6. Poems

**(B) TIMELINE**

Timeline of the life of Bahá'u'lláh
- Nov. 12, 1817 His Birth
- 1835 Bahá'u'lláh marries
- 1822 Father's dream
- 1853 Exiled to Baghdád

**(C) GOD'S TREASURE**

**(D) FISH MOBILE**

**(E) RIDVÁN ROSES**

*After the craft activities, dismiss the children for lunch and quiet time.*

★ ★ ★ ★ ★

Bahá'u'lláh: The Glory of God – Lesson #2

# (A) WRITING & DRAWING

These activities are designed to reinforce the material presented during class. When children have completed a project and cleaned up their work area, they may assist others who need help. Let students know that, out of respect, we do not draw pictures of Bahá'u'lláh or any of the other Manifestations of God. Remind them to label all projects with their names. Quiet music can be played in the background if desired.

## Project Ideas

1. Ridván greeting cards
2. Letter to Bahá'u'lláh
3. Decode Hidden Message (below)
4. Coloring pages
5. Student drawings, for example:

   - Fish from the dream of Bahá'u'lláh's father
   - Chains and rats from the Black Pit
   - The Ridván Garden

6. Student poems

## Materials Needed

- Paper (card stock, parchment or other fancy paper will add a special touch)
- Notebook paper (for writing letters or poems)
- Hidden Message ("Bahá'u'lláh declared in the Garden of Ridván")
- Coloring pages (the Prison at Akká; the Shrine of Bahá'u'lláh – included below)*
- Postcards or photos of the Prison and the Shrine (to serve as models)
- Rulers, pencils, pens, erasers, crayons, markers
- Construction paper, scissors, glue sticks
- Colorful stickers with appropriate designs
- Rubber stamps and stamp pad (optional)

\* Coloring pages are available online as part of the download packet for this teacher's guide: www.UnityWorksStore.com > Children's Classes > student handouts.

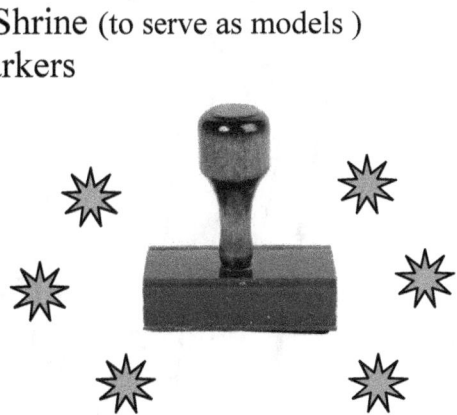

**Bahá'u'lláh: The Glory of God – Lesson #2**

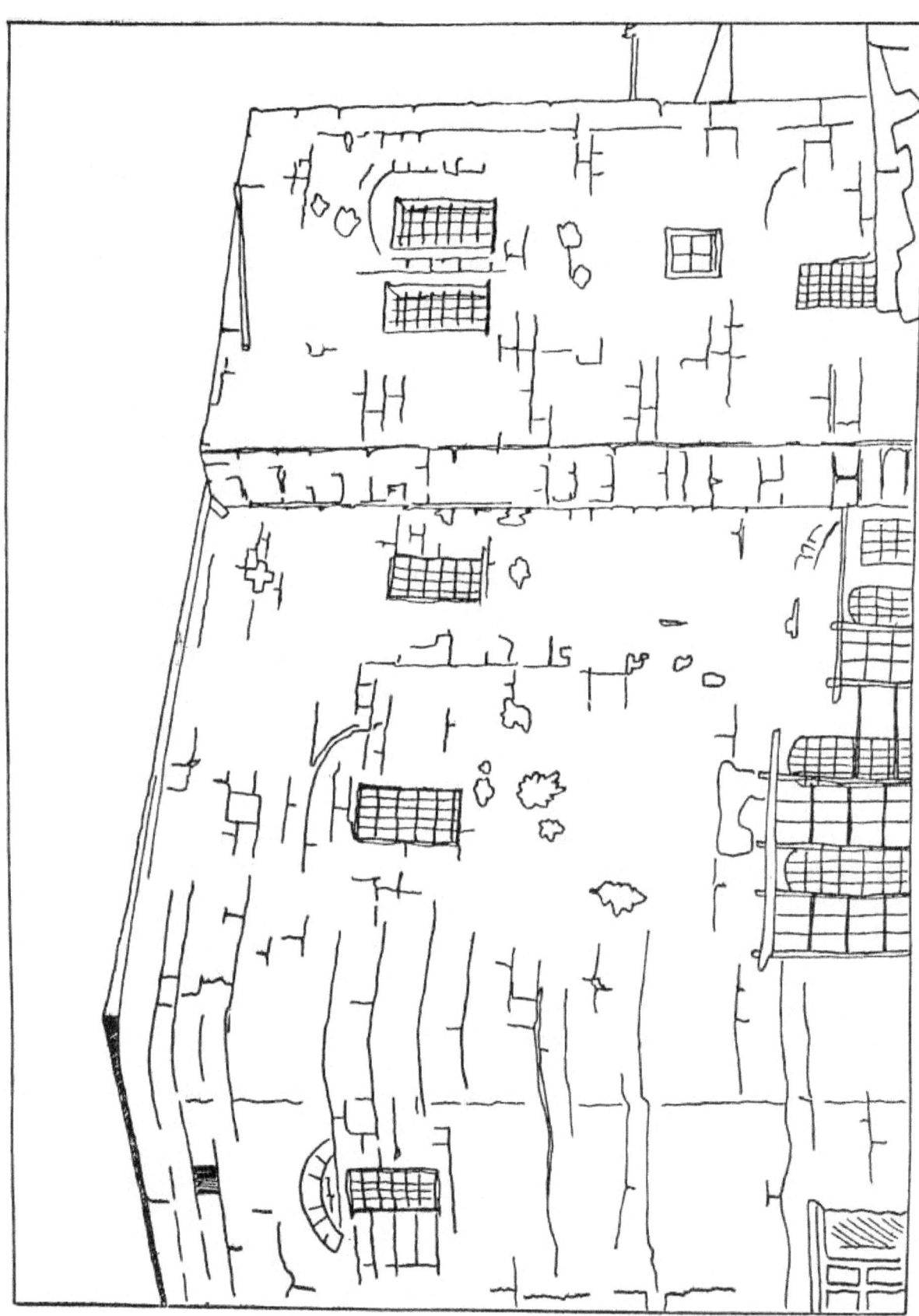

The Prison at Akká. Drawing by Dorrine Sadilek, from *A Bahá'í Coloring Book*, compiled by Evelyn Musacchia. (c) NSA of the Bahá'ís of the Hawaiian Islands. Used with permission.

Bahá'u'lláh: The Glory of God – Lesson #2

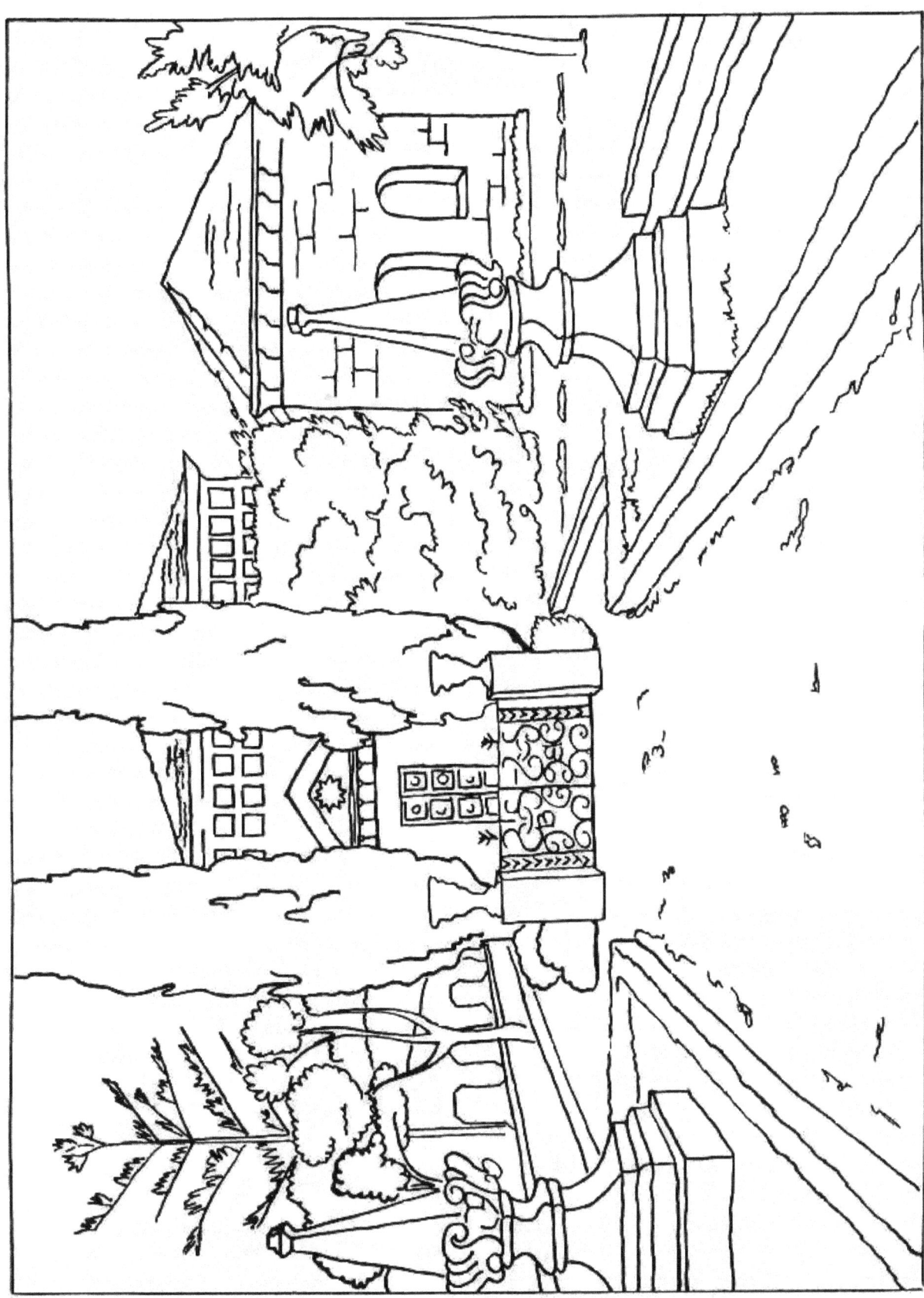

Bahá'í Children's Classes and Retreats: Theme 4, p. 41

Bahá'u'lláh: The Glory of God – Lesson #2

# Hidden Message *by Cathy Weber*

Bahá'u'lláh did not tell anyone who He was for ten years. Then the time came, in 1863, for Him to be exiled again, this time to Constantinople. He gathered His friends and went to an island in the river. They stayed in a garden called the "Garden of Ridván." For twelve days He disclosed that He was the Messenger of God for this day. We celebrate this time as the Festival of Ridván, from April 21st to May 2nd every year.

Here is a hidden message for you to solve about this special time. After you solve this, you can invent a hidden message that you can use to tell someone else about Bahá'u'lláh.

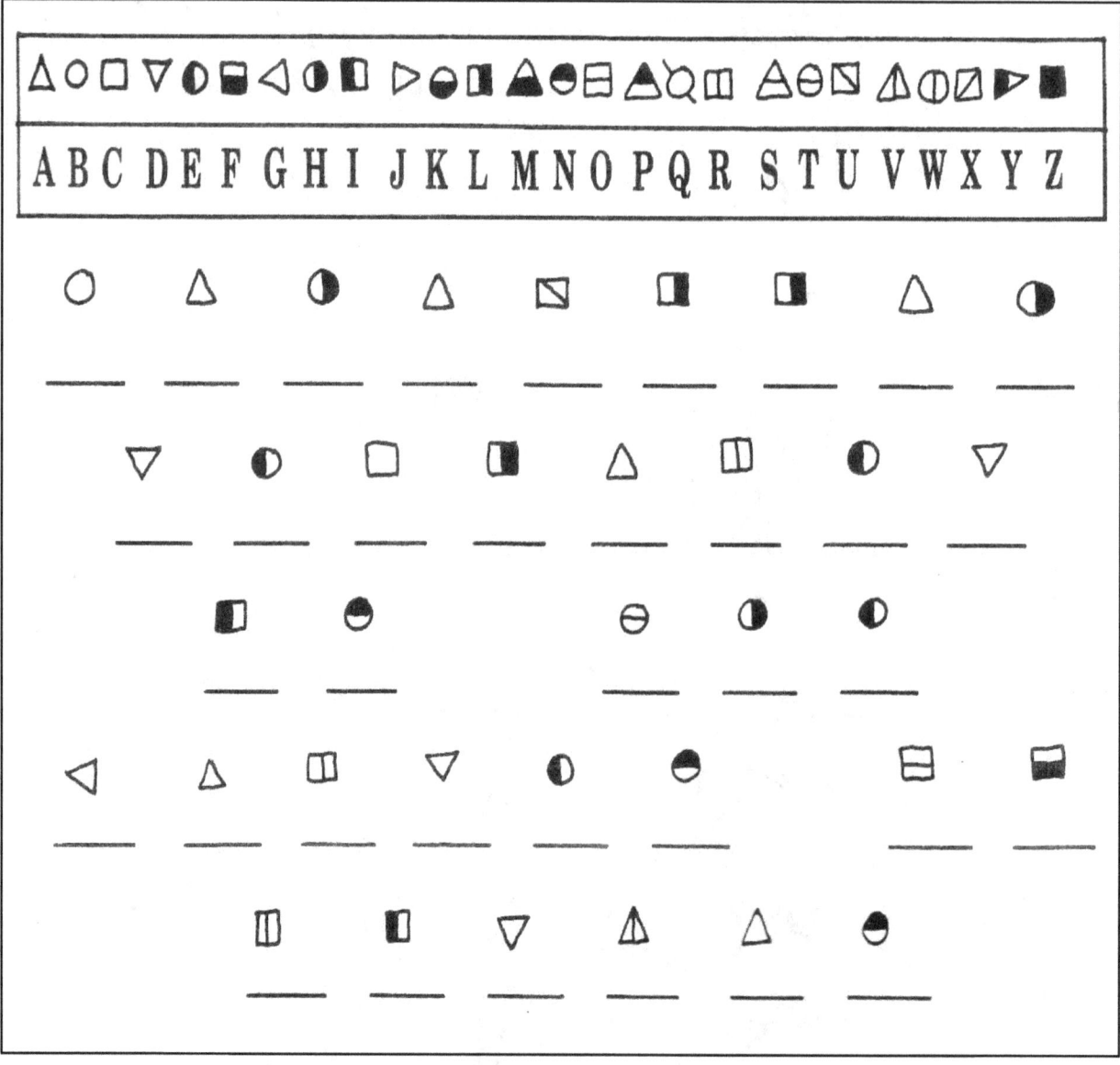

From *Brilliant Star*, Special Edition 1991, p. 26. Used with permission.

Bahá'u'lláh: The Glory of God – Lesson #2

# (B) TIMELINE OF BAHÁ'U'LLÁH'S LIFE

Adapted with permission from *Brilliant Star*, Special Edition 1991, p. 16-17

These activities are designed to reinforce the material presented during class. When children have completed a project and cleaned up their work area, they may assist others who need help. Remind them to label all projects with their names. Quiet music can be played in the background if desired.

## Materials Needed

- Scissors
- One page of timeline cards for each child
- Colored pencils or crayons
- Approximately 1 yard (1 meter) of ribbon for each timeline (about 1¼ inches or 3 cm. wide)
- White craft glue or glue sticks
- Push pins and bulletin board for displaying timelines

## Instructions

1. Color and cut out the cards on the next page.
2. Cut a piece of ribbon about 1 yard (1 meter) long.
3. Trim the ends of the ribbon with the point facing in.
4. Arrange the timeline cards in order by date.
5. Starting with the title, glue each card to the rough side of the ribbon from top to bottom.
6. Allow glue to dry.

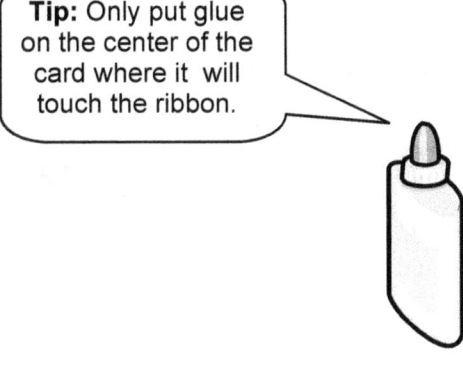

**Tip:** Only put glue on the center of the card where it will touch the ribbon.

*Copy the next page onto white cardstock to make one set of cards for each child.*

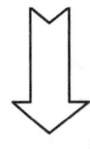

Bahá'u'lláh: The Glory of God – Lesson #2

*"Remember My days during thy days…"* Bahá'u'lláh

| | | |
|---|---|---|
| **Timeline of the life of Bahá'u'lláh** | Nov. 12 **1817** Bahá'u'lláh is born | **~1822** Father's dream of many fish |
| **1835** Bahá'u'lláh marries Navváb | May 23 **1844** 'Abdu'l-Bahá is born | May 23 **1844** The Báb declares |
| **1852** Bahá'u'lláh imprisoned in Síyáh-Chál | **1852** Receives Revelation from Maid of Heaven | **1853** Released from Síyáh-Chál, exiled to Baghdad |
| **1854** Travels to Kurdistan as a hermit | **1856** Returns from Kurdistan to Baghdad | April 21 – May 2 **1863** Declares in Ridván Garden |
| **1863** Exiled to Constantinople, then Adrianople | **1863-1873** Writes letters to kings and rulers | **1868** Banished to prison-city of Akká |
| **1870** Mírzá Midhí dies in fall | **1879** Bahá'u'lláh moves to mansion of Bahjí outside Akká | May 29 **1892** Passing of Bahá'u'lláh |

# (C) GOD'S TREASURE

These activities are designed to reinforce the material presented during class. When children have completed a project and cleaned up their work area, they may assist others who need help. Remind them to label all projects with their names. Quiet music can be played in the background if desired.

## Materials Needed

- Scissors
- Cards with Bahá'u'lláh's name <sup>A</sup>
- Half-squares of peel-and-stick linoleum floor tile <sup>B</sup>
- Glue, glitter-glue or glue sticks
- Glitter, sequins, plastic gemstones <sup>C</sup>

## Instructions

1. Glue Bahá'u'lláh's name onto the linoleum tile.
2. Glue on plastic gems to make a design around His name.
3. Add some glitter-glue to the letters to make them sparkle.

---

**A.** Copy the following page onto cardstock (use white and/or other colors). Cut on dotted lines and give one card to each child. Trim ends if desired.

**B.** Hardware stores often have free samples and inexpensive closeouts. Choose tiles with a solid color or simple background so the gems will stand out. Marble and wood-grain patterns look good. Mark tiles on the back side and cut them in half with a sharp scissors or paper cutter before class. Do not remove the paper backing. When the children return home, the paper can be removed and the tiles mounted on a piece of wood for a more finished look.

**C.** Shiny acrylic gemstones can be found at craft and aquarium supply stores, and sometimes at thrift shops or dollar stores. One side should be flat for gluing to the linoleum.

   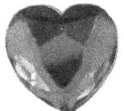

Bahá'u'lláh: The Glory of God – Lesson #2

# Bahá'u'lláh

# Bahá'u'lláh

# Bahá'u'lláh

# Bahá'u'lláh

# Bahá'u'lláh

Bahá'í Children's Classes and Retreats: Theme 4, p. 46

Bahá'u'lláh: The Glory of God – Lesson #2

## Lilita displays her "God's Treasure" craft

"Pointing with her finger unto My head, she addressed all who are in heaven and all who are on earth, saying: By God! This is the Best-Beloved of the worlds, and yet ye comprehend not. This is the Beauty of God amongst you, and the power of His sovereignty within you, could ye but understand. This is the Mystery of God and His <u>Treasure</u>, the Cause of God and His glory unto all who are in the kingdoms of Revelation and of creation, if ye be of them that perceive."

Bahá'u'lláh, *Summons of the Lord of Hosts*, p. 6 (emphasis added)

# (D) CRAFT MOBILE

# "A Dream of Many Fish"

> These activities are designed to reinforce the material presented during class. When children have completed a project and cleaned up their work area, they may assist others who need help. Remind them to label all projects with their names. Quiet music can be played in the background if desired.

## Materials

- Fish patterns (included below)
- Pens (for tracing patterns)
- Craft foam sheets* (for making 6-8 fish per child)
- Sharp scissors (one pair for every 2 children)
- Large paper clips (to hold fish halves together when cutting)
- Small paper clips (to make fish hooks; plastic-coated or metal; 6-8 per child)
- Glue sticks (one for every 2 children)
- Pipe cleaners* (approx. 6-8 per child—for an easier project) or
- Spool of light blue cotton crochet string
  (10 ft. or 3 meters per child—for a more challenging project)
- Plastic "pony" beads or other craft beads for decoration*
- Material to make fish eyes (e.g., self-adhesive craft rhinestones, white round stick-on hole reinforcers, or "googly" craft eyes)
- Small paper cups to hold beads, fish eyes, paper clips, etc. (one per child)
- Materials for base or hanger (see "Attaching Fish to a Base" below)

    * In an assortment of colors

**Tip:** Do not use sticky-back foam as it is harder to work with for this project.

## Optional Materials

- Permanent marker (for drawing eyes and scales on fish)
- Craft paste or tacky glue (for gluing on beads for eyes)
- Shells with a small hole (e.g., from an old shell necklace) for threading onto the crochet string (for decoration)
- Spool of royal blue curling ribbon (for decoration)

Bahá'u'lláh: The Glory of God – Lesson #2

## Teacher Preparation

1. Make fish patterns by tracing fish onto tag board or stiff vinyl placemat, then cutting out. (Make one set of patterns for every 4-5 children.)

2. Using a paper cutter or scissors, cut rectangles from different colors of craft foam.
   - Make the rectangles a little larger than the largest fish pattern.
   - Cut two rectangles for each fish needed (6-8 fish per child).

3. Set up clamps or vise grips to hold fish hangers in place while attaching lines.

4. Cover work surface with a tarp, and set out small containers on each table with foam rectangles, paper clips, beads, stickers, and other small parts, along with glue sticks, pens, patterns and scissors.

*Pipe cleaners or string for fishing line will be distributed later, depending on the interest and ability of each child.*

## Making the Fish

1. Select two foam rectangles of the same color. Place one on top of the other, and trace a fish pattern on the top piece.

2. Hold both pieces of foam together with a large paper clip, and using a pen, make a small dot on the outside of each piece.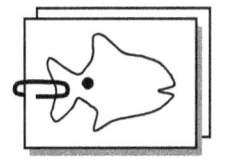

3. Cut out fish along the lines, cutting through both layers at once. *(Each layer will become one side of the fish.)*

4. Repeat steps 1-3 to make five or six whole fish, using a different color for each if desired.

5. Fold open a small paper clip and flatten to make a hook for each fish.

6. Then take the first fish and cover the entire "dot side" of each half with glue, all the way to the edge.

7. Make a "fish sandwich" by carefully matching up the two fish halves, with the hook in the middle as shown. *(The dots should be on the inside.)*

8. Press the glued sides together to make a whole fish (see below). Repeat for each fish.

Alignment of small paper clip

9. Add eyes to both sides of each fish. In order of difficulty, eyes can be:

   a. **Drawn on** (using permanent marker; easiest)
   b. **Stuck on** (hole reinforcers, self-stick gemstones or "googly" eyes)
   c. **Glued on** (beads, sequins, small circles of craft foam)
   d. **Sewn on** (see directions below)

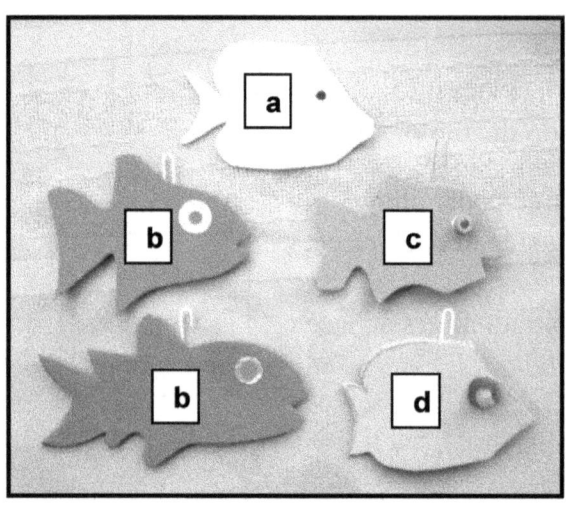

**To sew on eyes**
- Using a large open paper clip, poke a hole through the fish where the eye should be.
- Thread a 2-in. (5 cm.) length of pipe cleaner through the hole. (Pipe cleaner can easily be cut with scissors.)
- Slide a small bead onto each end of the pipe cleaner, and curl the ends back to lock beads in place.

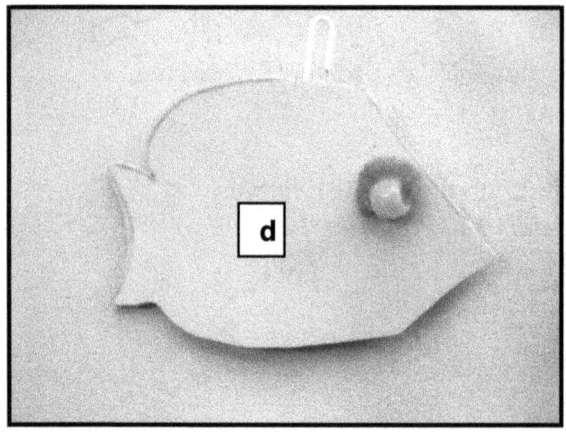

## Making the Fishing Line

1. Attach each fish to the end of a "fishing line" made out of pipe cleaner or string. Pipe cleaners are easier to use, especially for younger children.

   a. <u>Pipe cleaners</u>: Use pipe cleaners that are folded or cut in half, for attaching to a standing base. *(Whole pipe cleaners are too long to support the weight of the fish.)*

   b. <u>String</u>: Use strings cut to the same length (approx. 18 in. or 45 cm.) for attaching to a hanging mobile.

2. Add beads or shells to the "fishing line" for decoration if desired.

**Loop the string back through the bead to hold it in place.**

## Attaching Fish to a Base or Hanger

1. <u>Standing base</u> (easier)
   A standing base can be made from Styrofoam, modeling clay or other suitable material with a flat bottom. We have used inexpensive plastic ashtrays, each filled with a plastic mesh scouring pad (found at the discount store). Stick pipe cleaners into the mesh pad to hold them in place. Use masking tape to add the child's name to the bottom of the base.

2. <u>Hanger</u> (more challenging)
   Use an embroidery hoop or small tree branch (approx. 12 in. or 30 cm. long) as a hanger. Hold the hanger in a vise or clamp for stability while working.

   a. Attach fish by tying the "fishing line" around the hanger.
   b. Adjust spacing of fish so the mobile is balanced.
   c. Adjust the length of each line by wrapping the excess around the hanger.
   *(For a neater finish, cover the cut end of the string when wrapping.)*
   d. Attach another piece of string or pipe cleaner to the top for hanging the mobile.
   e. Add curly blue ribbon streamers if desired, to represent the ocean waves.

**Standing base**

Bahá'u'lláh: The Glory of God – Lesson #2

## Variations on a Theme

One ring of an embroidery hoop makes an excellent hanger for the fish mobile. The hoop can be hung from the wall or the ceiling.

**Ruby and Emily with their fish creations.**

Bahá'u'lláh: The Glory of God – Lesson #2

# Patterns for "A Dream of Many Fish" – Craft Mobile

*Cut patterns out of tag board or stiff vinyl placemat material.
Children will trace around the patterns and cut fish out of craft foam.*

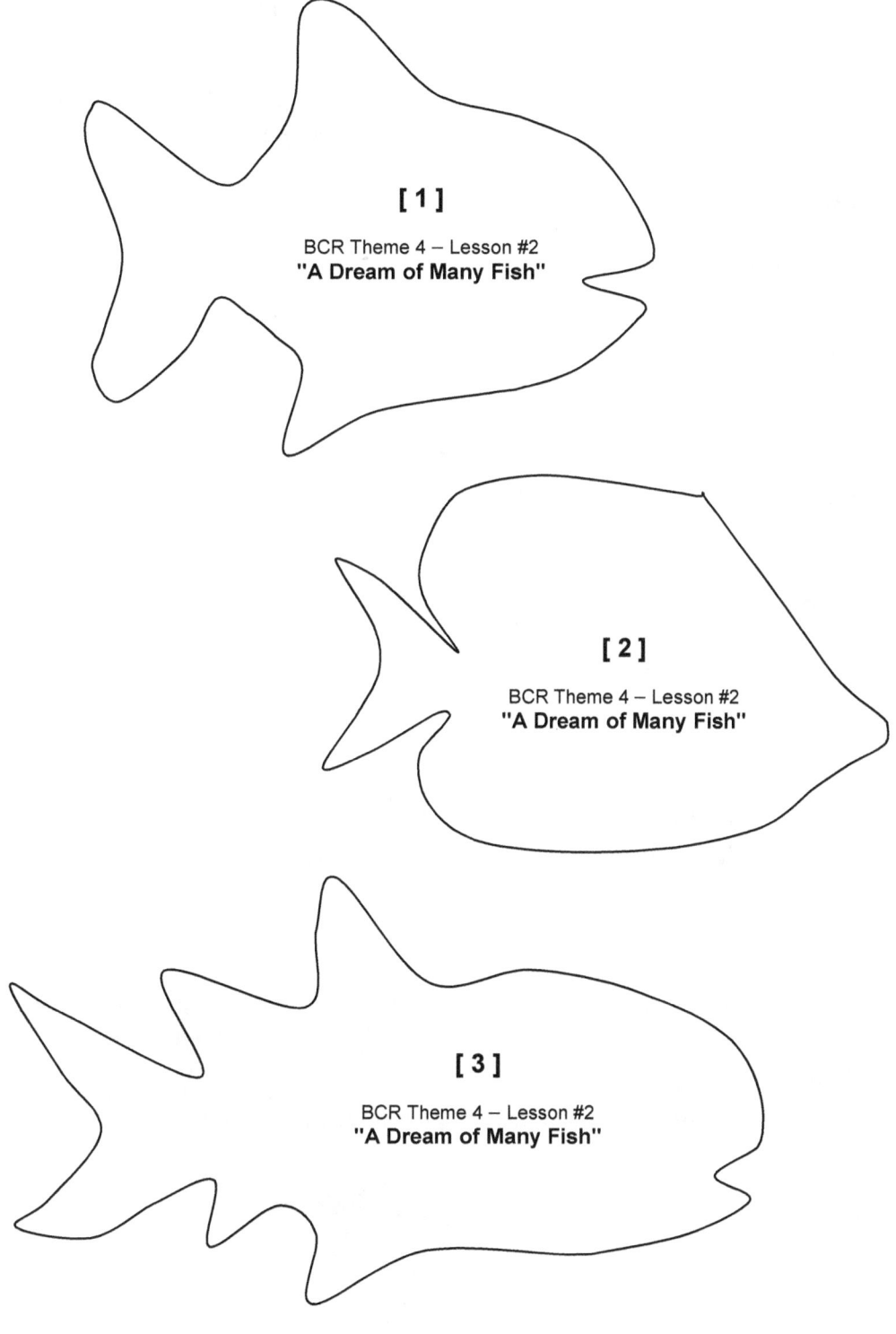

**[ 1 ]**
BCR Theme 4 – Lesson #2
**"A Dream of Many Fish"**

**[ 2 ]**
BCR Theme 4 – Lesson #2
**"A Dream of Many Fish"**

**[ 3 ]**
BCR Theme 4 – Lesson #2
**"A Dream of Many Fish"**

Bahá'u'lláh: The Glory of God – Lesson #2

# (E) RIDVÁN ROSES

These activities are designed to reinforce the material presented during class. When children have completed a project and cleaned up their work area, they may assist others who need help. Remind them to label all projects with their names. Quiet music can be played in the background if desired.

**Tissue paper roses can be prepared as decorations for the children's performance54. See illustrations on following page.**

## Materials

- Large sheets of tissue paper (red, pink or other rose colors)
- Small plate, circular lid or pattern to trace around (4-5 in. or 10-12 cm. in diameter)
- Awl or large needle (for poking holes in the paper)
- Green pipe cleaners (one per flower)
- Pencils for tracing circle
- Large paper clips
- Scissors

## Instructions

1. Fold tissue paper in half again and again until it is just larger than the circle pattern.
2. Draw or trace a circle on the tissue paper. (Larger circles will make larger flowers.)
3. Holding all the layers together with a paper clip, cut out the circle.
   (If too thick to cut, try cutting through half of the layers at a time.)
4. Stack 8-10 of the circles together and carefully poke two holes near the center.
5. Bend the pipe cleaner in half and insert each end through a different hole.
6. Gently pull tight and twist the ends together under the flower to make a stem.
7. Gently separate each circle starting with the top one. Crinkle upwards to form petals.

**For more detailed instructions with clear photo illustrations, see:**
http://foldingtrees.com/2008/08/flower-week-tissue-paper-carnations

**For more realistic looking roses, but a much more challenging project, see:**
http://www.curbly.com/DIY-Maven/posts/802-how-to-fold-a-paper-rose#jump

Bahá'í Children's Classes and Retreats: Theme 4, p. 54

Bahá'u'lláh: The Glory of God – Lesson #2

## Speed Method

1. Fold the tissue paper into a square eight layers thick.
2. Anchor with the pipe cleaner, then cut the circle freehand and open the petals.

**Brighton and his Ridván Rose**

Bahá'í Children's Classes and Retreats: Theme 4, p. 55

Bahá'u'lláh: The Glory of God – Lesson #2

# "The Promised One"

## Teacher's Guide, Script, and Patterns for Felt Lesson

**TO THE TEACHER:** This packet contains a script, instructions, and patterns for making a felt lesson on "The Promised One." In order to present the lesson, you will need either a felt board or carpet board (see instructions on following pages). A carpet board is more durable and has a more finished look. After preparing the board and cutting out the pattern pieces, read through the script and repeat the actions until you can present the lesson smoothly. The objectives of the lesson are listed below.

(1)
**To help children understand the concept of "The Promised One."**

(2)
**To familiarize them with the names of those promised by different religions.**

(3)
**To help them recognize Bahá'u'lláh as the One promised by <u>all</u> religions.**

Bahá'í Children's Classes and Retreats: Theme 4, p. 56

Bahá'u'lláh: The Glory of God – Lesson #2

Script for Felt Lesson

# "The Promised One"

| | NARRATION | ACTION |
|---|---|---|
| 1 | We're going to learn about a special promise made by all of God's Prophets or Messengers. Do you remember some of their names? (Students respond.) That's right. They all promised that a great teacher would come someday to bring peace to the world. Let's learn Who was promised by each Messenger of the past. | Distribute all the cards and arrows, except for the two column headings: "Prophet" and "Promised One." Give the reference chart to one student to refer to as needed. |
| 2 | First, let's review the Prophets. [Prophet] | Place "Prophet" heading in first column on board. |
| 3 | Do you remember which Prophet came first? (Students respond.) Even before that? Who came next? (Refer to chart as needed.) | As each Prophet is named, the child holding that card places it on the felt board in order. |
| 4 | Now let's put the heading in the second column, and an arrow after each Prophet's name. [Promised One] | Place the "Promised One" card in the second column and have students add the arrows. |
| 5 | Does anyone know who Jesus promised would come? That's right! His own return. (Continue in this manner for each Prophet, referring to the chart as necessary.) | Student places the "Return of Christ" card to the right of the arrow. (Etc.) |
| 6 | So we see that each Prophet of God promised that a great teacher would come to bring peace to the whole world. | Point to all the "Promised One" cards covering the board. |
| 7 | What does "pledge" mean? That's right, it means "promise". What does do you think Bahá'u'lláh means when He says: "Lo, the sacred Pledge hath been fulfilled, for He, the Promised One, is come!"* Yes! Bahá'u'lláh is the One promised by all the Prophets of God. (He **is** the Lord of Hosts, the 5th Buddha, etc.) | Place "Bahá'u'lláh" vertically on the felt board, covering the names of all the Promised Ones. |

\* Quoted in Shoghi Effendi, *The World Order of Bahá'u'lláh*, p. 104

| PROPHET | | PROMISED ONE |
|---|---|---|
| Krishna | → | Tenth Avatar |
| Moses | → | Messiah / Lord of Hosts |
| Zoroaster | → | Shah-Bahram |
| Buddha | → | Fifth Buddha |
| Jesus | → | Return of Christ |
| Muhammad | → | Great Announcement |
| The Báb | → | Him Whom God Shall Make Manifest |

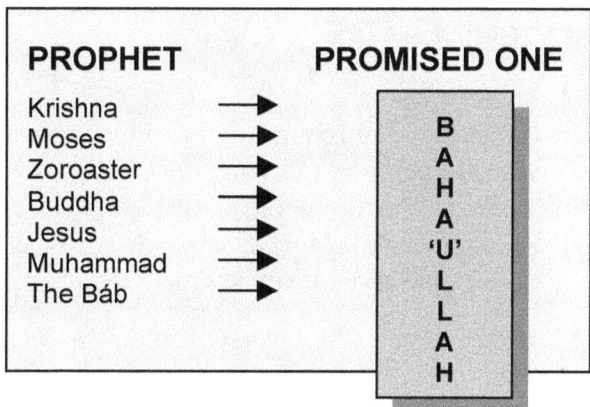

Bahá'í Children's Classes and Retreats: Theme 4, p. 57

Bahá'u'lláh: The Glory of God – Lesson #2

## Additional Activities for Felt Lesson

**Practice A:** Once all the cards have been placed on the board in order, ask students questions about the Prophets, for example: Who did Buddha promise would come? *(The 5th Buddha)* Who promised the Lord of Hosts? *(Moses)* Which Prophet came after Muhammad? *(The Báb)* Students can look at the board to help them answer the questions. Then have students ask similar questions of each other. For an extra challenge, have children answer without looking at the board.

**Practice B:** Redistribute all the cards and let student volunteers arrange them on the board without help. The cards are color-coded to make the task easier. Ask who might like to demonstrate this entire lesson for the children's performance. Make note of their names and have them practice later. (One can do the narration and two can place the cards.)

**Practice C:** Students can draw their own Promised One chart or fill in the blank chart at the end of this lesson..

### Instructions for Making Felt or Carpet Board

A felt board can be purchased at a teacher supply store, or one can be constructed by gluing a large piece of felt onto a stiff backing such as heavy cardboard, thin plywood or masonite. Spray glue gives the best results. A carpet board is constructed in the same way. Felt and glue are available at yardage and craft supply stores.

## MATERIALS

- ❑ Sharp scissors
- ❑ Large piece of felt or indoor-outdoor carpet* (choose beige or other neutral color, approx. 24 x 36 in. or 60 x 90 cm.)
- ❑ Backing board (same size as felt or carpet)
- ❑ Spray glue or white craft glue

\* If using carpet, test a piece of felt to be sure it sticks. Some types of carpeting may work better than others.

Bahá'u'lláh: The Glory of God – Lesson #2

## Instructions for Making Laminated Cards for Felt Lesson on "The Promised One"

This set includes rectangular pattern pieces for seven Prophets and seven Promised Ones. The **Prophet cards** are also found in theme book #2 on *The Manifestation of God* and can be re-used for this lesson. The **Promised One cards** use common names for the One expected by each religion. However, you may wish to prepare alternative cards with more familiar names, (e.g., Maitreya Buddha instead of Fifth Buddha or Qá'im rather than Great Announcement) as appropriate for your region.

### MATERIALS

- Paper cutter or sharp scissors
- Pattern pieces (on following pages)
- Nine different colors of paper (see chart below)
- Clear contact paper or laminating machine
- Stick-on velcro (plastic loop side)

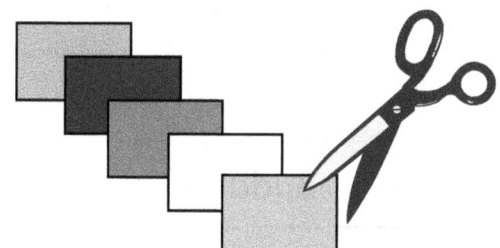

### Laminated Cards

1. Photocopy the pattern pieces onto different colors of paper (see suggested colors below).
2. Carefully cut out each card and laminate.
3. Trim edges, leaving a thin border of plastic, and cut off any sharp corners.
4. Stick a small piece of velcro on the back of each laminated piece, near the top. (Velcro can be found at yardage and craft supply stores.)
5. Store felt pieces with script in a zip-lock plastic bag for ease of use.

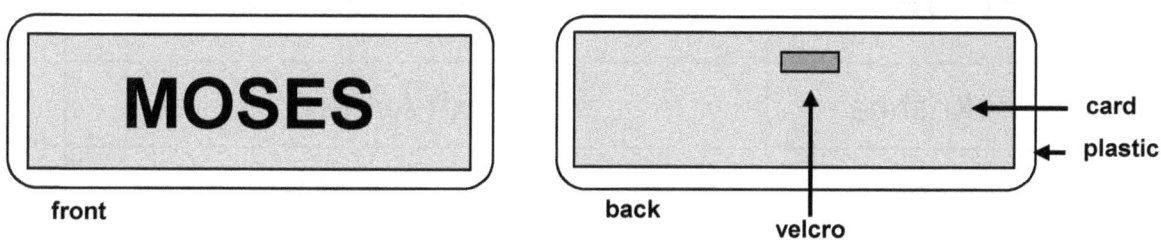

| PROPHET | PROMISED ONE | | CARD COLOR |
|---|---|---|---|
| Krishna | Tenth Avatar | 1 | red |
| Moses | Messiah | 2 | dark orange |
| Zoroaster | Shah-Bahram | 3 | light orange |
| Buddha | Fifth Buddha | 4 | yellow |
| Jesus | Return of Christ | 5 | light green |
| Muhammad | Great Announcement | 6 | dark green |
| The Báb | Him Whom God Shall Make Manifest | 7 | medium blue |
| (Long vertical card) | Bahá'u'lláh | 8 | turquoise |
| (Headings, charts, arrows) | | 9 | light blue |

Bahá'u'lláh: The Glory of God – Lesson #2

**Reference charts for felt lesson on "The Promised One" (color #9)**
(Laminate this page and cut out each chart, leaving a thin plastic border.)

| PROPHET | PROMISED ONE |
|---|---|
| Krishna | Tenth Avatar |
| Moses | Messiah / Lord of Hosts |
| Zoroaster | Shah-Bahram |
| Buddha | Fifth Buddha |
| Jesus | Return of Christ |
| Muhammad | Great Announcement / Qá'im |
| The Báb | Him Whom God Shall Make Manifest |

| PROPHET | PROMISED ONE |
|---|---|
| Krishna | Tenth Avatar |
| Moses | Messiah / Lord of Hosts |
| Zoroaster | Shah-Bahram |
| Buddha | Fifth Buddha |
| Jesus | Return of Christ |
| Muhammad | Great Announcement / Qá'im |
| The Báb | Him Whom God Shall Make Manifest |

Bahá'u'lláh: The Glory of God – Lesson #2

**Headings for felt lesson on "The Promised One" (color #9)**

Bahá'u'lláh: The Glory of God – Lesson #2

**Arrows for felt lesson on "The Promised One" (color #9)**
(A few extras are included as they tend to get lost.)

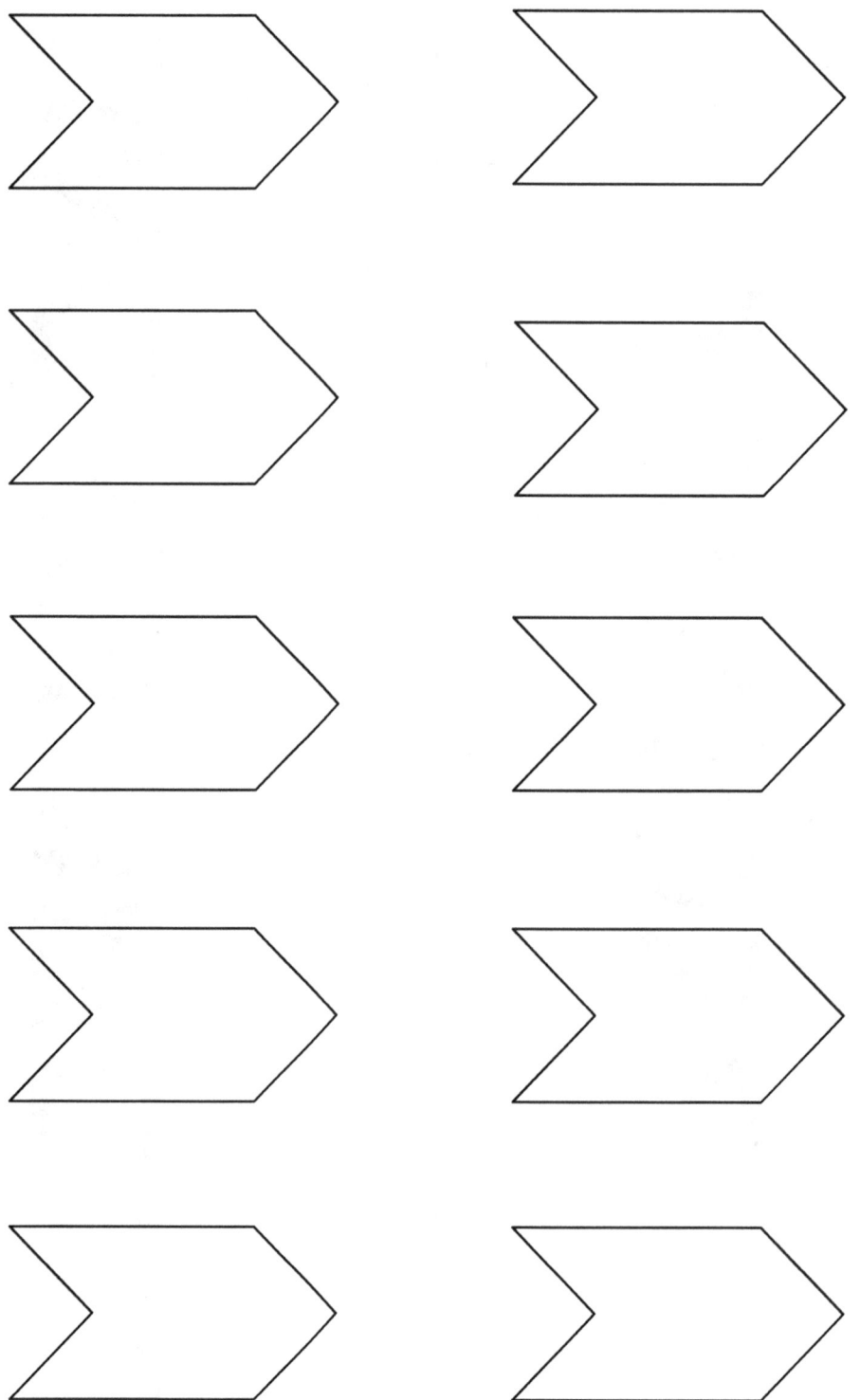

Bahá'u'lláh: The Glory of God – Lesson #2

**Cards for felt lesson on "The Promised One" (color #1)**

Krishna

Tenth Avatar

Bahá'í Children's Classes and Retreats: Theme 4, p. 63

Bahá'u'lláh: The Glory of God – Lesson #2

**Cards for felt lesson on "The Promised One" (color #2)**

# Moses

# Messiah

Bahá'u'lláh: The Glory of God – Lesson #2

**Cards for felt lesson on "The Promised One" (color #3)**

Zoroaster

Shah-Bahram

Bahá'u'lláh: The Glory of God – Lesson #2

**Cards for felt lesson on "The Promised One" (color #4)**

Buddha

Fifth Buddha

Bahá'í Children's Classes and Retreats: Theme 4, p. 66

Bahá'u'lláh: The Glory of God – Lesson #2

**Cards for felt lesson on "The Promised One" (color #5)**

Jesus

Return of Christ

Bahá'í Children's Classes and Retreats: Theme 4, p. 67

Bahá'u'lláh: The Glory of God – Lesson #2

**Cards for felt lesson on "The Promised One" (color #6)**

# Muhammad

# Great Announcement

Bahá'u'lláh: The Glory of God – Lesson #2

**Cards for felt lesson on "The Promised One" (color #7)**

- The Báb
- Him Whom God Shall Make Manifest

Bahá'u'lláh: The Glory of God – Lesson #2

**Patterns and instructions for making Bahá'u'lláh's name for felt lesson on "The Promised One" (color #8)**

## Instructions

1. Copy the following three pages onto full sheets of colored paper.
2. Cut along dotted lines to make three cards.
3. Laminate each card.
4. Line up the cards vertically to form Bahá'u'lláh's name.
5. Using clear, heavy-duty packing tape, connect all three cards together.
6. Trim off excess tape (do not fold tape over cards).
7. On the back of the first card, add a strip of velcro across the top.

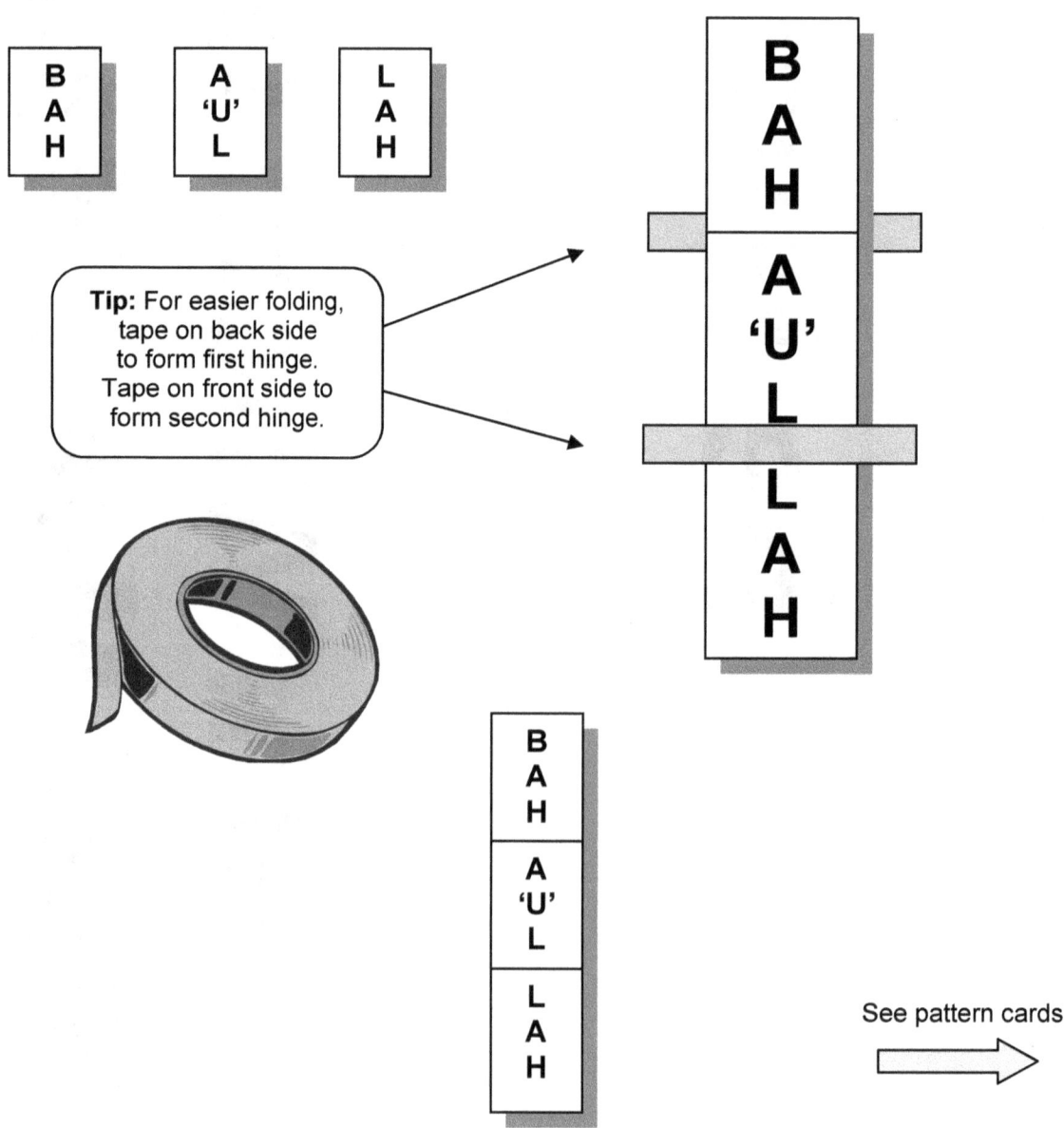

**Tip:** For easier folding, tape on back side to form first hinge. Tape on front side to form second hinge.

See pattern cards ⇨

Bahá'í Children's Classes and Retreats: Theme 4, p. 70

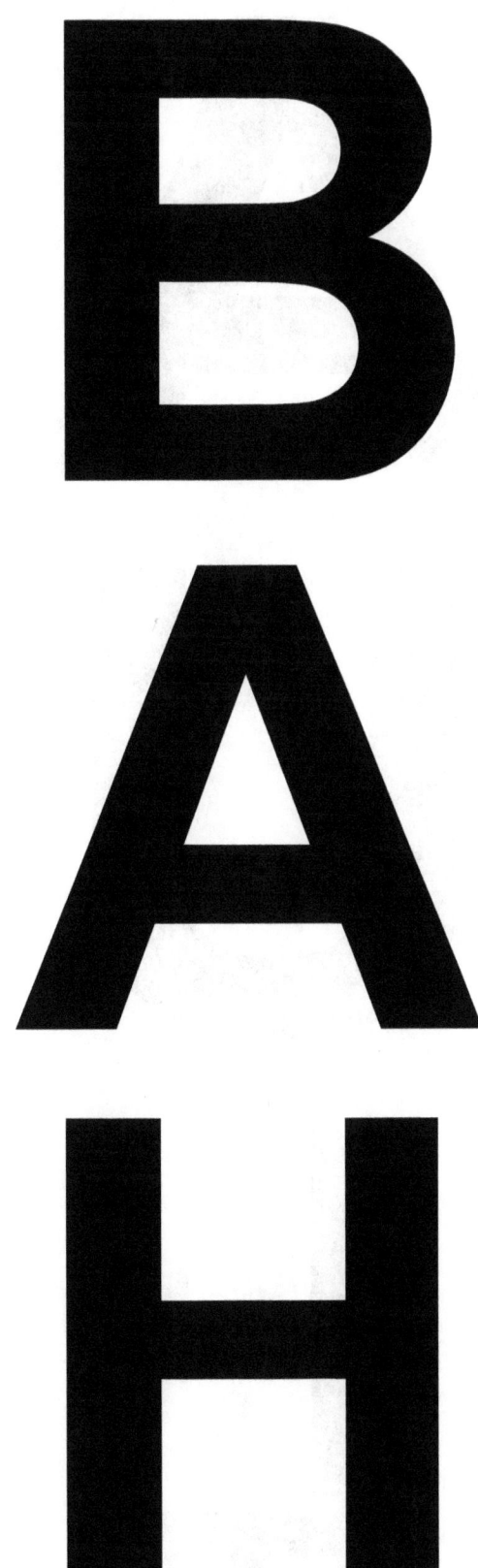

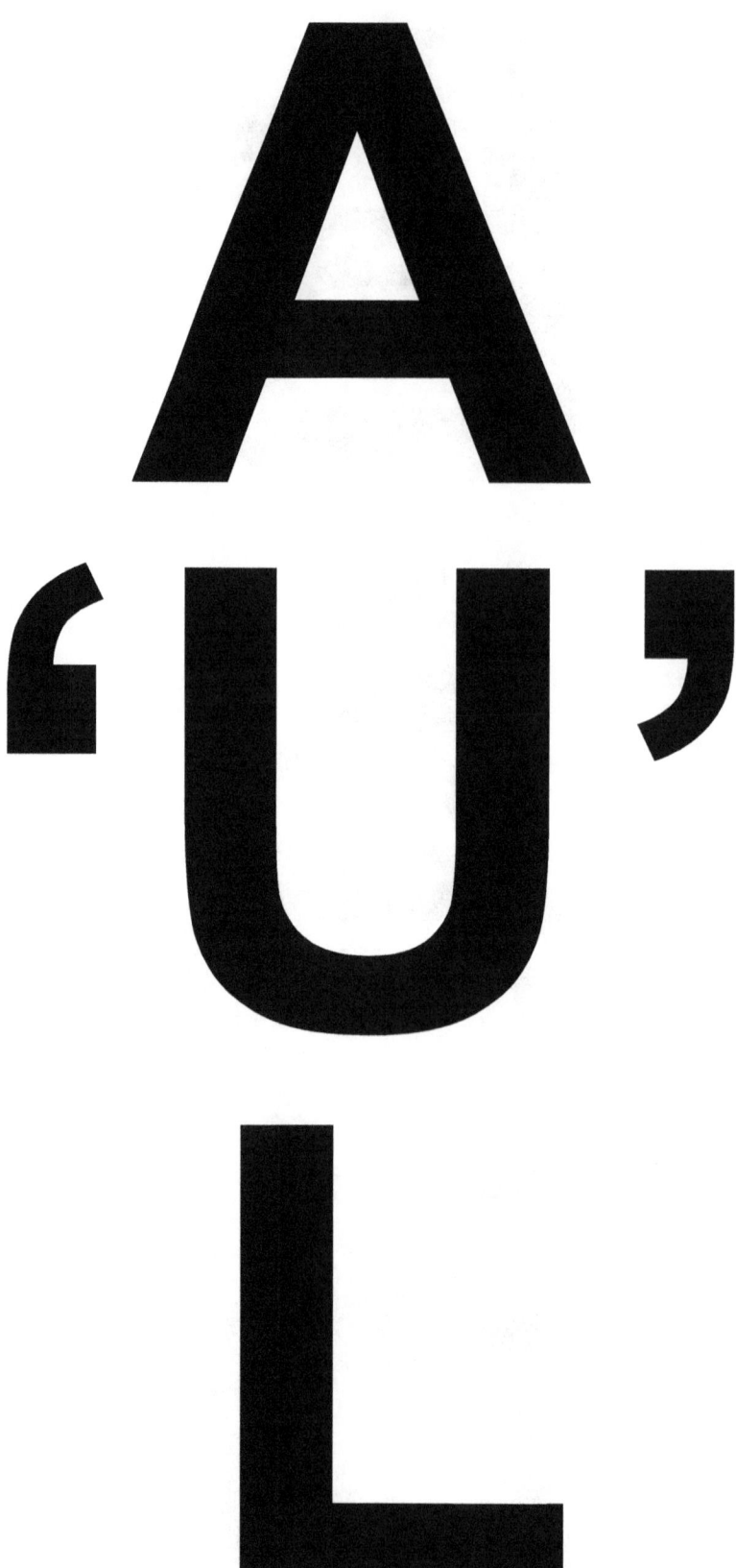

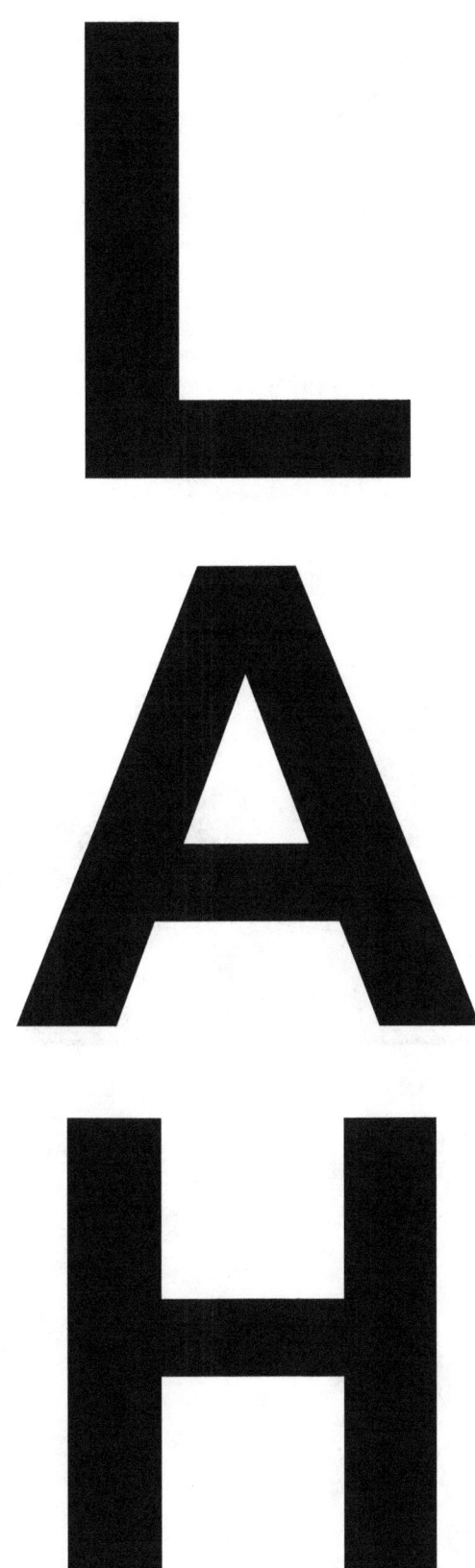

Bahá'u'lláh: The Glory of God – Lesson #2

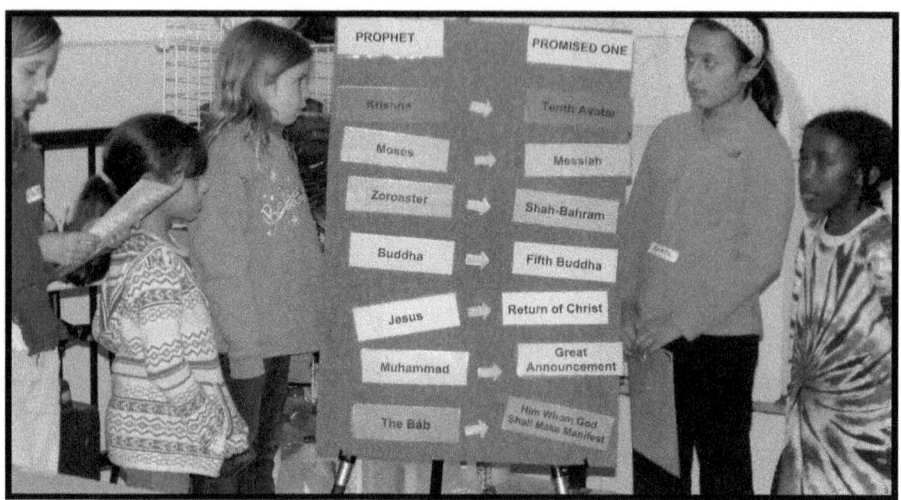

**Shiraz, Lilita, Ruby, Maleka and Emily teach a lesson on "The Promised One."**

Bahá'u'lláh: The Glory of God – Lesson #2    Name _____

# The Promised One

| Prophet | Promised One | Fulfilled |
|---|---|---|
| | ⇒ | |
| | ⇒ | |
| | ⇒ | |
| | ⇒ | |
| | ⇒ | |
| | ⇒ | |
| | ⇒ | |

For Activity #2 – Additional Activities

Bahá'u'lláh: The Glory of God – Lesson #2

# MATERIALS NEEDED

- ☐ White board, easel, markers, eraser
- ☐ Folders for each student
- ☐ Song sheets and page of quotations for each student [A]
- ☐ Handout on "Declaration of Bahá'u'lláh" (from story packet) [A]
- ☐ Dictionary and large world map
- ☐ Felt lesson on "The Promised One" (script and patterns included)
- ☐ Felt board and easel
- ☐ Treasure chest with treasure [B]
- ☐ Materials for craft activities (see separate lists), samples of each project, and page of instructions for the assistant at each station
- ☐ References for teachers (included at the end of this manual)

---

A. Included in the Handouts section of this manual.

B. An inexpensive box and its treasure can usually be found at a thrift shop or discount store. Strands of shiny plastic bead necklaces make excellent "jewels" and are easy to pick up in case of a spill. Fake coins and colored glass aquarium gemstones complete the illusion.

The treasure box should be placed in front of the room on a tall table or stool so it can easily be seen during the lesson. Cover the stool with a beautiful cloth to give it a decorative look.

\* \* \* \* \*

## LESSON #3

# Exiles and Imprisonment

Bahá'u'lláh: The Glory of God – Lesson #3

# Exiles and Imprisonment

**Objectives:** Students will be able to:
- Describe the Most Great Prison, the circumstances of Bahá'u'lláh's incarceration there, and the sacrifice of His son Mírzá Mihdí.
- Trace the path of His exiles.
- List some of His hardships.
- Describe His journey to Baghdad.

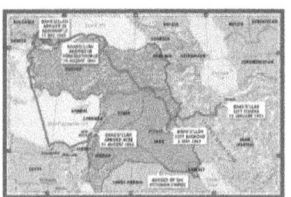

---

*Before class, prepare all instructional materials on the list at the end of this lesson. Set up the "Walk to Baghdad." Post the large map of Bahá'u'lláh's exiles and a photograph of His Shrine. Orient volunteer assistants. Distribute folders and red pens to each participant.*

---

### 1. INTRODUCTORY QUOTE (5 min.)

Have students take out their page of quotations and locate quote #17: *"Remember my days…"* Follow along as one student reads the full quote out loud, twice. Ask questions to help students understand the meaning of the words and encourage them to share their thoughts:

- Who wrote these words?
- What do you think they mean?
- Why does Bahá'u'lláh want us to remember all the things that happened to Him?
- What else does He want us to do?

Remember My days during thy days, and My distress and banishment in this remote prison.

Bahá'u'lláh

### 2. THE MOST GREAT PRISON (15-20 min.)

Have students turn to "The Most Great Prison" in their story packets (3 pages before the quiz). Give each student a small cup of salty water and some stale bread. (An assistant can help.) Explain:

*Hold on to this bread and water for now. Listen carefully to the story, and you will know when to eat and drink.*

Then read the story out loud, alternating paragraphs with an assistant. Point to the large map to show students the path of Bahá'u'lláh's exiles. At the end of the story, show them a picture of His Shrine.

If there is time and interest, have the class read the story aloud once again, each student reading one paragraph. After each paragraph, the reader can ask the other students one or two questions about that paragraph. Children should raise their hands to answer.

*Collect the cups.*

Bahá'í Children's Classes and Retreats: Theme 4, p. 78

Bahá'u'lláh: The Glory of God – Lesson #3

## 3. MAP ACTIVITY (15-20 min.)

A. Distribute the "Exiles of Bahá'u'lláh" map to each child. They should write their names at the bottom of the page.

B. On a large wall map, ask different students to point out the country you are in, then the state or province, then the city. (For example: the United States, Washington State, Yakima.)

C. Then on the large map, ask them to point out the country of Iran and its capital city of Tehran. Explain that this is the city of Bahá'u'lláh's birth and His imprisonment in the Black Pit.

D. Next, have students find the seven dots on their own maps and color them in with the red pen. They should not connect the dots yet.

E. After students have finished coloring the dots, ask: *"What are some of the important stories and events from Bahá'u'lláh's life that happened at point number one?"* A few answers are included below the map. Give children hints if they are uncertain about additional facts. (See story packet and teacher's map for answers.)

F. Have students connect the dots from #1 to #2, and ask: *"What happened at point two?"*

G. Do the same for dots #3 and #7. (There are no details listed for #4–6 as these haven't been studied yet.) Remind children that the line from #3 returns to #2 before going to #4. Bahá'u'lláh declared after returning to point #2.

H. If there is time, students may wish to lightly color in Iran and the countries to which Bahá'u'lláh was exiled.

I. Remind students that Bahá'u'lláh walked much of the way. By exiling Him, His enemies hoped to destroy the Faith of God, but they unintentionally helped it to spread.

*Note: If this activity is part of a longer class for older students, you may wish to leave country names off the map. Students can then look these up and write them in.*

## 4. QUIZ (15-20 min.)

Have students locate the "Quiz on the Life of Bahá'u'lláh" at the end of their story packets. The children should be familiar with the answers to most of the questions from reading through the stories in classes #1 and #2. The quiz serves as a review, and also provides the basis for a quiz show during the children's performance. Ask the questions quickly and have students raise their hands to answer. Repeat the correct answer to reinforce learning. (See the teacher's version at the end of this lesson.)

## 5. REVIEW (5-10 min.)

Divide children into small groups to brainstorm a list of Bahá'u'lláh's hardships and suffering (e.g., all possessions stolen, imprisoned, beaten, chained, rats, hungry, thirsty, cold, poisoned, exiled, son died, watched loved ones suffer). Then ask each group to share one item from their list. Write these on the board. Go around again until all the ideas have been shared.

## 6. SACRIFICE (20-30 min.)

Divide children into small groups and assign a youth or adult volunteer to each group. Give each volunteer a copy of the group questions on "Sacrifice." As group facilitators, they should ask the questions and encourage the children to share their thoughts. Walk around to observe the discussions. Groups can move to another room or outside if desired. Allow 15-20 minutes for them to work.
If there is time, allow an additional 10-15 minutes for groups to report back.

*As an additional activity, older students may wish to discuss and memorize quote #16, "The Ancient Beauty hath consented to be bound with chains..."*

## 7. WALK TO BAGHDAD (45 min.)

Keep children in the same small groups and have group leaders take them on a simulated "Walk to Baghdad." Plan out the route beforehand. (See sample instructions and list of materials on the following pages.) Stagger the trips so that each group leaves about five minutes after the previous one. Remind the children that only five family members accompanied Bahá'u'lláh on His long journey across the mountains.

For those who are waiting, you may wish to play the song "The Prisoner" by England Dan and John Ford Coley (see song sheet). They can also use the time to color in their maps if they haven't already done so. When the children return, they can join in the outdoor activities. The final group can collect the props.

*Note: If you live in an area where it snows, hold this class during the winter and have children walk through the snow for a more realistic experience.*

★ ★ ★ ★ ★

Bahá'u'lláh: The Glory of God – Lesson #3

# Walk to Baghdad

- Take small groups of 4–5 children on walk for activity #7.
- Make sure children use the bathroom beforehand and wash hands.
- Give each child two ice cubes to hold to represent the ice and snow, and an old washcloth to represent the clothes carried by the exiles.

On the way, remind children that when Bahá'u'lláh was released from the Black Pit, He and His wife, two small children, and two other family members walked to Baghdad over the steep, snow-covered mountains in the middle of winter. There were no cars, trains or airplanes to travel in. The journey took three months. They had to leave their baby behind. They were cold and hungry, and Bahá'u'lláh was still sick and weak from having been in prison.

**Sample Route** *(teachers should adapt these instructions to the local setting)*

1. Walk up the road, pass old stone house, and turn left onto gravel path.

2. Walk through "mini forest" behind the house, and pick up a stick to protect against any "wild animals" (the neighbor's dogs).

3. At the top of the hill, look out over the city of "Tehran" and imagine Bahá'u'lláh waving goodbye to family and friends whom He would never see again.

4. At the bottom of the hill, make a U-turn between gravel path and orchard to **bread-making station** at small wooden table.

    a. Have one child clean hands with wet wipes or hand sanitizer.
    b. In the bowl, mix 1 scoop of flour and ½ scoop of salt.
    c. Add a little water to make dough and mix together with the spoon.
    d. After tasting, throw out remaining mixture, clean the bowl and spoon with a paper towel, and put everything back for the next group.

    **(The final group should bring back all the props in the wheelbarrow.)**

5. Turn around and go back out to the gravel path and down the hill.

6. Turn left after 9th row of apple trees (at the Baghdad sign) and go through the orchard towards the Bahá'í Center.

7. Stop halfway through the orchard to offer prayers for a safe journey and feel free to pick an apple for each traveler.

8. Cross the dirt road and continue to the **clothes-washing station**.

    a. Have children take turns washing the old washcloths with soap.
    b. They should use the dipper to bring water from the yellow bucket to the wash basin.
    c. Bring wet cloths back with you as the exiles had no time to dry their clothes.

9. Return to the Bahá'í Center and join the outdoor activities.

Bahá'u'lláh: The Glory of God – Lesson #3

**Materials for Walk to Baghdad**

- Baghdad sign (set up along path)
- Bowl of ice cubes (two per child)
- Washcloths (one per child)
- Plastic bag for used washcloths
- Wheelbarrow to carry props

Randie and Jordan mark the trail.

**Clothes-Washing Station**
- Small table
- Washing basin
- Bucket of water
- Water dipper in bucket
- Bar of soap in soap dish

Chloe washes laundry on the road to Baghdad.

**Bread-Making Station**
- Small table
- Navváb's recipe
- Flour & salt in unmarked containers with lids
- Jar of water
- Mixing bowl & spoon
- Small measuring scoop
- Wet wipes or hand sanitizer
- Paper towels & trash bag

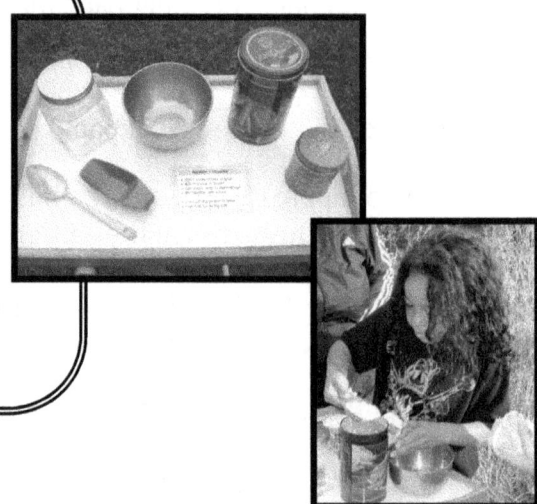

Takanga prepares Navvab's recipe.

Bahá'í Children's Classes and Retreats: Theme 4, p. 82

Bahá'u'lláh: The Glory of God – Lesson #3

# WALK TO BAGHDAD

*Photocopy this sign, add an arrow point, laminate if desired for durability,
and mount on a wooden stick or tack to a tree along the route.*

---

---

*Photocopy this recipe, cut out and laminate. Place on table at bread-making station.*

| Navváb's Mistake |
|---|
| • Add 1 scoop of flour to bowl<br>• Add ½ scoop of "sugar"<br>• Add a little water to make dough<br>• Mix together with spoon |
| • Pinch off tiny pieces to taste<br>• Clean up for next group |

Bahá'í Children's Classes and Retreats: Theme 4, p. 83

Bahá'u'lláh: The Glory of God – Lesson #3

Teacher's version of quiz for activity #2

# Quiz on the Life of Bahá'u'lláh

1. Why does God send us Messengers? *(To teach us about God, and how to live with each other.)*
2. Who was Bahá'u'lláh? *(The Messenger of God for today)*
3. What does "Bahá'u'lláh" mean? *(Glory of God)*
4. What name did His parents give Him? *(Husayn-'Alí)*
5. When and where was He born? *(Nov. 12, 1817, in Iran)*
6. What was Iran called at the time of Bahá'u'lláh? *(Persia)*
7. Was Bahá'u'lláh's family rich or poor? Explain.
   *(Very rich. Father was a nobleman in the court of the king.)*
8. Did Bahá'u'lláh go to school like other children?
   *(No. His teacher sent Him home saying there was nothing he could teach Him.)*
9. Where did His knowledge come from?
   *(God. A Prophet comes to teach people, not to learn from them.)*
10. What was Bahá'u'lláh like as a teenager?
    *(Wise, kind and trustworthy. He cared for the elderly, sick, orphans and the poor.)*
11. What did Bahá'u'lláh's father see in a dream, and what did it mean?
    *(Fish holding His hairs; great leader with many followers.)*
12. What did Bahá'u'lláh see in the puppet show, and what did it mean to Him?
    *(Powerful king ended up in a box; like this world, no permanence in material things.)*
13. What was the name of Bahá'u'lláh's wife, and what was she like?
    *(Navváb was tall, slender, black hair, blue eyes, beautiful, wise, gentle, courteous, queenly.)*
14. Why was Bahá'u'lláh arrested and put in prison? *(Follower of the Báb)*
15. What was the name of the prison and what was it like? *(Síyáh-Chál / Black Pit, awful)*
16. What wonderful thing happened to Bahá'u'lláh in the Black Pit? *(Received His Revelation)*
17. Why did the king of Persia exile Bahá'u'lláh? *(Fearful of growing influence)*
18. What was the journey like from Persia to Baghdad?
    *(3 months on foot, steep mountains, weak from prison, cold, hungry, hand laundry, salty cake)*
19. After reaching Baghdad, why did Bahá'u'lláh go to live in the mountains alone?
    *(To avoid disunity with His brother; to show the Bábís their true leader.)*
20. How long was He gone? *(2 years)*
21. How did Bahá'u'lláh's family find Him again? *(Heard stories of wise hermit.)*
22. How long did Bahá'u'lláh wait before telling people He was God's Messenger? *(10 years)*
23. When and where did He choose to tell them? *(Ridván Garden, outside Baghdad, April 21, 1863)*
24. When and where did the Bahá'í Faith begin? *(Bahá'u'lláh received Revelation in Síyáh-Chál, 1852; announced to followers in Ridván Garden, April 21, 1863)*
25. What does "Ridván" mean? *(Paradise)*
26. What was the Ridván Garden like? *(Paradise, springtime, trees, river, roses, birds)*
27. Compare the Ridván Garden to the Síyáh-Chál. *(Day and night; heaven and hell)*
28. Why is Bahá'u'lláh called the Promised One of all religions? *(He fulfills the promises of every major religion regarding the great Teacher to come: Messiah, Return of Christ, Fifth Buddha, etc.)*
29. When He came, were the people expecting Him? *(The Bábís expected Him Whom God Shall Make Manifest. Other religions also expected someone, but they didn't know it was Bahá'u'lláh.)*
30. What was Bahá'u'lláh's main message? *(He came to bring peace and unity to the world.)*

Bahá'u'lláh: The Glory of God – Lesson #3

Name: _____

# EXILES OF BAHA'U'LLAH

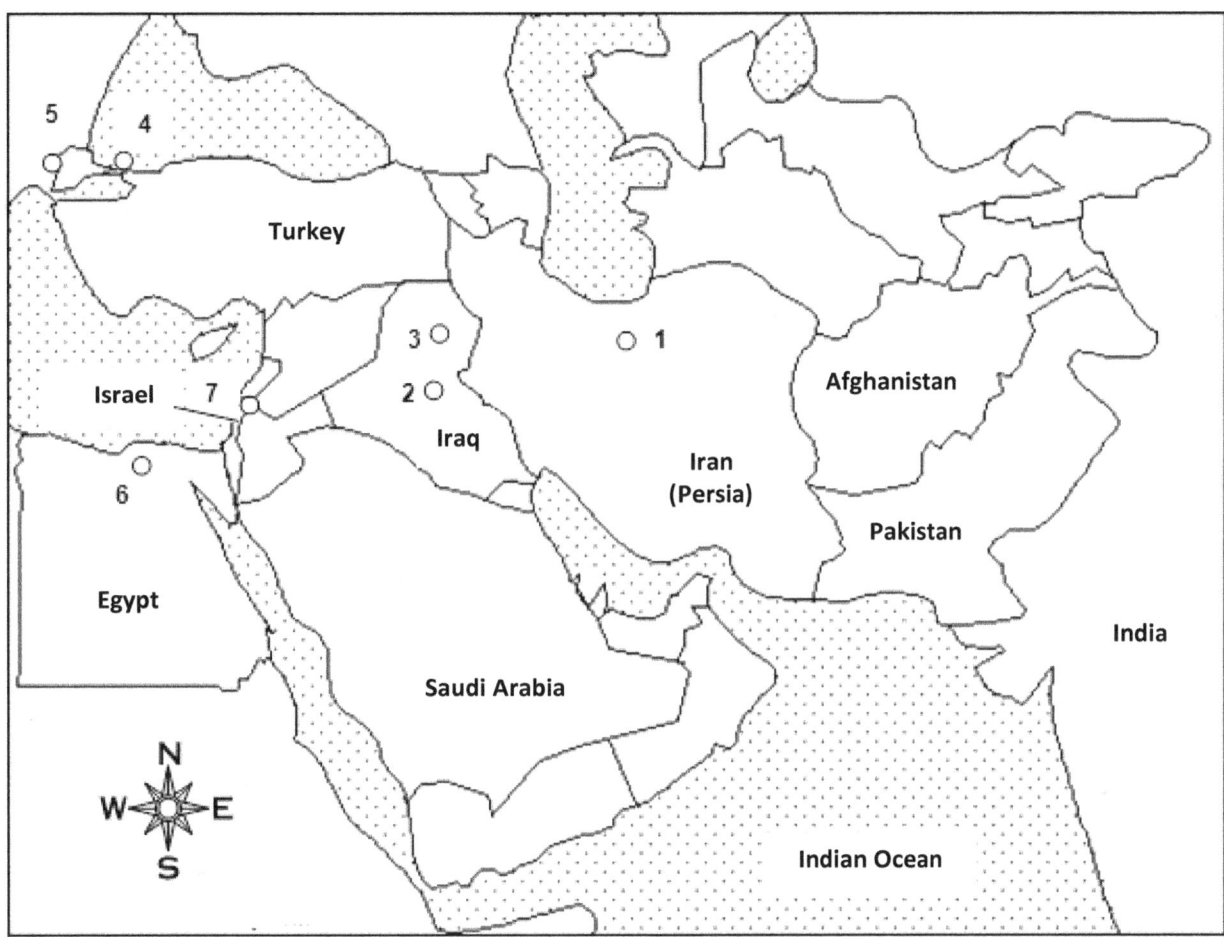

1. Bahá'u'lláh was born in Tehran, Iran (1817)

2. Exiled to Baghdad, Iraq (1853)

3. Lived alone in Kurdistan for two years (1854–1856), before returning to Baghdad

4. Exiled to Constantinople (now called Istanbul) in Turkey (1863)

5. Exiled to Adrianople (now called Edirne) in Turkey (1863–1868)

6. Taken to Alexandria, Egypt, on the way to Akká (1868)

7. Exiled to Akká in Palestine (now Israel) where He was a prisoner for 24 years (1868–1892)

Bahá'u'lláh: The Glory of God – Lesson #3

Teacher's version of map for activity #4

# EXILES OF BAHA'U'LLAH

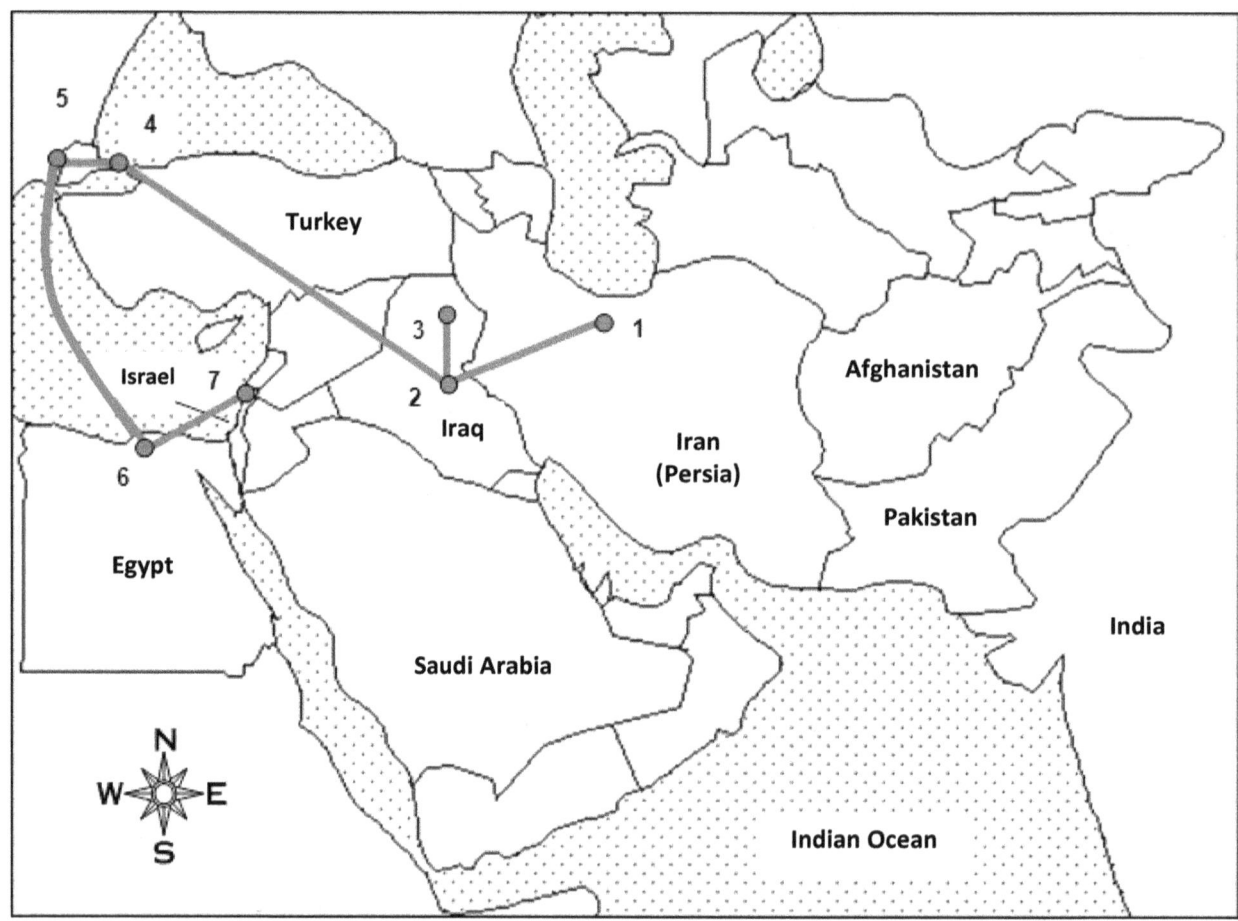

1. Bahá'u'lláh was born in Tehran, Iran (1817) *(Birth, fish dream, puppet show, marriage, children, Father of the Poor, Black Pit, received Revelation)*

2. Exiled to Baghdad, Iraq (1853) *(Winter walk across mountains, salty cake, many visitors, left to avoid disunity. He declared at the end of His second stay there—after point #3.)*

3. Lived alone in Kurdistan for two years (1854–1856), before returning to Baghdad *(Hermit, writing lesson)*

4. Exiled to Constantinople (now called Istanbul) in Turkey (1863)

5. Exiled to Adrianople (now called Edirne) in Turkey (1863–1868)

6. Taken to Alexandria, Egypt, on the way to Akká (1868)

7. Exiled to Akká in Palestine (now Israel) where He was a prisoner for 24 years (1868–1892) *(Waved at pilgrims, Mihdí died 1870, revealed many books, ascended, Shrine)*

Bahá'u'lláh: The Glory of God – Lesson #3

# *Sacrifice*

**Instructions for group leaders for activity #6**

Gather your small group and find a quiet place. You will have about 15 minutes to work. Your job is to ask the questions below and encourage all of the children to share their thoughts. Give hints and encouragement if needed, but don't answer for them. A child who is silent can be asked, "What do you think about this?" Do not allow the children to laugh at or tease each other. Take notes below. If there is time to report back, prepare the group to share a brief summary of their thoughts.

1. Bahá'u'lláh's family was rich, and He could have had an easy life. Why do you think He choose suffering, prison and exile instead? What would you have done?

2. Do you know of any other Prophets of God who have sacrificed or given up something for us?

3. What does the word "sacrifice" mean?

4. Have you ever experienced hardships or willingly made a sacrifice for someone you love?

5. Have you ever been teased, left out, or put down for being a Bahá'í, or for investigating the Faith?

6. How can we show our appreciation and love for Bahá'u'lláh today?

As an additional activity, some students may wish to discuss and memorize quote #16, "The Ancient Beauty hath consented to be bound with chains…"

Bahá'í Children's Classes and Retreats: Theme 4, p. 87

Bahá'u'lláh: The Glory of God – Lesson #3

# Sacrifice

Bahá'u'lláh's family was rich, and He could have had an easy life. The Russian and British governments offered to protect Bahá'u'lláh, but He refused to run away.
Why did He choose suffering, prison and exile instead?

*Sample answers from children during previous classes...*

- So our own hearts could be illumined.
- He accepted the Will of God.
- To give us an example of courage.
- To make our faith stronger.
- It was the only way to bring us the Word of God.
- No one else had the braveness to do it.
- To show that our tests are small by comparison.

**Youth volunteer, Kierra Haug, with her young charges.**

Bahá'í Children's Classes and Retreats: Theme 4, p. 88

Bahá'u'lláh: The Glory of God – Lesson #3

# MATERIALS NEEDED

- ❏ White board, easel, markers, eraser
- ❏ Folder and red pen for each student
- ❏ Dictionary
- ❏ Page of quotations for each student ᴬ
- ❏ Quiz on the Life of Bahá'u'lláh (from story packet) ᴬ
- ❏ Teacher's version of Quiz on the Life of Bahá'u'lláh
- ❏ The Most Great Prison (from story packet) ᴬ
- ❏ Dry bread ᴮ
- ❏ Small cups of salt water ᶜ
- ❏ Postcard or photo of Shrine of Bahá'u'lláh ᴰ
- ❏ Large map of Bahá'u'lláh's exiles ᴱ
- ❏ Exiles map for each student
- ❏ Colored pencils or crayons for coloring the map
- ❏ Teacher's version of exiles map
- ❏ Instructions for group leaders for activity #6 on Sacrifice (one copy for each volunteer)
- ❏ Materials for Walk to Baghdad (see previous pages)
- ❏ "The Prisoner" (optional) song by England Dan and John Ford Coley on the *Lift Up Your Voices* CD, Volume I. Available from: www.bahaibookstore.com. Also available for download from iTunes.
- ❏ References for teachers (included at the end of this manual)

---

A. Included in the Handouts section of this manual.

B. Prepare a bowl of dried bread cubes. Purchase croutons at the grocery store or cut fresh bread into small pieces and dry in a warm oven. Let cool.

C. To make salt water, mix approximately one teaspoon of salt in one cup (250 mL) of water. Pour a few sips of the salt water into a small cup (one per participant, including volunteers) and place cups on a sturdy tray.

D. Some Bahá'í bookstores carry pictures of the Shrine. You can also download it from http://media.bahai.org > Buildings & Places > Holy Places - Acre > Shrine of Bahá'u'lláh, or find it on Google > Images: type in "Shrine of Baha".

E. Bahá'u'lláh's exiles can be traced with a red marker on a large map of the Middle East, which can be posted on the wall.

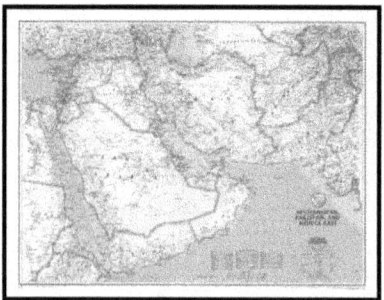

**Poster-size maps can be ordered from:**

- www.allposters.com
- http://shop.nationalgeographic.com

  (Enter "middle east map" in the search box.)

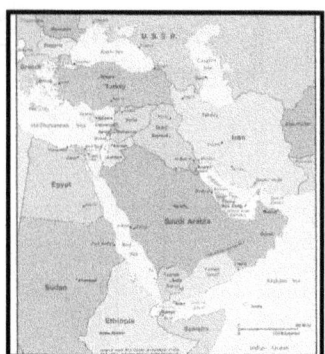

**Outline maps can be printed out or projected:**

- www.lib.utexas.edu/maps

  (Enter "Middle East political" in the search box. Then click on any of the Middle East maps.)

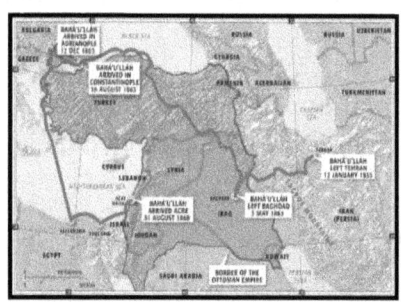

**Smaller maps showing Bahá'u'lláh's exiles can also be found online at:**

- http://bahai-library.com/visuals/travels (click on "printable image")
- http://media.bahai.org/img/ 7143/460/460/nc/Exile%20map2-460.jpg
- http://www.bahai.us/history

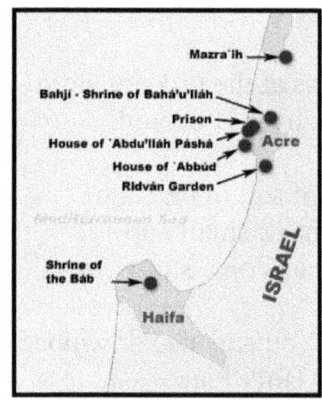

**Wikipedia has a map of Israel showing some of the places visited by Bahá'u'lláh:**

- http://en.wikipedia.org/wiki/Image: BahaiHaifaAkka.png

# LESSON #4

# Clouds of Glory

Bahá'u'lláh: The Glory of God – Lesson #4

# Clouds of Glory

The Shah of Iran

**Objectives:** Students will be able to:
- Explain the spiritual symbolism of clouds.
- List some reasons why people deny the Manifestation of God.
- Summarize Bahá'u'lláh's message to the kings.
- Describe His station as the King of kings.
- Tell someone who Bahá'u'lláh is.

---

*Before class, prepare all instructional materials on the list at the end of this lesson.
Set up craft activity centers. Post photos of the kings and rulers around the room.
Write the memory quote neatly on the board with one phrase on each line.
Orient volunteer assistants. Distribute folders to each participant.*

---

1. **SONG: "Can't You See the New Day"** (3 min.)

Have students take out their song sheets and sing along.
Ask the music coordinator for assistance if needed.

2. **INTRODUCTION** (2 min.)

*Hold up the sun and the cloud and demonstrate as you ask students:*

- If the sun is shining in the sky and a dark cloud passes in front of it, what happens? What if you're looking right at it and can't see it? Is the sun still there?

  *(Yes. Clouds can't stop the sun from shining.)*

- Just as the sun brings light to the physical world, the Messenger of God brings light to our souls. What are some examples of this spiritual light?

  *(Love, truth, justice, unity, knowledge, peace, etc.)*

- If Bahá'u'lláh is like the spiritual sun, what are some examples of spiritual clouds that prevent people from seeing the Light of God?

  *(Example of Mírzá Yahyá and religious leaders: pride, jealousy, prejudice, desire for leadership or power, prior knowledge, blind imitation, no personal investigation.)*

3. **PROCLAMATION TO THE KINGS** (15-20 min.)

   A. Have children take out their story packets and turn to "Proclamation to the Kings" on the next to last page. Remind them of the puppet show that Bahá'u'lláh saw when he was a young boy, and how the king treated people (story #3).

B. Ask for youth or capable student volunteers to read each paragraph. Have them ask the class one or two questions about what they just read. The other students should raise their hands to answer.

C. You should read the section which begins, "Bahá'u'lláh wrote to…." Pronounce the names of the rulers while pointing out the corresponding photos on the wall. You should also read the following paragraph, "Can you imagine…" and ask: *How would a prisoner usually speak to a king? Why? How do you think the kings replied to Bahá'u'lláh?* Then continue with student readers until the end of the story.

## 4. MEMORY QUOTE (5-10 min.)

Have students locate the quote, "*Ye are but vassals…*", at the end of the story on "Proclamation to the Kings." (It is also #5 on their page of quotations and should already be on the board.)

A. **Understanding**: Read the quote aloud slowly, then ask:

- Who said these words? *(Bahá'u'lláh)*
- What does "vassal" mean? *(servant)*
- Who is Bahá'u'lláh talking about and what does He mean?

*(Bahá'u'lláh is saying that He is greater than any earthly king. In comparison, they are like His servants.)*

B. **Repetition**: Read the quote again slowly and have students repeat after each phrase. Read it again, faster. Then read two phrases at a time as students repeat.

C. **Backwards Buildup**: Read the last phrase and have students repeat until it is memorized. Then add the previous phrase and read through to the end. Continue in this manner until you have reached the beginning. By that time, most children should have the entire passage memorized.

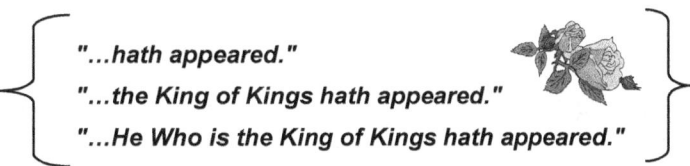

D. **Disappearing Act**: Then, using an eraser, swipe a diagonal path through the entire passage. This will leave a blank space on each line. Ask for student volunteers to read the passage again. Let everyone who wants to take a turn. Then make another eraser swipe and ask for another round of volunteers. Continue until the passage has completely disappeared.

E. **Recitation**: Ask for student volunteers to close their eyes and recite the quote from memory. Call on the most capable ones first so they can serve as models.

Bahá'u'lláh: The Glory of God – Lesson #4

### 5. CLOUDS OF GLORY (20-30 min.)

Explain to the students that they will be working in small groups to share their thoughts about why the kings refused to accept Bahá'u'lláh's message. Divide children into groups of 4-5 and assign a youth or adult volunteer to each group.

Give each volunteer a copy of the "Clouds of Glory" instruction sheet (included at the end of this lesson). As group facilitators, they should ask the questions and encourage the children to share their thoughts. Groups can move to another room or outside if desired. Allow about 15 minutes to work, and walk around to observe their progress. If time allows, call the groups back to share a summary of their discussions.

America, Chloe, Maleka

### 6. REVIEW (10-20 min.)

A. <u>Nine Important Facts</u>: Keeping the same small groups as above, ask each group to develop a list of nine or more important facts about Bahá'u'lláh and His life. Allow about five minutes to work. Reconvene the class and have each group share one fact. Write each fact briefly on the board. Continue in this way until all ideas have been shared. Then praise the students for what they have learned.

B. <u>Who Is Bahá'u'lláh?</u> Act out the following dialogue and have the same small groups prepare an answer. Give students about five minutes to work, then share the responses.

Your friend asks, *"What is a Bahá'í?"* and you say, *"A follower of Bahá'u'lláh."*
Your friend then asks, *"Who is Bahá'u'lláh?"* How do you respond?

**7. CLOSING THOUGHT:** Although Bahá'u'lláh was imprisoned and exiled for over 40 years, His Voice could not be silenced. From a dark underground prison, the Sun of Truth rose to spread the Light of God around the world.

### 8. SONG: "King of Kings" (5 min.)

### 9. CRAFT ACTIVITIES (45 min.)

See instructions for "Salt Dough Sun" and "Spiritual Light Switch" at the end of this lesson. These activities are designed to reinforce the concepts presented during class.

*Although Bahá'u'lláh was imprisoned and exiled for over forty years, His Voice could not be silenced. From a dark underground prison, the Sun of Truth rose to spread the Light of God around the world.*

*After the craft lesson, dismiss the children for outdoor activities.*

Bahá'u'lláh: The Glory of God – Lesson #4

BCR Theme 4 – Lesson #4
Activity #2

# SUN PATTERN

Photocopy onto heavy yellow paper.

Or copy on plain white paper, place copy on top of yellow poster board or construction paper, and cut through outer edge of pattern to make yellow sun.

For a bigger sun, enlarge the image while photocopying.

Bahá'u'lláh: The Glory of God – Lesson #4

**Násiri'd-Dín Sháh of Iran**
Used with permission – The Bettmann Archive

Bahá'u'lláh: The Glory of God – Lesson #4

**Sultán 'Abdu'l-Azíz of Turkey**
Used with permission – The Bettmann Archive

Bahá'í Children's Classes and Retreats: Theme 4, p. 98

Bahá'u'lláh: The Glory of God – Lesson #4

**Queen Victoria of England**
Used with permission – The Bettmann Archive

Bahá'í Children's Classes and Retreats: Theme 4, p. 99

Bahá'u'lláh: The Glory of God – Lesson #4

**Napoleon III of France**
Used with permission – The Bettmann Archive

Bahá'u'lláh: The Glory of God – Lesson #4

### Czar Alexander II of Russia
Used with permission – The Bettmann Archive

Bahá'u'lláh: The Glory of God – Lesson #4

**Kaiser Wilhelm I of Germany**
Used with permission – The Bettmann Archive

Bahá'í Children's Classes and Retreats: Theme 4, p. 102

Bahá'u'lláh: The Glory of God – Lesson #4

Emperor Francis Joseph of Austria
Used with permission – Ewing Galloway

**Pope Pius IX**
Used with permission – Ewing Galloway

Bahá'u'lláh: The Glory of God – Lesson #4

# Clouds of Glory

### Instructions for group leaders for activity #5

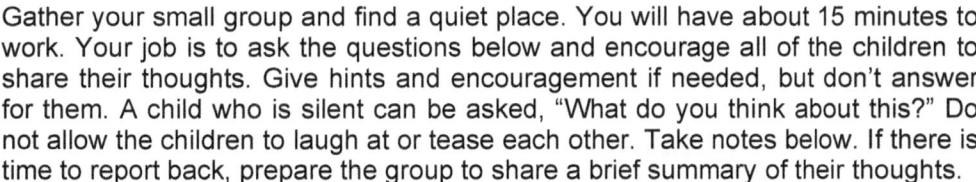

Gather your small group and find a quiet place. You will have about 15 minutes to work. Your job is to ask the questions below and encourage all of the children to share their thoughts. Give hints and encouragement if needed, but don't answer for them. A child who is silent can be asked, "What do you think about this?" Do not allow the children to laugh at or tease each other. Take notes below. If there is time to report back, prepare the group to share a brief summary of their thoughts.

1. Why didn't the kings accept Bahá'u'lláh's message?

2. Why did they deny Bahá'u'lláh and put Him in prison instead?

3. How would the world be different if the kings **had** recognized Bahá'u'lláh as the Messenger of God for today?

4. If all the Prophets of the past said Bahá'u'lláh would come, why didn't the **religious** leaders recognize Him when He finally did come?

5. The Bible says Christ will return in the clouds with great power and glory. What do you think this means? (Ref: Matthew 24:30, Mark 13:26)

Bahá'u'lláh: The Glory of God – Lesson #4

# Salt Dough Sun

**To remind us of Navváb's salty cake and also that Bahá'u'lláh is like the sun**

**Pre-heat oven to 250 degrees F (120 ºC).**

**Materials:** Flour, salt, food coloring, water, powdered alum (optional), vegetable oil (optional), measuring cup, mixing bowl, waxed paper, masking tape, rolling pin, cookie sheet.

**Mix dry ingredients in large bowl**
- 1 cup flour
- ½ cup salt
- 1 tablespoon powdered alum (to keep dough from getting moldy)
- Add color if desired (see box below).

**Add** about 1/3-cup warm water and mix until dough is like stiff putty. (A tablespoon of vegetable oil added to the water will make the dough more pliable and easier to knead.) Do not add too much water or the project won't hold together. Work dough with hands until smooth, then shape into a ball.

**Create**
- Tape waxed paper to a table or countertop for a work surface.
- Roll dough flat with a rolling pin, dowel or the side of a drinking glass.
- Make designs with cookie cutters, plastic knives, forks, toothpicks, straws, etc.

*Children can make a sun or other design of their choice. Remind them that, out of respect, we do not make sculptures or draw pictures of Bahá'u'lláh.*

- Dough can be braided, twisted or coiled.
- To make circles, cut around a small bowl or lid.
- Use the end of a pencil to punch a hole near the top for hanging.
- Children should label all projects with their names.
- Dough can be stored in a plastic container with a tight lid for future use.

**Bake**
About 2 hours at 250 degrees F (120 ºC) until hard, or more time if project is thick. If it starts to turn brown, cover with aluminum foil. When done, turn oven off and let project cool slowly in oven to prevent hairline cracks, or allow to air dry for 2-3 days.

**When dry:** Shellac or varnish with acrylic gloss to seal project for longer life (optional).

**Coloring:** If you want to color the dough, you have several choices:

1. Add a few drops of food coloring to the water before adding to flour mixture.
2. Add powdered Cool-Aid or Jell-O to the flour mixture before adding water.
3. Add natural color: cinnamon, curry, paprika, cocoa powder, instant coffee.
4. After baking, let cool, then color with magic markers or poster paint.

Bahá'u'lláh: The Glory of God – Lesson #4

# Spiritual Light Switch

**To remind us that Bahá'u'lláh has come to bring light to our lives**

Idea from Mrs. Pasha Mohajerjasbi

## Materials

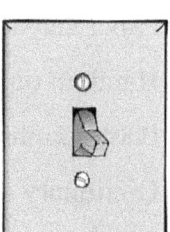

- Light switch covers (one cover for each child)
- Spray can of plastic primer
- Tarp to protect work table
- Fimo or Sculpey clay in a variety of colors*
- Cookie sheet covered with waxed paper
- Clay modeling tools (rolling pins, plastic knives, toothpicks, etc.)
- Polyurethane spray (optional; use only with adequate ventilation)

**Tip:** Before children arrive, spray one coat of plastic primer on the switch covers and let dry. This will prepare the surface so the clay will stick.

## Instructions

- Start with clean hands.
- Pre-heat oven to 250 degrees F (120 °C).  (Do not microwave.)
- Use pre-softened clay (e.g., Fimo or Sculpey) or knead firm clay until soft.
- Press different colors of clay onto the light switch cover to form a design. (Be sure to press firmly or clay pieces may pop off after baking.)
- Bake on cookie sheet at 250 degrees F (120 °C) for 30 minutes to harden clay.
- Let cool gradually in oven to prevent tiny cracks.
- Spray with polyurethane for a hard gloss finish if desired.

---

\* Fimo or Sculpey pre-softened modeling clay is ideal for children, as it is easy to knead and comes in an assortment of bright colors. Additional shades can be created by mixing colors. The clay can be found at craft supply stores and online at the following websites:

www.reuels.com/reuels/page317.html
www.artsuppliesonline.com/catalog.cfm?cata_id=8351
www.theclaystore.com  (or)  www.sculpey.com

Bahá'u'lláh: The Glory of God – Lesson #4

# MATERIALS NEEDED

- ❑ White board, easel, markers, eraser
- ❑ Folders for each student
- ❑ Song sheets and page of quotations for each student [A]
- ❑ Paper sun and cloud (patterns included)
- ❑ Handout on Proclamation to the Kings (from story packet) [A]
- ❑ Photographs of the Kings and Rulers [B]
- ❑ Dictionary and large map
- ❑ Instructions for group leaders for activity #5, Clouds of Glory (one copy per volunteer)
- ❑ Materials for craft activities (see separate lists), sample of each project, and page of instructions for the assistant at each station
- ❑ References for teachers (included at the end of this manual)

---

A. Included in the Handouts section of this manual.

B. Photographs of the Kings and Rulers are used with permission of the National Spiritual Assembly of the Bahá'ís of the United States, courtesy of the Bettmann Archive and Ewing Galloway.

The photos can be downloaded as part of the handout packet for this teacher's guide from: **www.UnityWorksStore.com** > Children's Classes > Bahá'u'lláh: The Glory of God > student handouts.

UnityWorks offers a colorful PowerPoint program on Bahá'u'lláh's tablets to the kings. Download it from: **www.UnityWorksStore.com** > PowerPoint Firesides > Proclamation of Bahá'u'lláh.

For an online version of Bahá'u'lláh's tablets to the kings:
< http://bahai-library.com/writings/bahaullah/pb >.

# Children's Performance

# CHILDREN'S PERFORMANCE*

## To the Coordinator

The children's performance provides students with an opportunity to demonstrate and reinforce what they have learned. This is often the highlight for children and adults. The fact that children will be performing in front of a live audience serves as excellent motivation for them to learn the material presented in class. The program consists of prayers, songs, stories, memorized passages, demonstrations to illustrate various concepts, a showing of crafts, a quiz show and a short play. The following pages include a detailed agenda for the event, rehearsal instructions, scripts and other materials. Feel free to modify the program to suit the needs of the participants.

As the coordinator, it will be helpful for you to sit in on classes and take notes on which children might be best suited for which type of presentation. Some will memorize quotes easily, others may be good at explaining a concept or telling a story, and still others might enjoy acting or saying a prayer. Assign parts or ask for volunteers. Be sure everyone is included.

One or two children should be asked to serve as Master or Mistress of Ceremonies (MC). Select children who are responsible, with strong voices and stage presence, who can keep the program moving forward. This places the children center stage and in charge of the presentation.

Before the rehearsal, gather any props and costumes, and remind the adult and youth volunteers that you will need their assistance. Determine their preferences for rehearsal groups. A copy of the agenda and the rehearsal groups should be given to each volunteer. Copies of the appropriate script or reading should be given to the adults and children who will be working on that part of the program.

## Rehearsal for the Show

During rehearsal time, the coordinator's tasks include:
- ❑ Meet together with all the participants to explain the nature of the program.
- ❑ Talk about program order, where to sit, use of strong voices so the audience can hear, eye contact, learning the parts rather than reading them, and how to use a microphone if needed.
- ❑ Assign adults and youth to work with each rehearsal group.
- ❑ Assign parts to each child depending on interest and ability.
- ❑ Distribute costumes and props as appropriate.
- ❑ Inform groups when the rehearsal time is almost over.
- ❑ Collect all props and set them out for the show.

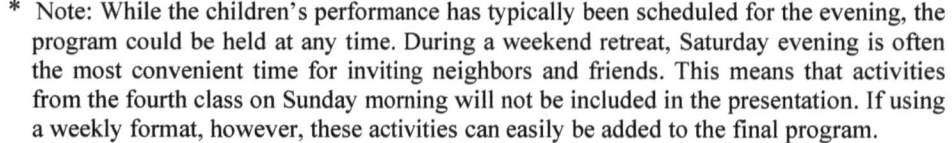

> \* Note: While the children's performance has typically been scheduled for the evening, the program could be held at any time. During a weekend retreat, Saturday evening is often the most convenient time for inviting neighbors and friends. This means that activities from the fourth class on Sunday morning will not be included in the presentation. If using a weekly format, however, these activities can easily be added to the final program.

Bahá'u'lláh – Children's Performance

# MATERIALS NEEDED

**Note: Items in italics are included with this section.
Children's artwork can be displayed on the walls.**

- *Agenda*
- *Rehearsal groups*
- Welcome sign (if desired)
- *Sample program* (for distributing to the audience)
- Persian music (can be played in the background as people are arriving)
- Microphone and sound system (if needed)
- Artwork display (some items can be pinned on a clothesline)
- Song sheets for all (including audience)
- Felt board and easel
- *Opening prayer* ("O God! Educate these children…")
- Memory quotes
- Stories From the Life of Bahá'u'lláh (handout packet, any props)
- *Heavy chain demo* (heavy item, scale)
- *The Promised One* (felt lesson script and cards)
- *Quiz on Bahá'u'lláh and quiz answers* (bells or other sound makers)
- Easel with large map of Bahá'u'lláh's exiles
- *The Promise* (play with script, cue cards, costumes and props)
- Craft samples
    - ___ Ridván cards, coloring pages and drawings
    - ___ Timeline of Bahá'u'lláh's Life
    - ___ God's Treasure
    - ___ Dream of Many Fish
    - ___ Ridván Roses
- Refreshments

**Note:** If this presentation is done after Lesson #4, you can include craft samples of the Salt Dough Sun and Spiritual Light Switch; the cloud and sun demonstration; photos of the Kings and Rulers with a summary of "Proclamation to the Kings"; the additional memory quote; and other activities from that lesson.

Bahá'u'lláh – Children's Performance

# SAMPLE AGENDA FOR MC (90 min.)

---

(1) **Welcome** to our program on **"BAHÁ'U'LLÁH: THE GLORY OF GOD"** (cell phones off)

(2) **Opening Music:** _____ **Prayer:** _____ **Music:** _____

(3) **Intro** (don't read): Bahá'ís believe there is only one God, the creator of the universe. God is invisible. Because we can't see Him, He sends us Special Messengers to tell us about Him and to teach us how to live. Bahá'u'lláh is the Messenger of God for this Day. We have been studying about Bahá'u'lláh all weekend, and tonight we are pleased to present what we have learned.

(4) **Introduce** each section and each presenter and thank them afterwards.

---

### BAHÁ'U'LLÁH: HIS EARLY LIFE & STATION (25 min.)
- ❑ Song of the Prophets (ALL)
- ❑ Introduction to Bahá'u'lláh _____
- ❑ Stories from the Life of Bahá'u'lláh ⟶
- ❑ Song: Shine Your Light (ALL)
- ❑ Heavy chain demo _____ _____
- ❑ Memory quote #16 (The Ancient Beauty) _____

> _____ 1) Baby Who Never Cried
> _____ 2) A Dream of Many Fish
> _____ 3) The Puppet Show
> _____ 4) Father of the Poor
> _____ 5) The Black Pit
> _____ 6) Banished to Baghdad
> _____ 7) Hermit in the Mountains
> _____ 8) The Writing Lesson

### DECLARATION OF BAHÁ'U'LLÁH (15 min.)
- ❑ Promised One (felt lesson) _____
- ❑ Declaration of Bahá'u'lláh (story) _____
- ❑ Memory quote #7 (Verily, I say) _____
- ❑ Show some crafts: _____ _____ _____
- ❑ Song: Can't You See the New Day (ALL)

### BAHÁ'U'LLÁH'S EXILES & IMPRISONMENT (15 min.)
- ❑ Most Great Prison (story) _____
- ❑ Exiles (large map) _____
- ❑ Song: El Rey de los Reyes (ALL)
- ❑ Memory quotes _____ _____
- ❑ Show remaining crafts: _____ _____ _____

### SONGS, QUIZ SHOW & PLAY (30 min.)
- ❑ Song: We Are the People of Bahá (ALL)
- ❑ Quiz show host _____ and panelists _____ _____ _____ _____
- ❑ Song: King of Kings (ALL)
- ❑ "The Promise" (a short play) ⟶ _____ _____ _____ _____ _____ _____ _____ _____
- ❑ Song: Bahá'u'lláh (ALL)
- ❑ Memory quotes: _____ _____
- ❑ Song: I Have Found Bahá'u'lláh (ALL STAND)
- ❑ **Say:** We hope you liked our program. Please join us for refreshments!

Bahá'u'lláh – Children's Performance

# REHEARSAL GROUPS

*Scripts and instructions are included on the following pages.*

**PROGRAM COORDINATOR**: _____

- ❏ Select and orient 1 or 2 MCs. Provide a clipboard, pencil and copy of the agenda.
- ❏ Divide children into 3-4 groups and assign adults to each group (6-8 adults total).
- ❏ Make sure each child has at least one part in addition to the group songs.
- ❏ One or two children can be asked to play a short musical selection to begin the program.
- ❏ Songs can be practiced all together after group rehearsals and again after dinner.

---

*Rehearse each part below with the children. The order will be different during the show.*

### GROUP #1: Stories from the Life of Bahá'u'lláh (storytelling, most difficult)
*(2 adults + 4 or more children)*

- ❏ Introduction to Bahá'u'lláh _____
- ❏ Stories

    1. Baby _____    5. Black Pit _____
    2. Fish _____    6. Banished _____
    3. Puppets _____  7. Hermit _____
    4. Poor _____    8. Writing _____

- ❏ If rehearsal or performance time is limited, you might select only 2-3 stories to share.
- ❏ Divide into two groups to practice, with one adult for each group.
- ❏ Each child should re-read one of the stories, then retell it in his/her own words.*
- ❏ Children should speak naturally rather than reading.
- ❏ They can make a sketch or write a few key words on a card as a memory aid.
- ❏ Have them practice in pairs until they can tell the story smoothly in 1-2 minutes.
- ❏ Use props if desired (e.g., mirror and sun, large map, cut-out fish, puppets, chains, etc.)

\* An exception might be story #3, The Puppet Show, which could be read by a narrator while the show is performed.

### GROUP #2: Quiz Show (short answers, medium difficulty)
*(1 adult + 5 children)*

- ❏ Select host: _____ and 4 panelists: _____ _____ _____ _____
- ❏ Line children up (standing or sitting) as if facing an audience.
- ❏ Using the "Quiz on Bahá'u'lláh," have the host ask the questions in order.
- ❏ Panelists can take turns answering, or can ring a bell or make another sound if they wish to be called on. (Practice and make it fun!)
- ❏ During the program, they can confer among themselves or ask an audience member for help if needed.

Bahá'u'lláh – Children's Performance

**GROUP #3: Play on "The Promise"** (very short parts, easier)
*(2 adults + 7 or 8 children)*

- ❏ Read through entire play together.
- ❏ Ask for volunteers or assign parts. ⟶
- ❏ Children should speak naturally rather than reading.
- ❏ Rehearse the entire play together.
- ❏ Distribute costumes and props.
- ❏ Practice again.
- ❏ Collect costumes and props, and set aside for the performance.

1. _____ (Hindu)
2. _____ (Jew)
3. _____ (Buddhist)
4. _____ (Christian)
5. _____ (Muslim)
6. _____ (Bahá'í)
7. _____ (Bahá'í)
8. _____ (Bahá'í)

**GROUP #4: Miscellaneous** (prayer, demos, crafts and memory quotes)
You can use children from the other groups after they have finished. Practice each part below.
*(2 adults + about 10 children)*

- ❏ Short opening prayer *("O God! Educate these children...")* _____
- ❏ Heavy Chain Demo (1-2 children) _____ _____

### HEAVY CHAIN DEMO

**Materials: bathroom scale, item weighing about 50 pounds***

1. Ask three audience members to come up, lift the item, and guess its weight.
2. Then weigh it and tell them the result.
3. Explain that Bahá'u'lláh was forced to wear a 100-pound chain (about twice as heavy as this weight) around His neck in the Black Pit. His feet were also in stocks. He was chained to the other prisoners, and He was kept there for 4 months.

\* The chain around Bahá'u'lláh's neck weighed about 51 kilos. If using the metric system, find an object weighing about 25 kilos and adapt the script accordingly.

- ❏ "The Promised One" felt lesson (2-4 children) _____ _____ _____ _____
- ❏ Memory quotes (#16, #7, etc.) _____ _____ _____ _____
- ❏ Trace Bahá'u'lláh's exiles on large map using explanations from small map _____
- ❏ Show each craft, explain how we made it and what it means (2-3 children each)

    Ridván cards/roses _____ _____ _____

    Coloring pages/drawings _____ _____ _____

    Timeline/Fish mobile _____ _____ _____

    God's Treasure _____ _____ _____

# Opening Prayer

*O God! Educate these children.
These children are
the plants of Thine orchard,
the flowers of Thy meadow,
the roses of Thy garden.*

*Let Thy rain fall upon them;
let the Sun of Reality
shine upon them with Thy love.*

*Let Thy breeze refresh them
in order that they may be trained,
grow and develop,
and appear in the utmost beauty.*

*Thou art the Giver.
Thou art the Compassionate.*

– 'Abdu'l-Bahá

# Bahá'u'lláh – Children's Performance

## Script for Felt Lesson
# "The Promised One"

| | NARRATION | ACTION |
|---|---|---|
| 1 | We're going to learn about a special promise made by all of God's Prophets or Messengers. Do you remember some of their names? (Students respond.) That's right. They all promised that a great teacher would come someday to bring peace to the world. Let's learn Who was promised by each Messenger of the past. | Distribute all the cards and arrows, except for the two column headings: "Prophet" and "Promised One." Give the reference chart to one student to refer to as needed. |
| 2 | First, let's review the Prophets. [Prophet] | Place "Prophet" heading in first column on board. |
| 3 | Do you remember which Prophet came first? Even before that? Who came next? | As each Prophet is named, the child holding that card places it on the felt board in order. |
| 4 | Now let's put the "Promised One" heading in the second column, and an arrow after each Prophet's name. [Promised One] | Place the "Promised One" card in the second column and have students add the arrows. |
| 5 | Does anyone know who Jesus promised would come? That's right! His own return. (Continue in this manner for each Prophet, referring to the chart as necessary.) | Student places the "Return of Christ" card to the right of the arrow. (Etc.) |
| 6 | So we see that each Prophet of God promised that a great teacher would come to bring peace to the whole world. | Point to all the "Promised One" cards covering the board. |
| 7 | What does "pledge" mean? That's right, it means "promise." What do you think Bahá'u'lláh means when He says: "Lo, the sacred Pledge hath been fulfilled, for He, the Promised One, is come!"* Yes! Bahá'u'lláh is the One promised by all the Prophets of God. (He is the Lord of Hosts, the 5th Buddha, etc.) | Place "Bahá'u'lláh" vertically on the felt board, covering the names of all the Promised Ones. |

\* Quoted in Shoghi Effendi, *The World Order of Bahá'u'lláh*, p. 104

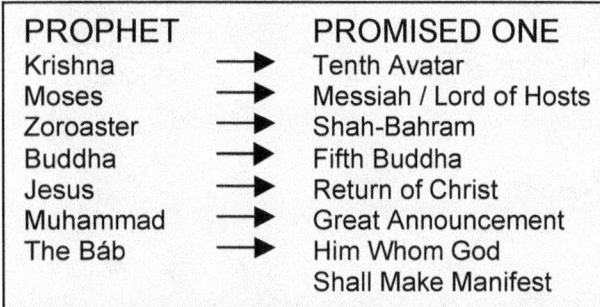

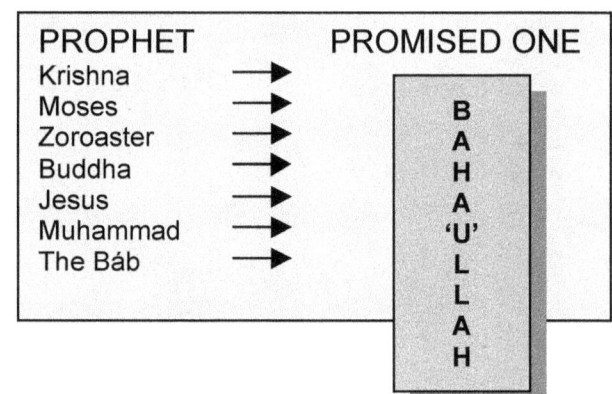

Bahá'í Children's Classes and Retreats: Theme 4, p. 116

Bahá'u'lláh – Children's Performance

# Quiz on the Life of Bahá'u'lláh

**Short version for the children's performance**

---

1. Why does God send us Messengers?
2. Who was Bahá'u'lláh?
3. What does "Bahá'u'lláh" mean?
4. What name did His parents give Him?

5. When and where was He born?
6. What was Irán called at the time of Bahá'u'lláh?
7. Was Bahá'u'lláh's family rich or poor?  Explain.

8. Did Bahá'u'lláh go to school like other children?
9. Where did His knowledge come from?
10. What did Bahá'u'lláh's father see in a dream, and what did it mean?

11. Why was Bahá'u'lláh arrested and put in prison?
12. What was the name of the prison and what was it like?
13. What wonderful thing happened to Bahá'u'lláh in the Black Pit?

14. Why did the king of Persia exile Bahá'u'lláh?
15. What was the journey like from Persia to Baghdad?

16. How long did Bahá'u'lláh wait before telling people He was God's Messenger?
17. When and where did He choose to tell them?
18. Compare the Riḍván Garden to the Síyáh-Chál.

19. Why is Bahá'u'lláh called the Promised One of all religions?
20. When He came, were the people expecting Him?
21. What was Bahá'u'lláh's main message?

Bahá'u'lláh – Children's Performance

# Answers to Quiz on the Life of Bahá'u'lláh

**Note: If one panelist is answering all the questions, the host should try to call on different ones.**

---

1. Why does God send us Messengers? *(To teach us about God, and how to live with each other.)*
2. Who was Bahá'u'lláh? *(The Messenger of God for today)*
3. What does "Bahá'u'lláh" mean? *(Glory of God)*
4. What name did His parents give Him? *(Husayn-'Alí)*

5. When and where was He born? *(Nov. 12, 1817, in Iran)*
6. What was Irán called at the time of Bahá'u'lláh? *(Persia)*
7. Was Bahá'u'lláh's family rich or poor? Explain.
   *(Very rich. Father was a nobleman in the court of the king.)*

8. Did Bahá'u'lláh go to school like other children?
   *(No. His teacher sent Him home saying there was nothing he could teach Him.)*
9. Where did His knowledge come from?
   *(God. A Prophet comes to teach people, not to learn from them.)*
10. What did Bahá'u'lláh's father see in a dream, and what did it mean?
    *(Fish holding His hairs; great leader with many followers.)*

11. Why was Bahá'u'lláh arrested and put in prison? *(Follower of the Báb)*
12. What was the name of the prison and what was it like? *(Síyáh-Chál / Black Pit, awful)*
13. What wonderful thing happened to Bahá'u'lláh in the Black Pit? *(Received His Revelation)*

14. Why did the king of Persia exile Bahá'u'lláh? *(Jealous and fearful of growing influence)*
15. What was the journey like from Persia to Baghdad? *(3 months on foot, steep mountains, weak from prison, cold, hungry, hand laundry, salty cake)*

16. How long did Bahá'u'lláh wait before telling people He was God's Messenger? *(10 years)*
17. When and where did He choose to tell them? *(Ridván Garden, outside Baghdad, April 21, 1863)*
18. Compare the Ridván Garden to the Síyáh-Chál. *(Like heaven and hell: springtime, roses, trees, rivers, birds—versus darkness, rats, chains, poison, etc.)*

19. Why is Bahá'u'lláh called the Promised One of all religions? *(He fulfills the promises of every major religion regarding the great Teacher to come: Messiah, Return of Christ, Fifth Buddha, etc.)*
20. When He came, were the people expecting Him? *(The Bábís expected Him Whom God Shall Make Manifest. Other religions also expected someone, but they didn't know it was Bahá'u'lláh.)*
21. What was Bahá'u'lláh's main message? *(He came to bring peace and unity to the world.)*

\* \* \* \* \*

# EXILES OF BAHA'U'LLAH

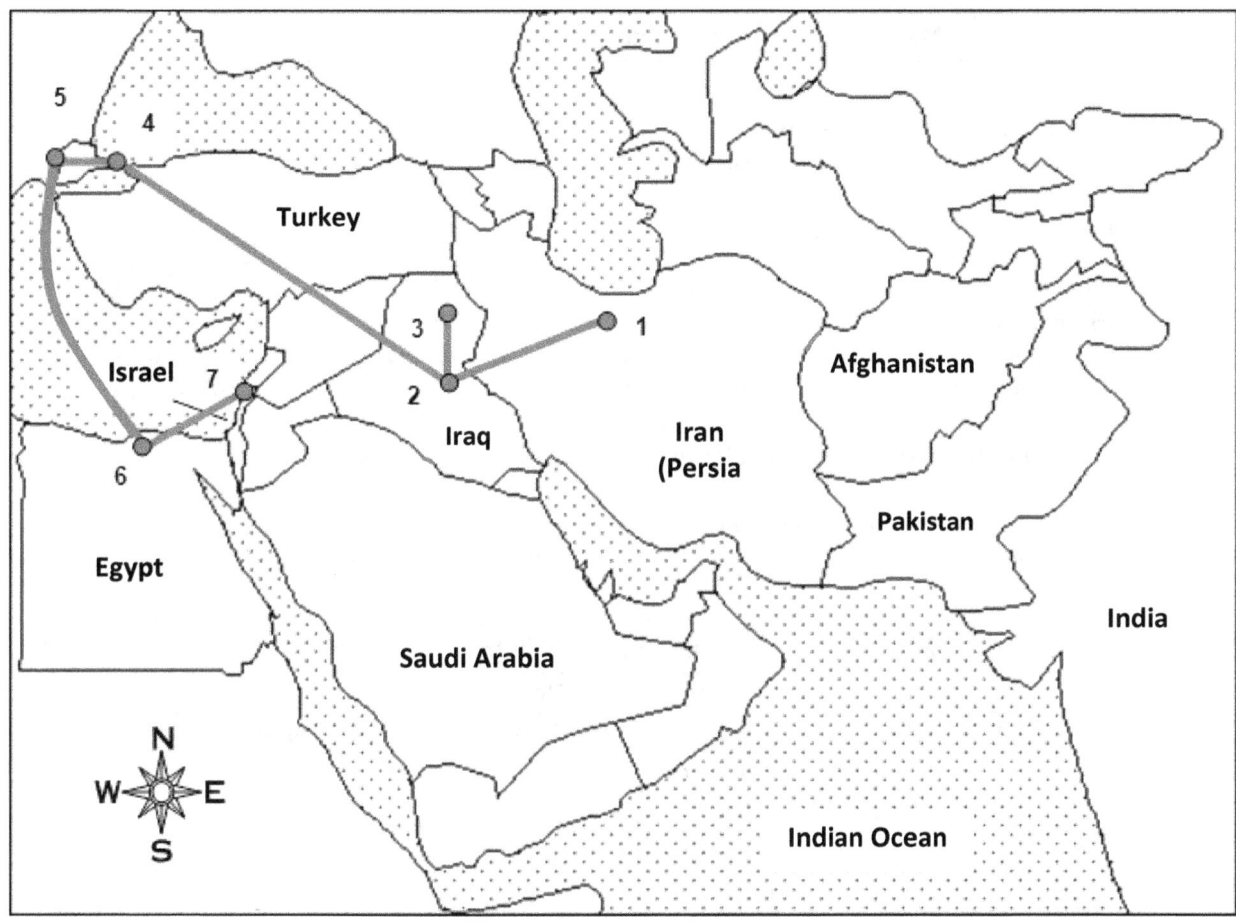

1. Bahá'u'lláh was born in Tehran, Iran (1817) *(Birth, fish dream, puppet show, marriage, children, Father of the Poor, Black Pit, received Revelation)*

2. Exiled to Baghdad, Iraq (1853) *(Winter walk across mountains, salty cake, many visitors, left to avoid disunity. He declared at the end of His second stay there—after point #3.)*

3. Lived alone in Kurdistan for two years (1854–1856), before returning to Baghdad *(Hermit, writing lesson)*

4. Exiled to Constantinople (now called Istanbul) in Turkey (1863)

5. Exiled to Adrianople (now called Edirne) in Turkey (1863–1868)

6. Taken to Alexandria, Egypt, on the way to Akká (1868)

7. Exiled to Akká in Palestine (now Israel) where He was a prisoner for 24 years (1868–1892) *(Waved at pilgrims, Mihdí died 1870, revealed many books, ascended, Shrine)*

Bahá'u'lláh – Children's Performance

# "THE PROMISE"

Note: This well-loved play has been performed in many countries over the years.

**Materials**: Holy Books and costumes for 7–8 children

(1) Five children representing five earlier religions are dressed in costume off stage. (See next page for costume ideas.) Each carries a Holy Book with reverence.

(2) The first child enters from stage right, faces the audience and says:

*I am a **Hindu**, a follower of **Krishna**. In my Holy Book, the **Bhagavad Gita**, it says that one day, a great Prophet will come to bring peace and justice to the world. He will be known as the **Tenth Avatar**. I sure hope He comes soon. We really need Him now.*

(3) That child then moves to stage left, looking through his/her book, sadly waiting.

(4) The other children enter, one at a time. They explain the promises from their own Holy Books (below), then join the others. They act suspicious of each other and some start to argue.

|   | ACTORS | RELIGION | PROPHET | BOOK | PROMISED ONE |
|---|--------|----------|---------|------|--------------|
| 1 |        | Hindu    | Krishna | Bhagavad Gita | Tenth Avatar |
| 2 |        | Jewish   | Moses   | Torah | Messiah / Lord of Hosts |
| 3 |        | Buddhist | Buddha  | Tripitaka | Fifth Buddha |
| 4 |        | Christian | Jesus  | Bible | Return of Christ |
| 5 |        | Muslim   | Muhammad | Qur'án | Great Announcement |
| 6 |        | Bahá'í   | Bahá'u'lláh |  |  |

(5) Then, one or more Bahá'ís enter and joyfully announce that the Promised One has come! His Name is Bahá'u'lláh. The Bahá'ís approach the followers of the other religions, one by one, and humbly share the good news:

*The One you are waiting for has come, and the promises in your Holy Book have all been fulfilled. Come and join us as we work together for unity and peace!*

(6) Each believer is led to center stage and is warmly welcomed by the others. Then they line up in order, face the audience, and each explains the fulfillment. For example:

*I am a **Hindu**, a follower of **Krishna**. We have been waiting for the **Tenth Avatar** who was promised in the **Bhagavad Gita**. He has finally come!*

(7) After the last one, they all link arms and proclaim in unison:

### *The Promised One of all religions has come! His name is Bahá'u'lláh.*

(8) All remain on stage and invite the audience to join in singing "Bahá'u'lláh" (see song sheet).

Bahá'u'lláh – Children's Performance

# "THE PROMISE"
### Sample costumes

Thrift stores are an excellent source of inexpensive robes, scarves, hats, vests and other items that can be fashioned into costumes to represent the different faiths. (Also see "I Am the Way" skit in Theme Book #2 on *The Manifestation of God*.)

Bahá'u'lláh – Children's Performance

# "THE PROMISE"
**Cue cards for the actors**

The cards below can be photocopied, cut out and taped onto the appropriate Holy Book (or any substitute book), to help children remember the main points. The children should speak naturally and with conviction, rather than reading or memorizing their lines. The exact wording is not important. The numbers show the order of appearance.

| NAME | PROPHET | BOOK | PROMISED ONE | |
|---|---|---|---|---|
| Hindu | Krishna | Bhagavad Gita | Tenth Avatar | 1 |

| NAME | PROPHET | BOOK | PROMISED ONE | |
|---|---|---|---|---|
| Jewish | Moses | Torah | Lord of Hosts | 2 |

| NAME | PROPHET | BOOK | PROMISED ONE | |
|---|---|---|---|---|
| Buddhist | Buddha | Tripitaka | Fifth Buddha | 3 |

| NAME | PROPHET | BOOK | PROMISED ONE | |
|---|---|---|---|---|
| Christian | Jesus | Bible | Return of Christ | 4 |

| NAME | PROPHET | BOOK | PROMISED ONE | |
|---|---|---|---|---|
| Muslim | Muhammad | Qur'án | Great Announcement | 5 |

Bahá'í Children's Classes and Retreats: Theme 4, p. 122

# Preparing for the children's performance

**Bahá'u'lláh – Children's Performance**

**Sample program for the audience**

Bahá'í Children's Class Performance

# Bahá'u'lláh: The Glory of God

"Verily I say, this is the Day in which mankind can behold the Face, and hear the Voice, of the Promised One." —Bahá'u'lláh

### Welcome

### Opening music and prayers

### Baha'u'llah: His Early Life and Station
- Song of the Prophets
- Introduction to Bahá'u'lláh
- Stories from the Life of Bahá'u'lláh
- Dream of Many Fish (craft)
- Shine Your Light on Me (song)
- The Heavy Chain (demo)
- Memory quote

### Declaration of Bahá'u'lláh
- The Promised One (felt lesson)
- Declaration of Bahá'u'lláh (story)
- Memory quote
- Ridván cards and roses (crafts)
- Can't You See the New Day (song)

### Baha'u'llah's Exiles and Imprisonment
- The Most Great Prison (story)
- Exiles of Bahá'u'lláh (map)
- El Rey de los Reyes (song)
- Memory quote
- Timeline and God's Treasure (crafts)

### Music, Quiz Show and a Play
- We Are the People of Bahá (song)
- The Life of Bahá'u'lláh (quiz show)
- King of Kings (song)
- The Promise (dramatic play)
- Bahá'u'lláh (song)
- Memory quote
- Closing song

### Refreshments and Campfire
(weather permitting)

# Handouts

For ease of photocopying, the handouts for these lessons are also available for downloading from: www.UnityWorksStore.com > Children's Classes > Bahá'u'lláh: The Glory of God > student handouts.

Bahá'u'lláh: The Glory of God

# HANDOUTS

### Orientation and All Lessons

| | |
|---|---:|
| Unity Bingo | 15 |
| Song Sheet | 127 |
| Quotations | 129 |
| Stories from the Life of Bahá'u'lláh (packet of readings) | 131 |

### LESSON #1: His Birth, Early Life and Station

| | |
|---|---:|
| Introduction to Bahá'u'lláh | 133 |
| The Baby Who Never Cried | 134 |
| A Dream of Many Fish | 135 |
| The Puppet Show | 136 |
| Father of the Poor | 137 |
| The Black Pit | 138 |
| Banished to Baghdad | 139 |
| The Hermit in the Mountains | 140 |
| The Writing Lesson | 141 |
| Stories from the Life of Bahá'u'lláh (instructions for group leaders) | 32 |

### LESSON #2: The Declaration of Bahá'u'lláh

| | |
|---|---:|
| The Declaration of Bahá'u'lláh (in story packet) | 142 |
| The Prison at Akká (coloring page) | 40 |
| The Shrine of Bahá'u'lláh (coloring page) | 41 |
| Hidden Message | 42 |
| Timeline Cards | 44 |
| Bahá'u'lláh's Name for "God's Treasure" Craft | 46 |
| The Promised One (blank chart) | 75 |

### LESSON #3: Exiles and Imprisonment

| | |
|---|---:|
| The Most Great Prison (in story packet) | 144 |
| Student Map | 85 |
| Quiz on the Life of Bahá'u'lláh (in story packet) | 147 |
| Sacrifice (instructions for group leaders) | 87 |
| Walk to Baghdad (instructions for group leaders) | 81 |

### LESSON #4: Clouds of Glory

| | |
|---|---:|
| Proclamation to the Kings (in story packet) | 146 |
| Clouds of Glory (instructions for group leaders) | 105 |

Bahá'u'lláh: The Glory of God

Name _____

# SONG SHEET

Note: Most of these songs are copyrighted and are used with permission.

### Shine Your Light (D-A7)
(by Greg Dahl)

Shine your light on me Bahá'u'lláh,
I am over here, Bahá'u'lláh.
Shine your light on me Bahá'u'lláh,
Glori-ay, glori-ay.

- Let me be a lamp...
- Help me light the world...
- Shine your light on me...

### God Is Sufficient (Em-B7-C)
(Words of Bahá'u'lláh, Dawn-Breakers:631)

God is sufficient unto me,
   He is the All-sufficing. (2x)
In Him let the trusting trust.
   Let the trusting trust. (4x)

### Bahá'u'lláh (D-G-Em-A)
(by Creadell Haley)

Bahá'u'lláh, Bahá'u'lláh,
Bahá, Bahá'u'lláh.

- The Glory of God...
- The Prince of Peace...
- The Lord of Hosts...
- The Spirit of Truth...
- The Promised One of all the ages...
- Bahá'u'lláh...

### We Are the People of Bahá (C-F-G7)
(by Donna Taylor)

We are the people of Bahá... (English)
Somos la gente de Bahá... (Spanish)
Nous sommes le peuple de Bahá... (French)
Má bandigáni Bahá... (Persian)

### Song of the Prophets (A-D-E)
(by Marvin Dryer)

Krishna, Buddha, Zoroaster,
Abraham, Moses, Christ,
Muhammad, the Báb, Bahá'u'lláh,
The spirit's the same.
Bahá'u'lláh teaches for today,
Tells us to look to the spirit,
Not to worship the name.

### El Rey de los Reyes (G-C-D)
(Spanish; composer unknown)

El es el Rey de los Reyes, (3x)
El es Bahá'u'lláh.

- El es el Sol Brillante...
- El es el Prometido...
- El es la Gloria de Dios...
- El es el Rey de los Reyes...

### Can't You See the New Day (A-E)
(Composer unknown)

Bahá'u'lláh has come,
   Can't you see the new day. } (3x)
He's the Glory of God.

- There is only one God.....
- All religions are one....
- Mankind is one....

Can't you see the new day,
   Bahá'u'lláh has come. } (3x)
He's the Glory of God.

### King of Kings (D-A)
(Slow, in a round; composer unknown)

King of Kings and Lord of Lords,
   Glory, Hallelujah! (2x)
Bahá'u'lláh, Glory, Hallelujah! (2x)

# Bahá'u'lláh: The Glory of God

## I Have Found Bahá'u'lláh  (G-C-D)

(by Nosisana Velem)

I have found Bahá'u'lláh,
In the early days of my life.
He is in my heart,
Now and forever.

Alláh'u'Abhá, Alláh'u'Abhá,
Alláh'u'Abhá, now and forever.

## The Nightingale  (C-G-F)

(by Chris Ruhe-Schoen)

The nightingale is singing
  all over the world. (2x)
The nightingale Bahá'u'lláh. (2x)
Lai, lai, lai...

The nightingale is singing
  that we are brothers...

The nightingale is singing
  that we are sisters...

## Prince of Peace  (Am-Dm-E-G-F)

(by Lloyd Haynes, with changes in italics)

There lived a Man across the ocean,
There lived a Man across the sea;
He spoke of love, He spoke of justice,
He spoke to *us* of unity.

**(chorus)**
They called Him the Prince of Peace.
They called Him the Prince of Peace.
From Constantinople to Adrianople,
To Akká the prison by the sea.

His teachings spread *to every nation,*
His teachings spread to all mankind,
His teachings took in all religions,
And left no helpless soul behind.

## Soon Will All  (echo song)  (Bm-A-F#)

(Words of Bahá'u'lláh, God Passes By: 184)

Soon will all that dwell on earth,
Be enlisted under these banners.
Yá-Bahá'u'l-Abhá. (4x)

## The Prisoner

(by England Dan and John Ford Coley)

Take us to the prisoner
Let us gaze into his eyes,
To see what kind of man
It takes a nation to despise.
Take us to the prisoner
Let us look upon his face,
To see why twenty thousand men
Would gladly take his place.
Won't someone give a drink to him?
Remove the chains and let him live,
Let him live.

Take us to the prisoner
Let us listen to his voice,
To see why worlds of wisdom's
In a cell without a choice.
Take us to the prisoner
Torn and bent beneath the chains,
We wonder if the world is really
Worthy of his name?
Won't someone give a drink to him?
Remove the chains and let him live,
Let him live.

We know where we're going
For we heard the new winds blowing
And we've got to know for ourselves.
It won't help to listen to someone else.

Take us to the prisoner
With his eyes so full of grace,
The priests have lied
And kings have died
Filled with their own disgrace.
Won't someone give a drink to him?
Remove the chains and let him live.

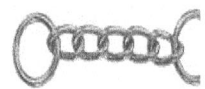 Let him live.
Let him live.
Let him live.

Bahá'u'lláh: The Glory of God

#  WORDS OF BAHÁ'U'LLÁH

### SHORTER

(1) O KINGS of the earth! Give ear unto the Voice of God... *(PB, p. 7)*

(2) Soon will all that dwell on earth be enlisted under these banners. *(Quoted in GPB, p. 184)*

(3) All the heavenly Scriptures of the past attest to the greatness of this Day... *(TB, p. 258)*

(4) Lo, the sacred Pledge hath been fulfilled, for He, the Promised One, is come! *(WOB, p. 104)*

(5) Ye are but vassals, O kings of the earth! He Who is the King of Kings hath appeared... *(G, p. 211)*

### MEDIUM LENGTH

(6) Hearts have they with which they understand not, and eyes have they with which they see not... *(Quoting the Qur'án, KI, p. 113)*

(7) Verily I say, this is the Day in which mankind can behold the Face, and hear the Voice, of the Promised One. *(G, p. 10)*

(8) Glory to Thee, O my God! But for the tribulations which are sustained in Thy path, how could Thy true lovers be recognized...? *(ESW, p. 94)*

(9) O YE RICH ONES ON EARTH! The poor in your midst are My trust; guard ye My trust, and be not intent only on your own ease. *(HW, Persian #54)*

(10) Incline your ears to the sweet melody of this Prisoner. Arise, and lift up your voices, that haply they that are fast asleep may be awakened. *(G, p. 213)*

(11) One night, in a dream, these exalted words were heard on every side: "Verily, We shall render Thee victorious by Thyself and by Thy Pen." *(ESW, p. 21)*

(12) All the heavenly Scriptures of the past attest to the greatness of this Day...Yet despite all this the people have remained heedless and are shut out as by a veil. *(TB, p. 258)*

(13) The time fore-ordained unto the peoples and kindreds of the earth is now come129. The promises of God, as recorded in the holy Scriptures, have all been fulfilled. *(PB, p. 109)*

(14) O KING! I was but a man like others, asleep upon My couch, when lo, the breezes of the All-Glorious were wafted over Me, and taught Me the knowledge of all that hath been. *(ESW, p. 11)*

## LONGER

(15) Recall thou to mind My sorrows, My cares and anxieties, My woes and trials, the state of My captivity, the tears that I have shed, the bitterness of Mine anguish, and now My imprisonment in this far-off land. *(G, p. 119)*

(16) The Ancient Beauty hath consented to be bound with chains that mankind may be released from its bondage, and hath accepted to be made a prisoner within this most mighty Stronghold that the whole world may attain unto true liberty. *(G, p. 99)*

(17) Remember My days during thy days, and My distress and banishment in this remote prison. And be thou so steadfast in My love that thy heart shall not waver, even if the swords of the enemies rain blows upon thee and all the heavens and the earth arise against thee. *(BP, p. 210)*

(18) Pointing with her finger unto My head, she addressed all who are in heaven and all who are on earth, saying: "By God! This is the Best-Beloved of the worlds, and yet ye comprehend not. This is the Beauty of God amongst you… This is the Mystery of God and His Treasure…" *(GPB, p. 102)*

## LONGEST

(19) Behold how…the worthless and foolish have fondly imagined that by such instruments as massacre, plunder and banishment they can extinguish the Lamp which the Hand of Divine power hath lit… How utterly unaware they seem to be of the truth that such adversity is the oil that feedeth the flame of this Lamp! Such is God's transforming power. He changeth whatsoever He willeth; He verily hath power over all things... *(G, p. 72)*

(20) VERILY I say, this is the Day in which mankind can behold the Face, and hear the Voice, of the Promised One. The Call of God hath been raised, and the light of His countenance hath been lifted up upon men. It behoveth every man to blot out the trace of every idle word from the tablet of his heart, and to gaze, with an open and unbiased mind, on the signs of His Revelation, the proofs of His Mission, and the tokens of His glory. *(PB, p. 109)*

### References

| | |
|---|---|
| BP | Bahá'í Prayers |
| ESW | Epistle to the Son of the Wolf |
| G | Gleanings from the Writings of Bahá'u'lláh |
| GPB | God Passes By |
| HW | Hidden Words |
| KI | Kitáb-i-Iqán |
| PB | Proclamation of Bahá'u'lláh |
| TB | Tablets of Bahá'u'lláh |
| WOB | World Order of Bahá'u'lláh |

# Stories from the Life of Bahá'u'lláh

Name: _____

**Bahá'u'lláh: The Glory of God**

**These stories, along with full-page color pictures designed to accompany the stories, are available for download from: www.UnityWorksStore.com.**

Note: The images on the following pages are intended to help children remember events in the life of Bahá'u'lláh. It would not be appropriate to represent the Manifestation of God in any human form, "whether pictorially, in sculpture or in dramatic representation…" (On behalf of The Universal House of Justice, Lights of Guidance, p. 99)

# Introduction to Bahá'u'lláh

God is invisible. Because we can't see Him, He sends us Messengers to tell us about Him and to teach us how to live. Bahá'u'lláh is the Messenger of God for this Day.

These Messengers are like perfect mirrors reflecting God's light to mankind. Bahá'u'lláh is reflecting God's light for today. When we look at Him, it's like looking at God. When we love and obey Him, it's the same as loving and obeying God.

Bahá'u'lláh was also a person like us in many ways. He had a mother and father, brothers and sisters. He ate and slept. Sometimes He was hungry and sometimes He was sad.

Bahá'u'lláh was born in Persia (Iran) almost 200 years ago. Even as a baby, His parents knew there was something special about Him. Did you know that Bahá'u'lláh's family was very rich? His father had a high position in the court of the king. When Bahá'u'lláh grew up, He married and had children. For a time, the family was very happy together.

However, every Prophet of God has enemies who don't like the new teachings He brings. Bahá'u'lláh had enemies too. They put Him in prison, stole all of His belongings and even tried to kill Him.

But His enemies were unable to stop the advance of His teachings, and today the Faith of Bahá'u'lláh has spread all around the world.

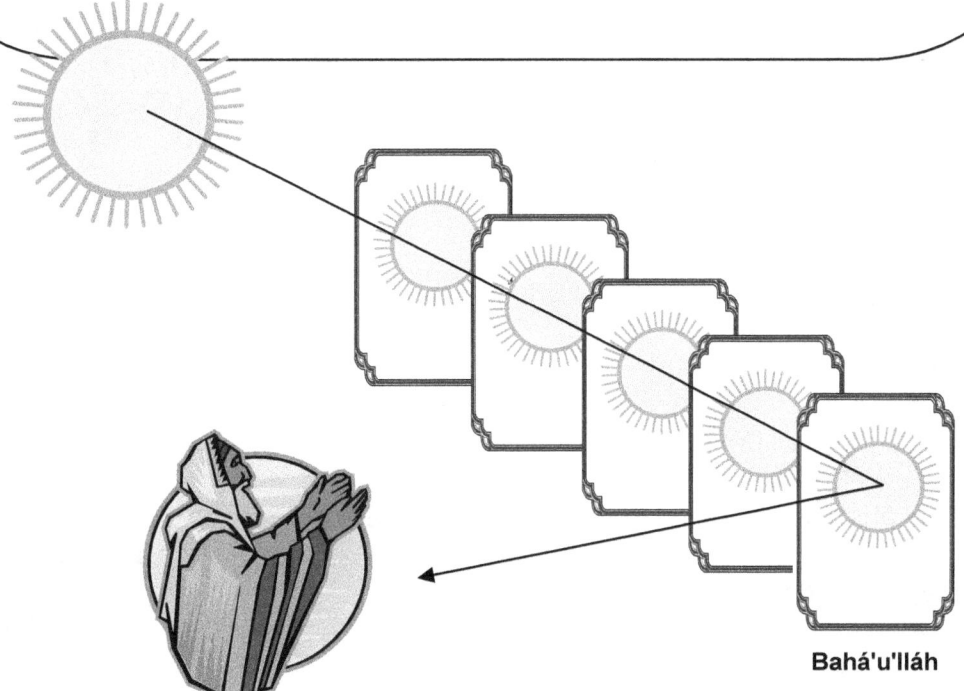

**Bahá'u'lláh**

Bahá'u'lláh: The Glory of God

## 1 The Baby Who Never Cried

Almost 200 years ago, in the land of Persia (Iran), a very special baby was born. His parents named Him Husayn-'Alí. He was later known as Bahá'u'lláh, which means the "Glory of God." The date of His birth was November 12, 1817.

Bahá'u'lláh's family was very rich and they lived in a beautiful mansion. His father was a nobleman* in the court of the king.

Bahá'u'lláh was different from other children. He was always kind and generous, and His mother said that, even as a baby, He never cried.

When He was still a child, people could see that Bahá'u'lláh was very smart. His parents sent Him to school, but his teachers were amazed by His knowledge and wisdom. There was nothing they could teach Him, so they sent Him home.

Just like the other Messengers of God, Bahá'u'lláh did not need to go to school like we do. His knowledge came from God and He was sent to be a teacher for all mankind.

By the time Bahá'u'lláh was fourteen years old, He was known throughout the land for his wisdom and kindness. He was loved and trusted by everyone. He helped people who were sad or in trouble. He looked after the elderly, took care of orphans, and gave food and money to the poor.

* **nobleman:** A man of high rank and privilege; just under the king in status; a member of the ruling class who often has land, money, power

## Study Questions

1. When and where was Bahá'u'lláh born?

2. What does the name "Bahá'u'lláh" mean?

3. What name did His parents give Him?

4. How do we spell "Bahá'u'lláh"?

5. What was Bahá'u'lláh like as a child?

6. Why did His teachers send Him home from school?

7. What was He like as a teenager?

8. Why do you think the Messenger of God starts out as a baby?

## 2 A Dream of Many Fish

One night, when Bahá'u'lláh was a small boy, His father had a strange dream. He dreamed that his Son was swimming in a wide ocean. Bahá'u'lláh's face was shining with light. Rays of light were streaming from His head in all directions. The light was so bright that the water all around Him glowed.

Bahá'u'lláh's long black hair floated out into the water as He swam. As His father watched in the dream, many fish appeared and gathered around his Son. Each fish took the end of one strand of Bahá'u'lláh's hair tightly in its mouth and swam along with Him.

There were a great number of fish, but they did not harm Bahá'u'lláh or slow Him down at all. He swam freely, and whichever way He turned, the fish followed Him.

The dream seemed so real, that Bahá'u'lláh's father decided to ask a wise man what it meant. The wise man told him that the ocean represented* the world and the fish were all the people.

Many people would be attracted to the light of God shining from Bahá'u'lláh, and they would follow Him. This meant that Bahá'u'lláh would have followers from all over the world.

* **represented:** Stood for, symbolized

## Study Questions

1. What did Bahá'u'lláh's father dream?

2. What was the meaning of this dream?

3. What did the light represent?

4. What are the followers of Bahá'u'lláh called today?

5. How can we be like the fish in the dream?

# 3. The Puppet Show

One day, when Bahá'u'lláh was still a child, He saw a puppet show. When the curtain rose, some puppets entered and announced with excitement that the king was about to arrive. "His Majesty is coming! Arrange the seats at once!" More puppets came on stage to prepare for the king. They swept the floor and sprinkled water on the ground.[1]

At last, the king entered. He was dressed in magnificent clothing with a golden crown on his head and shining jewels around his neck. As he walked on stage, the sound of guns and trumpets could be heard from behind the curtain, and smoke filled the air. With great pride, the king walked slowly and majestically to his throne and the entire court bowed with respect.

When the king was seated, some guards entered with a thief. The king ordered that the thief should be beheaded. Immediately, the chief executioner cut off the thief's head, and fake red blood gushed out of the puppet's neck.

Then another puppet ran on stage with the news that some people had rebelled[2] against the king. This made the king angry and he ordered his solders to find the rebels and shoot them at once. Again, the sound of guns was heard!

Bahá'u'lláh was greatly amazed by this scene. After the show had ended, He saw a man leaving with a large box under his arm. Bahá'u'lláh asked about the box, and the man explained that it contained all of the puppets: the king and his ministers, the princes and guards, the thief, the executioner, and everything from the show.

When He heard this, Bahá'u'lláh realized that the world is just like a puppet show. Its riches, power and glory only last for a short time, yet people are willing to fight and kill for them. If people stopped to think, they would realize that when we die, we end up in a box just like the puppets, and all the treasures of the world are worth nothing to us then.

Some years later, when Bahá'u'lláh was a young man, the king of Persia offered Him a high position in the government, but Bahá'u'lláh refused. He was not interested in fame and fortune. He knew that He had more important work to do.

1. **sprinkled water:** Probably to keep the dust down
2. **to rebel:** To go against, fight back, resist, disobey

## Study Questions

1. What was the puppet show about?
2. How did people treat the king?
3. How did the king treat other people?
4. How did the king feel about himself?
5. What was in the box?
6. How is the box similar to the world?
7. What kind of box do people end up in when they die?
8. What could be more important than working for the king?

# 4  Father of the Poor

Bahá'u'lláh had a handsome face and a kind smile. He rode on horseback and was brave and strong. He was also known for his beautiful calligraphy.[1] When Bahá'u'lláh was almost eighteen, He married a young lady of noble birth, called Navváb.

Navváb was tall and slender, with black hair and dark blue eyes. She was very beautiful and also very wise. Navváb had a kind and gentle nature, a courteous tongue, and a pure heart. She was like a queen, and Bahá'u'lláh loved her very much. Together they had seven children, but only three survived. The oldest was 'Abdu'l-Bahá.

Navváb also came from a wealthy family. When she married Bahá'u'lláh, her wedding treasures were so great that it took forty mules to carry them to her new home. Even the buttons on her dresses were made of gold.

The newlyweds lived in a great palace and had many servants. Their home was always open, and many important people came to visit them. Bahá'u'lláh and Navváb were kind to everyone they met, but especially to the poor. To those who were cold, they offered warm clothes. To the hungry, they provided food. To the homeless, they offered shelter. To the sad and lonely, they shared words of comfort and love.

Navváb was like a mother to all of the women and children. She was known as the Mother of Consolation.[2] Bahá'u'lláh was so kind and generous that He was called the Father of the Poor. Everyone loved Bahá'u'lláh and Navváb, and the family was very happy together.

In later years, when Bahá'u'lláh was unfairly thrown into prison and the family lost everything they had, Navváb never complained. She stayed with Bahá'u'lláh for the rest of her life, through forty years of poverty, prison and hardship. And she still treated everyone with courtesy and love. Bahá'u'lláh was at her side when she died, and He promised that she would be His companion forever, in all the worlds of God.

1. **calligraphy:** A beautiful, artistic style of handwriting
2. **consolation:** Providing comfort, support, assistance

## Study Questions

1. How old was Bahá'u'lláh when He married?
2. What was the name of Bahá'u'lláh's wife and what was she like?
3. Did Bahá'u'lláh and His wife have children?
4. Why were they called Mother of Consolation and Father of the Poor?
5. Do you think Bahá'u'lláh and Navváb were unusual for rich people? Explain.

# 5 The Black Pit

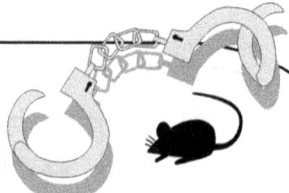

When Bahá'u'lláh was about 27 years old, He received a letter from the Báb, saying that soon God would send a new Messenger to the world. Although they never met, Bahá'u'lláh immediately became a follower of the Báb and began to share His teachings. From that time on, His life was filled with pain and sorrow.

The leaders of Persia were afraid of the growing influence of the Báb and they treated His followers with great cruelty. Thousands were thrown into prison or killed. Although Bahá'u'lláh was innocent of any crime, His palace was taken away and all His possessions were stolen. He was arrested and forced to walk for fifteen miles,[1] barefoot and in chains, to a terrible prison called the Black Pit. On the way to the prison, people at the side of the road laughed and threw stones at Him.

The Black Pit was underground, at the end of a dark hallway and down three flights of stairs. The prison was icy cold, damp, and swarming with rats. Bahá'u'lláh was surrounded by 150 thieves and murderers, and a few followers of the Báb. It was crowded and the prisoners were chained together. Most of the men had no clothes and not even a mat to sleep on. There were no toilets either, so the prison was filthy and the smell was horrible. Bahá'u'lláh's feet were in stocks[2] and there was a huge metal chain around His neck that weighed over 100 pounds.[3]

For the first three days and nights, He had nothing to eat or drink. Later, when His family was able to send food, His enemies mixed it with poison, which made Him very sick. Bahá'u'lláh and His friends were forced to stay in the Black Pit for four months.

But in that horrible place, something wonderful happened. One night, as Bahá'u'lláh lay in the dark, weighted down with chains, a heavenly maiden (like an angel) appeared in the air above Him. She pointed to Bahá'u'lláh and in a sweet voice, called out saying that He was the next Messenger of God—the One promised by the Báb. At that moment, Bahá'u'lláh knew He had a special mission in this world, but it wasn't time to tell people just yet.

1. **fifteen miles:** About 24 kilometers
2. **stocks:** A wooden frame with holes, like handcuffs for the legs; used as a punishment
3. **over 100 pounds:** It weighed about 51 kilos.
(Ref: Taherzadeh, Child of the Covenant, p. 56)

## Study Questions

1. What did Bahá'u'lláh do after reading the letter from the Báb?
2. Why was Bahá'u'lláh arrested and put into prison? Did He do something wrong?
3. What was the name of the prison, and what was it like?
4. In this country, why are people put in prison and how are they usually treated there?
5. Why do you think the leaders of Persia were afraid of the Báb and His followers?
6. What wonderful thing happened to Bahá'u'lláh in the prison?
7. Why don't you think He wanted to tell people yet?

Bahá'u'lláh: The Glory of God

## 6  Banished to Baghdad

As soon as Bahá'u'lláh was released from prison, the king of Persia ordered Him to take His family and leave the country at once. Bahá'u'lláh was exiled, which meant He had to leave His native land forever. The king thought that by sending Him far, far away, they could stop Him from teaching the Faith of the Báb.

So Bahá'u'lláh, His wife and two small children left Persia and set out for the city of Baghdad. 'Abdu'l-Bahá was only nine years old, and His little sister, Bahíyyih, was only six. Their baby brother, Mírzá Mihdí, was too small to make the trip, so he stayed behind with his grandmother. The whole family was sad because they loved Mihdí very much.

It was a long, hard journey to Baghdad. There were no airplanes or cars in those days, so the family traveled mostly on foot. They walked for three months, crossing the steep, snow-covered mountains in the middle of winter. Bahá'u'lláh was weak from being in prison. He was sick from the poison in His food. His back was bent and His neck was swollen from the weight of the prison chains.

Since all of their belongings had been stolen, the family started out on their journey with almost nothing. They did not even have enough money to buy warm clothes. They were cold and hungry. Bahá'u'lláh said that sometimes it was so cold they were unable to speak, and there was so much ice and snow, it was impossible to move.

On their journey, the travelers sometimes spent the night in a caravanserai,¹ where the whole family would stay in one small room with no beds or lights. At other times, they camped in the wilderness. Bahá'u'lláh's wife washed their few clothes by hand. Her delicate fingers became sore and her skin cracked because of the cold, but she never complained.

One time, she tried to make a sweet cake for Bahá'u'lláh and the children, but in the dark, she accidentally added salt instead of sugar. 'Abdu'l-Bahá said that, after eating that salty cake, His mouth burned all night. Finally, after three months of hardship, the family reached Baghdad.

Bahá'u'lláh's enemies thought that now, things would settle down in Persia, and the Faith of the Báb would die out. They didn't realize that by banishing² Bahá'u'lláh, they were actually helping to carry out God's Plan. Wherever He went, more and more people learned about the Faith, and it began to spread.

---

1. **caravanserai:** A simple roadside inn where travelers could rest
2. **banish:** To exile, send away, cast out, deport

## Study Questions

1. What does "exile" mean?
2. Why was Bahá'u'lláh exiled?
3. Who went with Him and where did they go?
4. Describe their journey. How long did it take and why was it so hard?
5. What happened when Bahá'u'lláh's wife tried to make a sweet cake for her family?
6. How did God turn hardship and exile into something positive?
7. Has anything bad or unfair ever happened to you that led to something positive?

Bahá'u'lláh: The Glory of God

# 7  The Hermit in the Mountains

When Bahá'u'lláh and His family arrived in Baghdad, the Faith of the Báb seemed to be falling apart. The Báb and thousands of His followers had been killed. Others had been thrown into prison and the few remaining Bábís were sad and afraid. Bahá'u'lláh began to encourage them, and the little community grew stronger once again. They loved Bahá'u'lláh and listened to His teachings.

This made Mírzá Yahyá jealous. Mírzá Yahyá was Bahá'u'lláh's own brother, and he wanted to be the leader of the Bábís. He was a mean person who told lies and tried to stir up trouble against Bahá'u'lláh. Most people paid no attention to him, but others were confused.

So Bahá'u'lláh decided to leave Baghdad. He did not want to cause disunity or bring sorrow to any heart. Also, that way, the Bábís would find out who their true leader was. If Mirzá Yahyá was a good leader, the people would want to follow him.

With great sadness, Bahá'u'lláh left His home and family. Without telling anyone, He went to live 200 miles[1] away in the remote[2] mountains of Kurdistan. He was gone for two years. Even His own family didn't know where He was. His only companions were the birds and animals in the wilderness.

Bahá'u'lláh disguised Himself as a poor hermit and lived alone on the top of a rough mountain. Sometimes He stayed in an old stone hut, where He could pray and be at peace. Other times He slept in caves or under the stars. He lived in poverty, eating only a little bread, rice and goat's milk. Some days He had no food at all.

Bahá'u'lláh was sad because of what Mírzá Yahyá had done, but He was also content because He was far away from His enemies and He felt close to God. He was getting ready for the great work that God wanted Him to do.

Once in a while, Bahá'u'lláh would meet shepherds and hunters living in the mountains. He answered their questions and helped them with their problems. Little by little, the mountain people got to know Bahá'u'lláh and grew to love Him. Soon stories about a wise and holy man spread throughout the land.

When His family learned about the hermit in the mountains, they knew it was Bahá'u'lláh and begged Him to return. The Bábís also wanted Him to come back and they were ready to follow Him. Bahá'u'lláh did return, and for a time, His family and friends were happy again.

1. **200 miles:** About 320 kilometers
2. **remote:** Far away from civilization

## Study Questions

1. Why were the Báb's followers so discouraged?
2. Who was Mírzá Yahyá and why was he jealous of Bahá'u'lláh?
3. Why did Bahá'u'lláh leave Baghdad and where did He go?
4. What was His life like in the mountains and how long did He stay?
5. What made Him happy and what made Him sad during that time?
6. Why do you think Bahá'u'lláh didn't tell anyone where He was going?
7. Why did He go back to Baghdad?

# 8 The Writing Lesson

Bahá'u'lláh lived like a dervish* for two years in the mountains of Kurdistan. One day, He saw a little boy crying on his way to school. Bahá'u'lláh stopped the boy and asked what was wrong.

The child had been punished by his teacher for having bad handwriting. Then the teacher had written out a special lesson so the boy could practice his letters. He was supposed to copy it for homework, but the writing lesson had gotten lost. The teacher would be angry and the boy was afraid. Tears filled his eyes once again.

Bahá'u'lláh comforted him and told him not to cry. He wrote another lesson in the boy's notebook and showed him how to copy the letters with great care. The child practiced again and again. Finally, he was able to write the letters almost perfectly. He thanked Bahá'u'lláh and went back to school with a smile on his face and a happy heart.

The teacher was amazed when he saw Bahá'u'lláh's beautiful handwriting. "Where did you get this?" he exclaimed. The boy told him about the dervish in the mountains. "This writing is not from a dervish," said the teacher, "but a royal person from the court of the king."

The story spread, and soon many people came to visit Bahá'u'lláh. They knew He was a great person, and they grew to love Him, but they didn't yet know who He really was.

* **dervish:** Muslim religious group whose followers live like hermits in extreme poverty

## Study Questions

1. Why was the boy crying?

2. How did Bahá'u'lláh help the boy?

3. How did the teacher know that Bahá'u'lláh was not a dervish?

4. Describe a time when you helped someone else, or someone helped you.

#  The Declaration of Bahá'u'lláh

Ten years had passed since Bahá'u'lláh was released from prison and exiled to Baghdad. He still had not told anyone He was a Messenger of God. The king of Persia was hoping that people would forget about Him and that the Faith of the Báb would fade away.

But the citizens of Baghdad had grown to love Bahá'u'lláh. He was wise and kind, and many came to Him for help and advice. When the king of Persia heard about His rising power, he was afraid and decided to send Him even farther away.

News spread that Bahá'u'lláh would soon be exiled to the city of Constantinople, and the people of Baghdad were very sad. Many came to say goodbye: friends and strangers, young and old, princes and beggars, merchants, orphans, Arabs, Persians, Kurds, Muslim leaders and government officials. Even the governor of Baghdad was there.

Bahá'u'lláh's friends were sobbing with grief. One small child grabbed His robe, and crying loudly, begged Him not to go. The streets and rooftops were crowded with people who had gathered for one last look at such a good and holy man.

Bahá'u'lláh's house was too small to hold all of these people, so He gathered His friends in a beautiful garden, by a river outside the city. It was called the Garden of Ridván, which means *paradise*.

Bahá'u'lláh crossed the river in a small boat, set up His tent in the garden, and prepared to welcome the stream of visitors from Baghdad.

It was springtime and the garden was in full bloom. The pathways were lined with trees and flowers. The rippling water made a peaceful sound. A gentle breeze whispered through the leaves. Roses perfumed the air and nightingales sang sweet melodies in the moonlight, creating an atmosphere of enchantment.

Every day before the sun rose, the gardeners picked hundreds of roses from the garden and piled them in the middle of Bahá'u'lláh's tent. When His friends came in for tea, the pile of roses was so high they couldn't see over it. When they left, Bahá'u'lláh gave them roses as gifts for His friends in the city.

Bahá'u'lláh stayed in the Ridván Garden for twelve days. During that time, He told His friends that He was the Messenger of God promised by the Báb and by all the religions of the past. He had come to bring peace and unity to the world. Ten years had gone by since Bahá'u'lláh first received His revelation in a dark underground prison. He had kept it a secret for all these years.
**Now it was time to tell His friends the good news.**

All sadness disappeared and His friends were filled with joy!
From that day on, they were called Bahá'ís, which means "followers of Bahá'u'lláh." The Divine Springtime had come! The Bahá'í Faith had been born. The date was April 21, 1863.

Once again, God had changed crisis into victory. Bahá'u'lláh's enemies thought that banishing Him would harm His Cause and bring sorrow to His followers. Instead it became a time of great joy. Now, every year, Bahá'ís around the world celebrate the Festival of Ridván, remembering Bahá'u'lláh's declaration as the Promised One.

# The Most Great Prison

After Bahá'u'lláh's declaration in the Garden of Ridván, many more people became His admirers. This made the king very angry, and Bahá'u'lláh was exiled once again. After only four months in Constantinople, He was sent even farther away to Adrianople, and finally to Akká, in the Holy Land. Bahá'u'lláh was a prisoner in Akká for twenty-four years.

In those days, the entire city of Akká was a prison, and the worst criminals in the land were sent there. Akká was dark and dirty, swarming with fleas, and surrounded by a high wall with guards at the gate. No one could go in or out without permission. The water was filthy, and the air was so smelly that people said if a bird flew over Akká, it would die. The king hoped Bahá'u'lláh would die there too, and that His teachings would be forgotten.

When Bahá'u'lláh arrived, the people of Akká were very cruel. They laughed at the prisoners, threw stones at them and called them names.

The Most Great Prison[1]

Bahá'u'lláh and almost seventy companions (including women and children) were imprisoned in two small rooms. There was no furniture and the floor was covered with mud. The prisoners were hungry and thirsty. **They were given salty water to drink and stale bread to eat.** With the dirty water and bad air, almost all of them got sick, and three people died. Bahá'u'lláh spent over two years in the prison there.

When the Bahá'í's of Persia found out where Bahá'u'lláh was, many walked all the way to Akká just to see Him. It was a long and dangerous journey, taking over four months to cross the mountains and deserts on foot. When they arrived, the guards wouldn't let them into the city.

A few pilgrims[2] managed to reach the outer wall of the prison. Some stood outside the wall for days, hoping for a glimpse of Bahá'u'lláh. If they were lucky, they would see Him waving through the prison window. This was enough to give His followers hope and courage. They forgot how tired they were, and walked all the way back to Persia to tell their friends.

One night, something very tragic happened. Bahá'u'lláh's son Mírzá Mihdí was saying his prayers on the prison roof, when he accidentally fell through a skylight[3] and was killed. He was only 22 years old.

Bahá'u'lláh was so sad. Perhaps this is one reason He called the prison in Akká the Most Great Prison. It was even worse than being chained underground in the Síyáh-Chál. Mírzá Mihdí's last wish was that his life could be a sacrifice, so the prison doors would open and the friends could see Bahá'u'lláh again.

A few months later, Mírzá Mihdí's wish came true. The Bahá'ís were let out of the prison and went to live in a small house nearby. Bahá'u'lláh was still a prisoner of the king, but after many years, the people of Akká began to admire Him, and the government officials allowed Him to move to a nicer home in the country. It had been nine years since the Messenger of God had seen any grass or flowers or trees or anything green. During those final years, Bahá'u'lláh revealed[4] many books, giving us the laws and teachings of God for today.

Bahá'u'lláh's home in the country[1]

## The Passing of Bahá'u'lláh

Bahá'u'lláh was now almost 75 years old. After a lifetime of hardship and suffering in order to bring us the Message of God, His mission on earth was coming to an end. He gathered His friends and family and told them He was pleased with them all. He said they should remain united and raise up the Cause of God.

Shrine of Bahá'u'lláh[5]

His blessed spirit returned to the Kingdom of God on May 29, 1892. The Sun of Bahá had set. His body was buried in a beautiful shrine outside the city of Akká. Today, people come from all over the world to pray at this holiest spot on earth. You too may visit it someday.

1. **photo:** Courtesy of David Haslip
2. **pilgrim:** One who travels to visit a sacred place or person for religious reasons
3. **skylight:** A window in the roof
4. **reveal:** To make known the Word of God
5. **photo:** By Steven Gottlieb

# Proclamation to the Kings

In the time of Bahá'u'lláh, kings had power over all the people. Whatever they ordered had to be obeyed immediately. Bahá'u'lláh had been banished and imprisoned by two of those kings. During His exiles, He wrote to them and to the other rulers of the earth as well.

Bahá'u'lláh told them that He was the Prophet of God for today, and called on them to accept His message. He said God wanted them to rule with justice and to treat their people with kindness. He told them to end slavery, to care for the poor, to stop making wars, and to work together for unity.

**Bahá'u'lláh wrote to:**

- Násiri'd-Dín Sháh, the King of Iran
- Sultán 'Abdu'l-Azíz of Turkey
- Queen Victoria of England
- Napoleon III of France
- Czar Alexander II of Russia
- Kaiser Wilhelm I of Germany
- Emperor Francis Joseph of Austria
- Presidents of the American republics
- Pope Pius IX and other religious leaders

Can you imagine a prisoner writing to a king, and telling him what to do? Bahá'u'lláh even wrote to the Pope to say that Christ had returned!

Bahá'u'lláh wanted the human race to be happy and at peace. He warned the kings that if they didn't listen, they would lose their power and the world would fall into a time of war and great troubles. That is exactly what happened.

When Napoleon read his letter, he said proudly, "If this man is God, I am two gods!"[1] Of all the rulers Bahá'u'lláh wrote to, only the Queen had a kind reply, and hers is the only throne that still stands today. The rest have disappeared.

"Ye are but vassals,[2] O kings of the earth!
He Who is the King of Kings hath appeared…"

(Bahá'u'lláh)

**1. Ref:** Promised Day Is Come, p. 51
**2. vassals:** Servants

Bahá'u'lláh: The Glory of God

# Quiz on the Life of Bahá'u'lláh

1. Why does God send us Messengers?
2. Who was Bahá'u'lláh?
3. What does "Bahá'u'lláh" mean?
4. What name did His parents give Him?
5. When and where was He born?
6. What was Iran called at the time of Bahá'u'lláh?
7. Was Bahá'u'lláh's family rich or poor? Explain.
8. Did Bahá'u'lláh go to school like other children?
9. Where did His knowledge come from?
10. What was Bahá'u'lláh like as a teenager?
11. What did Bahá'u'lláh's father see in a dream, and what did it mean?
12. What did Bahá'u'lláh see in the puppet show, and what did it mean to Him?
13. What was the name of Bahá'u'lláh's wife, and what was she like?
14. Why was Bahá'u'lláh arrested and put in prison?
15. What was the name of the prison and what was it like?
16. What wonderful thing happened to Bahá'u'lláh in the Black Pit?
17. Why did the king of Persia exile Bahá'u'lláh?
18. What was the journey like from Persia to Baghdad?
19. After reaching Baghdad, why did Bahá'u'lláh go to live in the mountains alone?
20. How long was He gone?
21. How did Bahá'u'lláh's family find Him again?
22. How long did Bahá'u'lláh wait before telling people He was God's Messenger?
23. When and where did He choose to tell them?
24. When and where did the Bahá'í Faith begin?
25. What does "Ridván" mean?
26. What was the Ridván Garden like?
27. Compare the Ridván Garden to the Síyáh-Chál.
28. Why is Bahá'u'lláh called the Promised One of all religions?
29. When He came, were the people expecting Him?
30. What was Bahá'u'lláh's main message?

# Music

"The art of music is divine and effective. It is the food of the soul and spirit.
Through the power and charm of music the spirit of man is uplifted.
It has wonderful sway and effect in the hearts of children,
for their hearts are pure, and melodies have great influence in them."

'Abdu'l-Bahá, The Promulgation of Universal Peace, p. 52

Bahá'u'lláh: The Glory of God – Music

# Music Program

*"A wonderful song giveth wings to the spirit and filleth the heart with exaltation."*
'Abdu'l-Bahá, Bahá'í World Faith, p. 334

## To the Music Coordinator

Singing brings people together for an enjoyable activity. It uplifts the souls and connects the hearts. It is also an excellent tool for memorizing information and for teaching and reinforcing new ideas.

The songs included in this teacher's guide have been selected to help children learn about Bahá'u'lláh. The students should all have song sheets in their folders. As the music coordinator, your job is to help them learn some of these songs.

If the children's classes are held during a weekend retreat format, a morning sing-a-long has been scheduled each day for this purpose. There are also opportunities for singing after lunch and in the evenings. Classroom teachers may ask for your assistance with music that is part of their class. In addition, the music coordinator should help with the children's performance and the rehearsal. Check with the organizers for a schedule with the exact times.

As the song leader, you should be enthusiastic, confident and encouraging. Be patient with children who are shy or who don't catch on right away. When teaching a song for the first time, you will need to sing slowly, with a lot of repetition. If you play an instrument, you can bring it with you to accompany the singing and to keep the beat.

Be sure to learn the songs and the correct meaning and pronunciation of all the words beforehand, and arrive early so your session starts on time. Bring a music stand if available. A song sheet and musical scores are included on the following pages. Some of the selections have been simplified and shortened for group singing with children. If you know a different melody for a particular song, use the version you feel most comfortable with.

Songs in other languages have been included and may be used if desired. *The Prince of Peace* and *The Prisoner* do not need to be learned, but are included because they relate to the theme and might be interesting for the children to hear if a recording is available.

To start a sing-a-long session:

- Ask the children to take out their song sheets and find the first song.
- Ask them what they think the song is about, and explain if necessary.
- Pronounce and define any difficult words.
- Play the song through once, encouraging those who know it to sing with you.
- If necessary, have children repeat each line in a speaking voice before trying to sing.
- Give the starting note and play or clap out the rhythm while everyone sings.
- Practice several times before going on to the next song.

## Transposing a Song

> Idea from Dick Grover

If the notes of a song are too high or too low to sing comfortably, you can easily change the song to a new key—called *transposing*. On a guitar, the easiest way to change the key is by using a capo. You can also follow the steps below.

1. Start by determining the original key (usually the first chord on the sheet music). Play that chord and sing a few lines of the song. If it is too high or too low, you will need to find a more comfortable key.

2. Play a different chord and try singing the song in that key. If it feels comfortable, you have found the right key. If not, play another chord and sing a few lines until you have found a comfortable key to sing in. You will transpose the song to that key. For example, if the song is too low in the original key of D but feels just right in the key of G, you will transpose the entire song to the key of G.

3. Using the chart and moving clockwise, count the number of steps from the original chord to the transposed chord. For example, there are five steps from D to G.

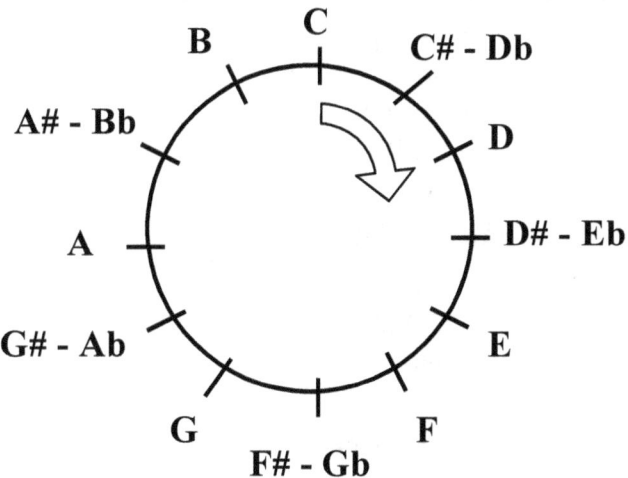

4. Then go through the entire song, changing all the chords by the same number of steps. Based on our example, you would raise all the D chords to G. All the E chords would change to A. An A7 would become a D7, etc. Write the new chord directly over the syllable you will be singing with that chord, or you will be out of rhythm when you play the song.

---

**#** means "sharp" (It raises that note by a half step.)

**b** means "flat" (It lowers that note by a half step.)

C# and Db are the same note and count together as one step.
This is also true for D# and Eb, F# and Gb, G# and Ab, A# and Bb.

Bahá'u'lláh: The Glory of God – Music

# SONG SHEET

Name _____

Note: Most of these songs are copyrighted and are used with permission.

### Shine Your Light (D-A7)

(by Greg Dahl)

Shine your light on me Bahá'u'lláh,
I am over here, Bahá'u'lláh.
Shine your light on me Bahá'u'lláh,
Glori-ay, glori-ay.

- Let me be a lamp...
- Help me light the world...
- Shine your light on me...

### God Is Sufficient (Em-B7-C)

(Words of Bahá'u'lláh, Dawn-Breakers:631)

God is sufficient unto me,
   He is the All-sufficing. (2x)
In Him let the trusting trust.
   Let the trusting trust. (4x)

### Bahá'u'lláh (D-G-Em-A)

(by Creadell Haley)

Bahá'u'lláh, Bahá'u'lláh,
Bahá, Bahá'u'lláh.

- The Glory of God...
- The Prince of Peace...
- The Lord of Hosts...
- The Spirit of Truth...
- The Promised One of all the ages...
- Bahá'u'lláh...

### We Are the People of Bahá (C-F-G7)

(by Donna Taylor)

| | |
|---|---|
| We are the people of Bahá... | (English) |
| Somos la gente de Bahá... | (Spanish) |
| Nous sommes le peuple de Bahá... | (French) |
| Má bandigáni Bahá... | (Persian) |

### Song of The Prophets (A-D-E)

(by Marvin Dryer)

Krishna, Buddha, Zoroaster,
Abraham, Moses, Christ,
Muhammad, the Báb, Bahá'u'lláh,
The spirit's the same.
Bahá'u'lláh teaches for today,
Tells us to look to the spirit,
Not to worship the name.

### El Rey de los Reyes (G-C-D)

(Spanish; composer unknown)

El es el Rey de los Reyes, (3x)
El es Bahá'u'lláh.

- El es el Sol Brillante...
- El es el Prometido...
- El es la Gloria de Dios...
- El es el Rey de los Reyes...

### Can't You See the New Day (A-E)

(Composer unknown)

Bahá'u'lláh has come,
   Can't you see the new day. } (3x)
He's the Glory of God.

- There is only one God...
- All religions are one...
- Mankind is one...

Can't you see the new day,
   Bahá'u'lláh has come. } (3x)
He's the Glory of God.

### King of Kings (D-A)

(Slow, in a round; composer unknown)

King of Kings and Lord of Lords,
   Glory, Hallelujah! (2x)
Bahá'u'lláh, Glory, Hallelujah! (2x)

## I Have Found Bahá'u'lláh  (G-C-D)
(by Nosisana Velem)

I have found Bahá'u'lláh,
In the early days of my life.
He is in my heart,
Now and forever.

Alláh'u'Abhá, Alláh'u'Abhá,
Alláh'u'Abhá, now and forever.

## The Nightingale  (C-G-F)
(by Chris Ruhe-Schoen)

The nightingale is singing
   all over the world. (2x)
The nightingale Bahá'u'lláh. (2x)
Lai, lai, lai...

The nightingale is singing
   that we are brothers…

The nightingale is singing
   that we are sisters…

## Prince of Peace  (Am-Dm-E-G-F)
(by Lloyd Haynes, with changes in italics)

There lived a Man across the ocean,
There lived a Man across the sea;
He spoke of love, He spoke of justice,
He spoke to *us* of unity.

**(chorus)**
They called Him the Prince of Peace.
They called Him the Prince of Peace.
From Constantinople to Adrianople,
To Akká the prison by the sea.

His teachings spread *to every nation,*
His teachings spread to all mankind,
His teachings took in all religions,
And left no helpless soul behind.

## Soon Will All  (echo song) (Bm-A-F#)
(Words of Bahá'u'lláh, God Passes By: 184)

Soon will all that dwell on earth,
Be enlisted under these banners.
Yá-Bahá'u'l-Abhá. (4x)

## The Prisoner
(by England Dan and John Ford Coley)

Take us to the prisoner
Let us gaze into his eyes,
To see what kind of man
It takes a nation to despise.
Take us to the prisoner
Let us look upon his face,
To see why twenty thousand men
Would gladly take his place.
Won't someone give a drink to him?
Remove the chains and let him live,
Let him live.

Take us to the prisoner
Let us listen to his voice,
To see why worlds of wisdom's
In a cell without a choice.
Take us to the prisoner
Torn and bent beneath the chains,
We wonder if the world is really
Worthy of his name?
Won't someone give a drink to him?
Remove the chains and let him live,
Let him live.

We know where we're going
For we heard the new winds blowing
And we've got to know for ourselves.
It won't help to listen to someone else.

Take us to the prisoner
With his eyes so full of grace,
The priests have lied
And kings have died
Filled with their own disgrace.
Won't someone give a drink to him?
Remove the chains and let him live.

 Let him live.
Let him live.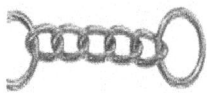
Let him live.

## SONGS ABOUT BAHA'U'LLAH

1. Bahá'u'lláh ................................................. 155
2. Can't You See the New Day ............................. 156
3. God Is Sufficient Unto Me ............................... 157
4. I Have Found Bahá'u'lláh ................................ 158
5. King of Kings and Lord of Lords ...................... 159
6. The Nightingale ............................................. 160
7. Prince of Peace ............................................. 161
8. El Rey de los Reyes ....................................... 162
9. Shine Your Light ........................................... 163
10. Song of the Prophets ..................................... 164
11. Soon Will All That Dwell on Earth .................... 165
12. We Are the People of Bahá ............................. 166

---

### Acknowledgements

Our deepest gratitude goes to Roger Olsen for transcribing the music for these songs; to Jonathan Gottlieb and Fran Gregory for their assistance; and to Tony Lee of Kalimát Press for permission to use those songs that first appeared in *Building Bridges: A Bahá'í Songbook* (compiled by Peggy Caton and Dale Nomura, for the U.S. Bahá'í National Education Committee, published by Kalimát Press: Los Angeles, 1984). In some cases, the songs have been simplified and shortened for the purpose of group singing with children.

Marvin Dryer's "Song of the Prophets," originally titled "Bahá'í Talking Blues," can be found with additional lyrics on the music CD "We Are Bahá'ís," available from the U.S. Bahá'í Distribution Service: www.bahaibookstore.com, (800) 999-9019. "The Nightingale" by Chris Ruhe, is available on the "Fruits of the Spirit" CD, while supplies last, from Louhelen Bahá'í School bookstore: Louhelen@usbnc.org. No score has been included for "The Prisoner" by England Dan and John Ford Coley. The song can be heard on the "Lift Up Your Voices" CD, vol. I, available from www.bahaibookstore.com.

While most of the songs included here are used with permission, a few have passed into the realm of Bahá'í folk songs and their origins have been lost. We would be pleased to hear from any artists we have been unable to locate and acknowledge.

# Baha'u'llah

Words and music by
Creadell Haley

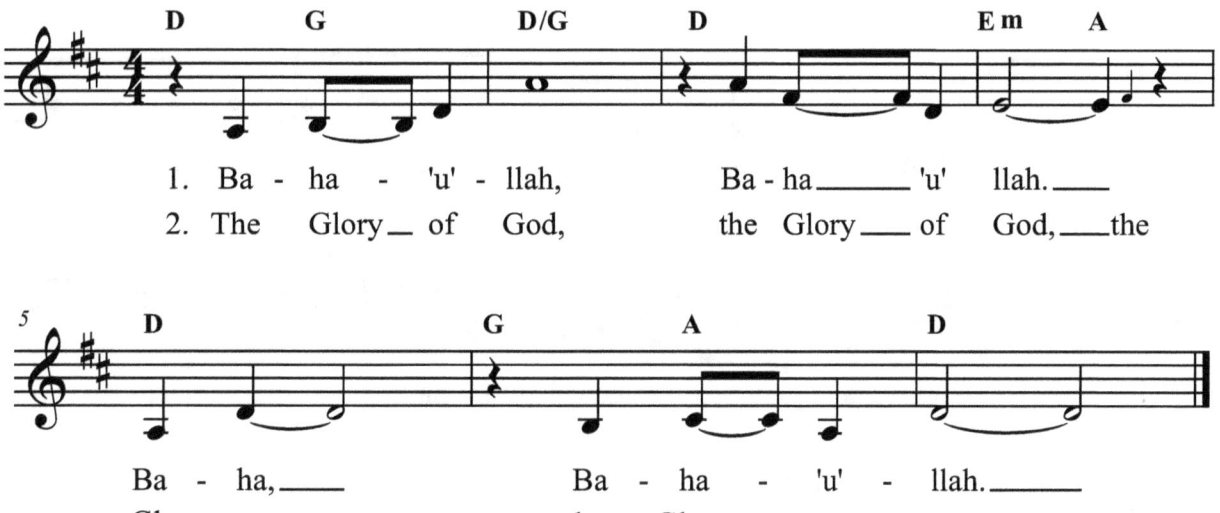

3. The Prince of Peace...

4. The Lord of Hosts...

5. The Spirit of Truth...

6. The Promised One of all the ages...

7. Baha'u'llah...

# Can't You See the New Day

From the Southern USA, early 1970's
Composer Unknown

Ba-ha-'u'-llah has come, Can't you see the new day;— Ba-ha-'u'-

llah has come, Can't you see the new day: Ba-ha-'u'-llah has come, Can't you

see the new day;— He's the Glo - ry of God.

2. There is only one God....

3. All religions are one...

4. Mankind is one...

5. Can't you see the new day, Baha'u'llah has come (3x)
   He's the Glory of God.

Note: This song can be done as a call and response.
The leader sings the first phrase: "Baha'u'llah has come."
The group responds: "Can't you see the new day."
Repeat this three times, then all sing: "He's the Glory of God."

# I Have Found Baha'u'llah

by Nosisana Velem

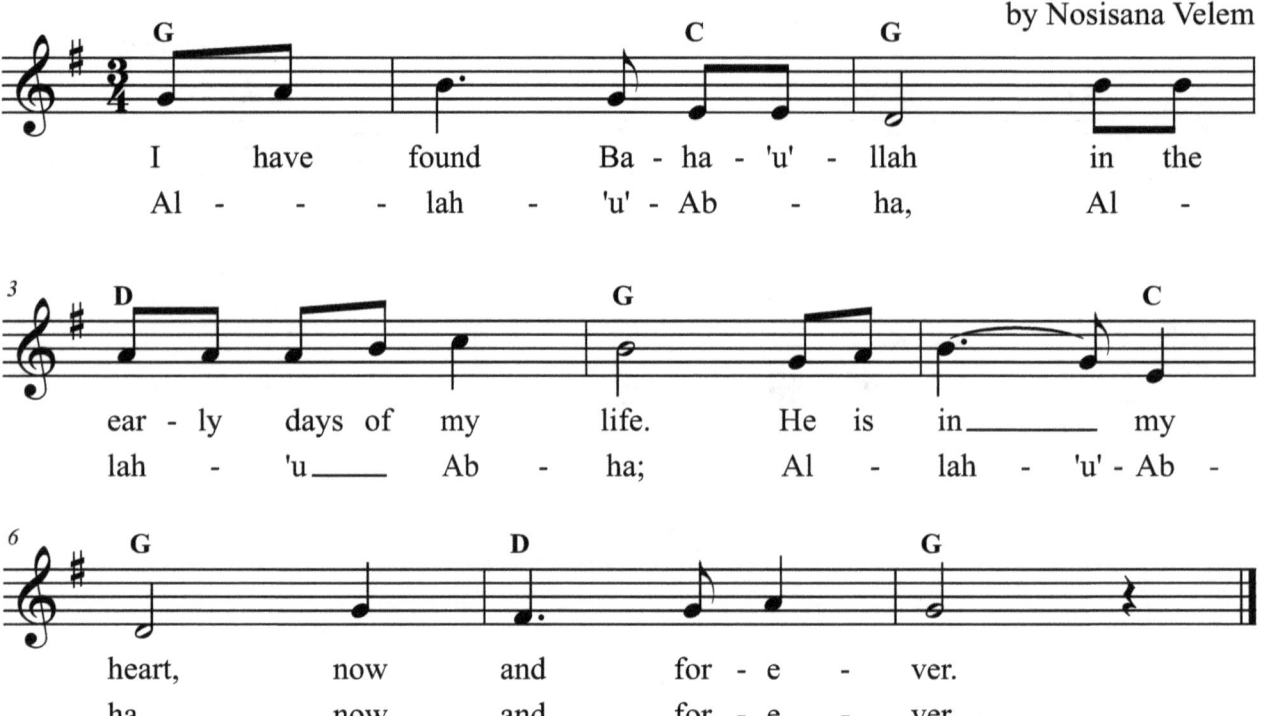

# King of Kings

Composer Unknown

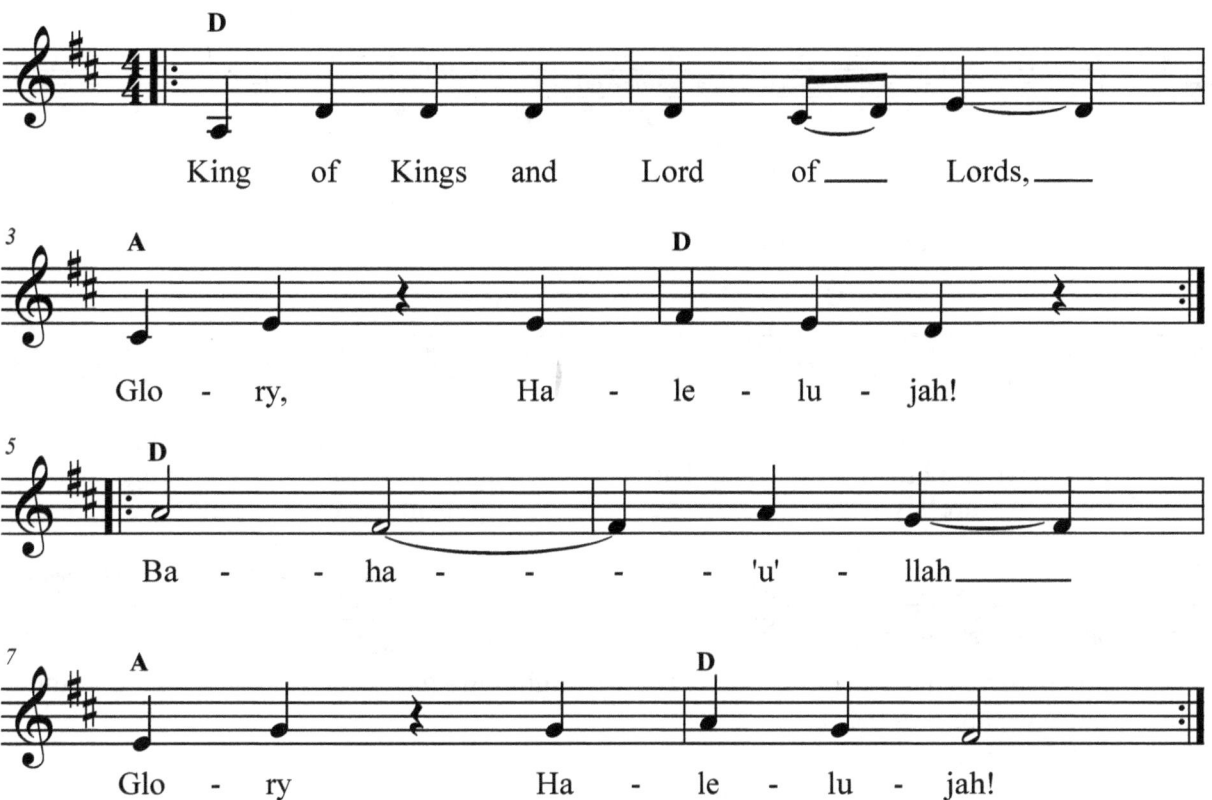

Note: This song may be sung as a round.
The first group sings the first four measures, twice.
When they start on measure #5, the second group begins.

# The Nightingale

by Chris Ruhe-Schoen
Used with permission

# The Prince of Peace

by Lloyd Hanes

Bahá'í Children's Classes and Retreats: Theme 4, p. 161

# El Rey de los Reyes

Composer Unknown

3. El es el Pro-me-ti-do...

4. El es la Glo-ria de Dios...

5. El es el Rey de los Re-yes...

# Shine Your Light

Greg Dahl
From *Building Bridges* songbook
Used with permission

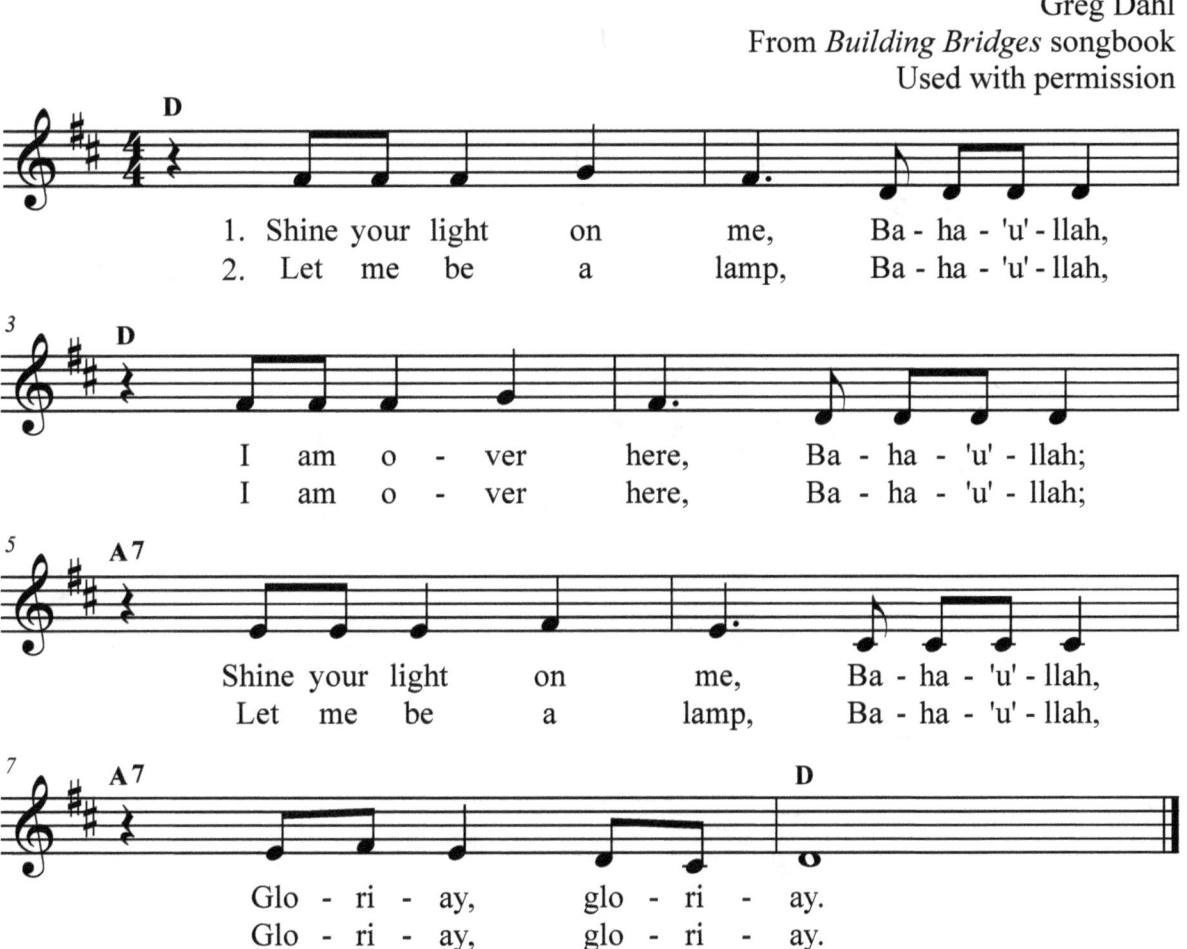

3. Help me light the world, Baha'u'llah...

4. Help me teach your Cause, Baha'u'llah...

5. Shine your light on me, Baha'u'llah...

# Song of the Prophets

by Marvin Dryer
Used with permission

Krish-na, Bud-dha, Zo-ro-as-ter, Ab-raham, Mo-ses, Christ, Mu-

hammad, the Bab, Ba-ha-'u'-llah, The spi-rit's the same - Ba-

ha-'u'-llah teach-es for to-day, Tells us to look to the spi-

- - rit, not to wor-ship the name.

# Soon Will All That Dwell on Earth

Words of Baha'u'llah  
*God Passes By*, p. 184  
Music by Van Gilmer  
Used with permission

Divide the class into two groups.

Group #1 sings the first line, then holds the last note ("earth") while group #2 sings the first line.

Group #1 then sings the second line, while group #2 holds their last note.

Continue in this manner for the whole song.

# We Are the People of Baha

by Donna Taylor
From *Building Bridges* songbook
Used with permission

(English)  We are the people of Baha...

(Spanish)  Somos la gente de Baha...

(French)  Nous sommes le peuple de Baha...

(Persian)  Ma bandigani Baha...

Bahá'u'lláh: The Glory of God

# CLOSING ACTIVITIES

At the end of the retreat or after the final class session on this theme, the organizers may wish to plan some closing activities for the participants. We have found the following schedule to be very effective. After the cleanup, call everyone together for a celebration of their achievements.

1. Begin with singing and prayers.

2. Ask for volunteers to recite any individual memory quotes learned.
   Then recite the main quotes together as a group, for example:

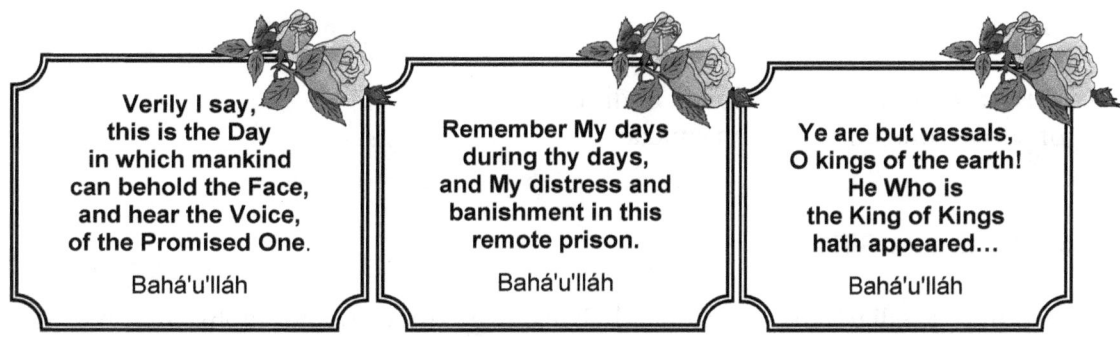

> Verily I say, this is the Day in which mankind can behold the Face, and hear the Voice, of the Promised One.
> Bahá'u'lláh

> Remember My days during thy days, and My distress and banishment in this remote prison.
> Bahá'u'lláh

> Ye are but vassals, O kings of the earth! He Who is the King of Kings hath appeared…
> Bahá'u'lláh

3. Conduct a short oral evaluation of the activities. Go around the room and ask each child, youth and adult to share brief thoughts on the three items to the right, which should be written on the board. Anyone may pass his or her turn. Suggestions can be considered in planning for the next class or retreat. An adult should take notes.

   ➢ I liked…
   ➢ I learned…
   ➢ I suggest…

4. The organizers can then share any closing comments regarding the importance of teachers (see sample quotes below) and present small gifts of appreciation to the teachers, youth volunteers, musicians, cooks and other helpers. Ask capable children to read the quotes. (The second quote usually gets a good laugh!)

> "Among the greatest of all services that can possibly be rendered by man to Almighty God is the education and training of children…It is, however, very difficult to undertake this service, even harder to succeed in it." (Selections from the Writings of 'Abdu'l-Bahá, p. 133)
>
> "If, in this momentous task, a mighty effort be exerted, the world of humanity will shine out with other adornings…The very demons will change to angels…the wild-dog pack to gazelles…and ravening beasts to peaceful herds…" (Selections from the Writings of 'Abdu'l-Bahá, p. 130)
>
> "It followeth that whatever soul shall offer his aid to bring this about will assuredly be accepted at the heavenly Threshold, and extolled by the Company on high." (Selections from the Writings of 'Abdu'l-Bahá, p. 134)
>
> "If one should, in the right way, teach and train the children, he will be performing a service than which none is greater at the Sacred Threshold." ('Abdu'l-Bahá, Bahá'í Education, p. 32)

# Bahá'u'lláh: The Glory of God

5. Follow-up suggestions and any messages from the sponsoring Institution can also be shared at this time (see next page for ideas).

6. A simple ceremony with diplomas (see Retreat Manual), can be held to recognize those children who will be "graduating" to the Junior Youth Spiritual Empowerment Program.

7. Logistical announcements (lost-and-found items, rides home, etc.)

8. Closing song ("I Have Found Bahá'u'lláh" is a favorite way to end this retreat.)

9. Group photo

10. Dessert (We have a well-loved tradition of serve-yourself ice cream sundaes.)

**Ideas for Thank-you Gifts**

- The Bahá'í Media Bank (http://media.bahai.org) offers photographs of some of the places visited by Bahá'u'lláh. Click on Buildings & Places > Holy Places - Acre. The images can be downloaded and printed on cardstock or laminated.

- A wall poster of the Mansion at Bahjí is also available from the Eesar Gallery (http://store.eesargallery.com). Enter "Bahjí" in the search box.

- Special Ideas offers postcards with the Short Obligatory Prayer and the name "Bahá'u'lláh." Visit: www.bahairesources.com and enter "PC-A3" in the search box.

- UnityWorks (www.UnityWorksStore.com) has produced two colorful PowerPoint programs which would make very nice gifts. The first is on the Central Figures of the Bahá'í Faith, and includes a section on Bahá'u'lláh. The second introduces Bahá'u'lláh's tablets to the kings and rulers of the world. Click on PowerPoint Firesides.

There is also a short (5-minute), very beautiful slide show with music, "Meditation on the Titles of Bahá'u'lláh" by Anne Gordon Perry, that can be shown to close the retreat. It is currently available as a PowerPoint presentation, and may soon be offered in DVD format. Contact: < unity9@sbcglobal.net >.

# FOLLOW-UP ACTIVITIES

**Teachers and sponsoring institutions can help children apply their new knowledge and skills by providing a variety of opportunities for practice. Some examples are listed below:**

- Ask the children to share during Feast what they have learned.

- Encourage them to recite memorized passages during a devotional meeting.

- Invite them to teach a class for younger children and to share stories from the life of Bahá'u'lláh.

- Ask them to talk about Bahá'u'lláh during a home visit.

- Encourage them to teach their friends and invite them to children's classes.

- Organize a children's fireside on "The Promised One" or "Clouds of Glory" and have children invite their family, friends and neighbors.

- Finished craft projects can be used as teaching tools to share stories from Bahá'u'lláh's life and to explain His station.

- Skits and demonstrations from the lessons can be performed during Holy Days, Unit Convention or Cluster Reflection Meetings.

- Teachers could also write a brief report of the children's class activities and submit this with photos to the local paper.

Bahá'u'lláh: The Glory of God

# References for Teachers

# References for Teachers

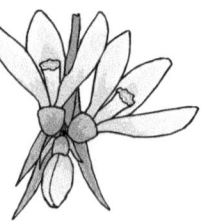

### LESSON #1: Birth of Bahá'u'lláh, Early Life and Station
The Puppet Show .................................................................................... 173
The Síyáh-Chál ....................................................................................... 175
The Maid of Heaven ............................................................................... 177

### LESSON #2: Declaration of Bahá'u'lláh
Departure from Baghdad ........................................................................ 179
Declaration of Bahá'u'lláh's Mission ...................................................... 180
The Promised One .................................................................................. 183

### LESSON #3: Exiles and Imprisonment
Exile to Constantinople .......................................................................... 184
Tribulations ............................................................................................ 185
Arrival in Akká ....................................................................................... 186
The Most Great Prison ........................................................................... 188
The Death of Mírzá Mihdí ...................................................................... 189

### LESSON #4: Clouds of Glory
Denial ..................................................................................................... 191
Response to Opposition ......................................................................... 192
Proclamation to the Kings and Rulers ................................................... 192
To Sultán 'Abdu'l-Azíz ........................................................................... 194
To Násiri'd-Dín Sháh ............................................................................. 194
To Napoleon III ..................................................................................... 194
Second Tablet to Napoleon III ............................................................... 195
To Kaiser Wilhelm I ............................................................................... 195
To Czar Alexander II ............................................................................. 195
To Queen Victoria .................................................................................. 196
To Emperor Francis Joseph ................................................................... 196
To the Rulers of America ....................................................................... 196
To the World's Religious Leaders .......................................................... 197
To Pope Pius IX ..................................................................................... 197

### ADDITIONAL REFERENCES
Station and Titles of Bahá'u'lláh ............................................................ 199
Photographic Narrative of the Life of Bahá'u'lláh ................................. 202

# LESSON #1

## His Birth, Early Life and Station

*Teachers may wish to study the following references in order to
gain a deeper understanding of the material presented in each lesson.*

### The Puppet Show

When I was still a child and had not yet attained the age of maturity, My father made arrangements in Tihrán for the marriage of one of My older brothers, and as is customary in that city, the festivities lasted for seven days and seven nights. On the last day it was announced that the play "Shah Sultan Salim" would be presented. A large number of princes, dignitaries, and notables of the capital gathered for the occasion. I was sitting in one of the upper rooms of the building and observing the scene. Presently a tent was pitched in the courtyard, and before long some small human-like figures, each appearing to be no more than about a hand's span in height, were seen to emerge from it and raise the call: "His Majesty is coming! Arrange the seats at once!" Other figures then came forth, some of whom were seen to be engaged in sweeping, others in sprinkling water, and thereafter another, who was announced as the chief town crier, raised his call and bade the people assemble for an audience with the king. Next, several groups of figures made their appearance and took their places, the first attired in hats and sashes after the Persian fashion, the second wielding battleaxes, and the third comprising a number of footmen and executioners carrying bastinados. Finally there appeared, arrayed in regal majesty and crowned with a royal diadem, a kingly figure, bearing himself with the utmost haughtiness and grandeur, at turns advancing and pausing in his progress, who proceeded with great solemnity, poise and dignity to seat himself upon his throne.

At that moment a volley of shots was fired, a fanfare of trumpets was sounded, and king and tent were enveloped in a pall of smoke. When it had cleared, the king, ensconced upon his throne, was seen surrounded by a suite of ministers, princes, and dignitaries of state who, having taken their places, were standing at attention in his presence. A captured thief was then brought before the king, who gave the order that the offender should be beheaded. Without a moment's delay the chief executioner cut off the thief's head, whence a blood-like liquid came forth. After this the king held audience with his court, during which intelligence was received that a rebellion had broken out on a certain frontier. Thereupon the king reviewed his troops and despatched several regiments supported by artillery to quell the uprising. A few moments later cannons were heard booming from behind the tent, and it was announced that a battle had been engaged.

This Youth regarded the scene with great amazement. When the royal audience was ended, the curtain was drawn, and, after some twenty minutes, a man emerged from behind the tent carrying a box under his arm.

"What is this box," I asked him, "and what was the nature of this display?"

"All this lavish display and these elaborate devices," he replied, "the king, the princes, and the ministers, their pomp and glory, their might and power, everything you saw, are now contained within this box."

I swear by My Lord Who, through a single word of His Mouth, hath brought into being all created things! Ever since that day, all the trappings of the world have seemed in the eyes of this Youth akin to that same spectacle. They have never been, nor will they ever be, of any weight and consequence, be it to the extent of a grain of mustard seed. How greatly I marveled that men should pride themselves upon such vanities, whilst those possessed of insight, ere they witness any evidence of human glory, perceive with certainty the inevitability of its waning. "Never have I looked upon any thing save that I have seen extinction before it; and God, verily, is a sufficient witness!"

It behoveth everyone to traverse this brief span of life with sincerity and fairness. Should one fail to attain unto the recognition of Him Who is the Eternal Truth, let him at least conduct himself with reason and justice. Erelong these outward trappings, these visible treasures, these earthly vanities, these arrayed armies, these adorned vestures, these proud and overweening souls, all shall pass into the confines of the grave, as though into that box. In the eyes of those possessed of insight, all this conflict, contention and vainglory hath ever been, and will ever be, like unto the play and pastimes of children. Take heed, and be not of them that see and yet deny.

Our call concerneth not this Youth and the loved ones of God, for they are already sore-tried and imprisoned and expect nothing from men such as thee. Our purpose is that thou mayest lift up thy head from the couch of heedlessness, shake off the slumber of negligence, and cease to oppose unjustly the servants of God. So long as thy power and ascendancy endure, strive to alleviate the suffering of the oppressed. Shouldst thou judge with fairness and observe with the eye of discernment the conflicts and pursuits of this transient world, thou wouldst readily acknowledge that they are even as the play which We have described.

Hearken unto the words of the one true God and pride thyself not in the things of this world. What hath become of those like unto thee who falsely claimed lordship on earth, who sought to quench the light of God in His land and to destroy the foundation of His mighty edifice in His cities? Where are they to be seen now? Be fair in thy judgement and return unto God, that perchance He might cancel the trespasses of thy vain life. Alas, We know that thou shalt never attain unto this, for such is thy cruelty that it hath made hell to blaze and the Spirit to lament, and hath caused the pillars of the Throne to shake and the hearts of the faithful to tremble.

O peoples of the earth! Incline your inner ears to the call of this Wronged One and pause to reflect upon the story that We have recounted. Perchance ye may not be consumed by the fire of self and passion, nor allow the vain and worthless objects of this nether world to withhold you from Him Who is the Eternal Truth. Glory and abasement, riches and poverty, tranquillity and tribulation, all will pass away, and all the peoples of the earth will erelong be laid to rest in their tombs. It behoveth therefore every man of insight to fix his gaze upon the goal of eternity, that perchance by the grace of Him Who is the Ancient King he may attain unto the immortal Kingdom and abide beneath the shade of the Tree of His Revelation.

Though this world be fraught with deception and deceit, yet it continually warneth all men of their impending extinction. The death of the father proclaimeth to the son that he, too, shall pass away. Would that the inhabitants of the world who have amassed riches for themselves and have strayed far from the True One might know who will eventually lay hand on their treasures; but, by the life of Bahá, no one knoweth this save God, exalted be His glory.

(Bahá'u'lláh, *The Summons of the Lord of Hosts,* p. 165-170)

---

## The Síyáh-Chál

We were consigned for four months to a place foul beyond comparison. As to the dungeon in which this Wronged One and others similarly wronged were confined, a dark and narrow pit were preferable. Upon Our arrival We were first conducted along a pitch-black corridor, from whence We descended three steep flights of stairs to the place of confinement assigned to Us. The dungeon was wrapped  in thick darkness, and Our fellow prisoners numbered nearly a hundred and fifty souls: thieves, assassins and highwaymen. Though crowded, it had no other outlet than the passage by which We entered. No pen can depict that place, nor any tongue describe its loathsome smell. Most of these men had neither clothes nor bedding to lie on. God alone knoweth what befell Us in that most foul-smelling and gloomy place!

…One night, in a dream, these exalted words were heard on every side: "Verily, We shall render Thee victorious by Thyself and by Thy Pen. Grieve Thou not for that which hath befallen Thee, neither be Thou afraid, for Thou art in safety. Erelong will God raise up the treasures of the earth—men who will aid Thee through Thyself and through Thy Name, wherewith God hath revived the hearts of such as have recognized Him."

…During the days I lay in the prison of Tihrán, though the galling weight of the chains and the stench-filled air allowed Me but little sleep, still in those infrequent moments of slumber I felt as if something flowed from the crown of My head over My breast, even as a mighty torrent that precipitateth itself upon the earth from the summit of a lofty mountain. Every limb of My body would, as a result, be set afire. At such moments My tongue recited what no man could bear to hear.

(Bahá'u'lláh, *Epistle to the Son of the Wolf,* p. 20-22)

---

Bahá'u'lláh's feet were placed in stocks, and around His neck were fastened the Qará-Guhar chains of such galling weight that their mark remained imprinted upon His body all the days of His life. "A heavy chain," 'Abdu'l-Bahá Himself has testified, "was placed about His neck by which He was chained to five other Bábís; these fetters were locked together by strong, very heavy, bolts and screws. His clothes were torn to pieces, also His headdress. In this terrible condition He was kept for four months." For three days and three nights, He was denied all manner of food and drink. Sleep was impossible to Him. The place was chill and damp, filthy, fever-stricken, infested with vermin, and filled with a noisome stench. Animated by a relentless hatred His enemies went even so far as to intercept and poison His food, in the hope of obtaining the favor of the mother of their sovereign, His most implacable foe—an attempt which, though it impaired His health for years to come, failed to achieve its purpose. "'Abdu'l-Bahá," Dr. J. E. Esslemont records in his book, "tells how, one day, He was allowed to enter the prison yard to see His beloved Father, where He came out for His daily exercise. Bahá'u'lláh was terribly altered, so ill He could hardly walk, His hair and beard unkempt, His neck galled and swollen from the pressure of a heavy steel collar, His body bent by the weight of His chains."

(Shoghi Effendi, *God Passes By,* p. 72)

---

The Síyáh-Chál, into which Bahá'u'lláh was thrown, originally a reservoir of water for one of the public baths of Tihrán, was a subterranean dungeon in which criminals of the worst type were wont to be confined. The darkness, the filth, and the character of the prisoners, combined to make of that pestilential dungeon the most abominable place to which human beings could be condemned. His feet were placed in stocks, and around His neck were fastened the Qará-Guhar chains, infamous throughout Persia for their galling weight. For three days and three nights, no manner of food or drink was given to Bahá'u'lláh. Rest and sleep were both impossible to Him. The place was infested with vermin, and the stench of that gloomy abode was enough to crush the very spirits of those who were condemned to suffer its horrors. Such were the conditions under which He was held down that even one of the executioners who were watching over Him was moved with pity. Several times this man attempted to induce Him to take some tea which he had managed to introduce into the dungeon under the cover of his garments. Bahá'u'lláh, however, would refuse to drink it. His family often endeavoured to persuade the guards to allow them to carry the food they had prepared for Him into His prison. Though at first no amount of pleading would induce the guards to relax the severity of their discipline, yet gradually they yielded to His friends' importunity. No one could be sure, however, whether that food would eventually reach Him, or whether He would consent to eat it whilst a number of His fellow-prisoners were starving before His eyes. Surely greater misery than had befallen these innocent victims of the wrath of their sovereign, could hardly be imagined.

(Shoghi Effendi, translator and editor, *The Dawn-Breakers,* p. 608-609)

---

"If sometime thou shouldst happen to visit the prison of His Majesty the Shah, ask thou the director and chief of that place to show thee those two chains, one of which is known as Qará-Guhar and the other as Salásil. I swear by the Day-star of Justice, that during four months, I was weighted and tormented by one of these chains. 'The sorrow of Jacob paleth before my sorrow; and all the afflictions of Job were but a part of my calamities.'"

(Bahá'u'lláh, quoted in *The Dawn-Breakers,* footnote, p. 608-609)

In a prayer revealed by Him at that time, Bahá'u'lláh, expatiating upon the woes and trials He had endured in the Síyáh-Chál, thus bears witness to the hardships undergone in the course of that "terrible journey": "My God, My Master, My Desire!... Thou hast created this atom of dust through the consummate power of Thy might, and nurtured Him with Thine hands which none can chain up.... Thou hast destined for Him trials and tribulations which no tongue can describe, nor any of Thy Tablets adequately recount. The throat Thou didst accustom to the touch of silk Thou hast, in the end, clasped with strong chains, and the body Thou didst ease with brocades and velvets Thou hast at last subjected to the abasement of a dungeon. Thy decree hath shackled Me with unnumbered fetters, and cast about My neck chains that none can sunder. A number of years have passed during which afflictions have, like showers of mercy, rained upon Me... How many the nights during which the weight of chains and fetters allowed Me no rest, and how numerous the days during which peace and tranquillity were denied Me, by reason of that wherewith the hands and tongues of men have afflicted Me! Both bread and water which Thou hast, through Thy all-embracing mercy, allowed unto the beasts of the field, they have, for a time, forbidden unto this servant, and the things they refused to inflict upon such as have seceded from Thy Cause, the same have they suffered to be inflicted upon Me, until, finally, Thy decree was irrevocably fixed, and Thy behest summoned this servant to depart out of Persia, accompanied by a number of frail-bodied men and children of tender age, at this time when the cold is so intense that one cannot even speak, and ice and snow so abundant that it is impossible to move."

(Shoghi Effendi, *God Passes By,* p. 108-109)

---

## The Maid of Heaven

While engulfed in tribulations I heard a most wondrous, a most sweet voice, calling above My head. Turning My face, I beheld a Maiden—the embodiment of the remembrance of the name of My Lord—suspended in the air before Me. So rejoiced was she in her very soul that her countenance shone with the ornament of the good pleasure of God, and her cheeks glowed with the brightness of the All-Merciful. Betwixt earth and heaven she was raising a call which captivated the hearts and minds of men. She was imparting to both My inward and outer being tidings which rejoiced My soul, and the souls of God's honoured servants.

Pointing with her finger unto My head, she addressed all who are in heaven and all who are on earth, saying: By God! This is the Best-Beloved of the worlds, and yet ye comprehend not. This is the Beauty of God amongst you, and the power of His sovereignty within you, could ye but understand. This is the Mystery of God and His Treasure, the Cause of God and His glory unto all who are in the kingdoms of Revelation and of creation, if ye be of them that perceive. This is He Whose Presence is the ardent desire of the denizens of the Realm of eternity, and of them that dwell within the Tabernacle of glory, and yet from His Beauty do ye turn aside.

(Bahá'u'lláh, *The Summons of the Lord of Hosts,* p. 5-6)

O Maid of Heaven! Step forth from the chambers of paradise and announce unto the people of the world: By the righteousness of God! He Who is the Best-Beloved of the worlds—He Who hath ever been the Desire of every perceiving heart, the Object of the adoration of all that are in heaven and on earth, and the Cynosure of the former and the latter generations—is now come!

(Bahá'u'lláh, *The Summons of the Lord of Hosts*, p. 53)

---

O ye beloved of God! O ye children of His Kingdom! Verily, verily, the new heaven and the new earth are come. The holy City, new Jerusalem, hath come down from on high in the form of a maid of heaven, veiled, beauteous, and unique, and prepared for reunion with her lovers on earth. The angelic company of the Celestial Concourse hath joined in a call that hath run throughout the universe, all loudly and mightily acclaiming: "This is the City of God and His abode, wherein shall dwell the pure and holy among His servants. He shall live with them, for they are His people and He is their Lord."

…He is Alpha and Omega. He is the One that will give unto him that is athirst of the fountain of the water of life and bestow upon the sick the remedy of true salvation.

…Rejoice, then, O ye beloved of the Lord and His chosen ones, and ye the children of God and His people, raise your voices to laud and magnify the Lord, the Most High; for His light hath beamed forth, His signs have appeared and the billows of His rising ocean have scattered on every shore many a precious pearl.

('Abdu'l-Bahá, *Selections from the Writings of 'Abdu'l-Bahá*, p. 12)

# LESSON #2

## Declaration of Bahá'u'lláh

*Teachers may wish to study the following references in order to gain a deeper understanding of the material presented in each lesson.*

### Departure from Baghdad

By the following day the Deputy-Governor had delivered to Bahá'u'lláh in a mosque, in the neighborhood of the governor's house, 'Alí Páshá's letter, addressed to Námiq Páshá, couched in courteous language, inviting Bahá'u'lláh to proceed, as a guest of the Ottoman government, to Constantinople, placing a sum of money at His disposal, and ordering a mounted escort to accompany Him for His protection. To this request Bahá'u'lláh gave His ready assent, but declined to accept the sum offered Him. On the urgent representations of the Deputy that such a refusal would offend the authorities, He reluctantly consented to receive the generous allowance set aside for His use, and distributed it, that same day, among the poor.

The effect upon the colony of exiles of this sudden intelligence was instantaneous and overwhelming. "That day," wrote an eyewitness, describing the reaction of the community to the news of Bahá'u'lláh's approaching departure, "witnessed a commotion associated with the turmoil of the Day of Resurrection. Methinks, the very gates and walls of the city wept aloud at their imminent separation from the Abhá Beloved. The first night mention was made of His intended departure His loved ones, one and all, renounced both sleep and food.... Not a soul amongst them could be tranquillized. Many had resolved that in the event of their being deprived of the bounty of accompanying Him, they would, without hesitation, kill themselves.... Gradually, however, through the words which He addressed them, and through His exhortations and His loving-kindness, they were calmed and resigned themselves to His good-pleasure."

…on a Wednesday afternoon (April 22, 1863), thirty-one days after Naw-Rúz, on the third of Dhi'l-Qa'dih, 1279 A.H., He set forth on the first stage of His four months' journey to the capital of the Ottoman Empire. That historic day, forever after designated as the first day of the Ridván Festival, the culmination of innumerable farewell visits which friends and acquaintances of every class and denomination, had been paying him, was one the like of which the inhabitants of Baghdad had rarely beheld. A concourse of people of both sexes and of every age, comprising friends and strangers, Arabs, Kurds and Persians, notables and clerics, officials and merchants, as well as many of the lower classes, the poor, the orphaned, the outcast, some surprised, others heartbroken, many tearful and apprehensive, a few impelled by curiosity or secret satisfaction, thronged the approaches of His house, eager to catch a final glimpse of One Who, for a decade, had, through precept and example, exercised so potent an influence on so large a number of the heterogeneous inhabitants of their city.

Leaving for the last time, amidst weeping and lamentation, His "Most Holy Habitation," out of which had "gone forth the breath of the All-Glorious," and from which had poured forth, in "ceaseless strains," the "melody of the All-Merciful," and dispensing on His way with a lavish hand a last alms to the poor He had so faithfully befriended, and uttering words of comfort to the disconsolate who besought Him on every side, He, at length, reached the banks of the river, and was ferried across, accompanied by His sons and amanuensis, to the Najíbíyyih Garden, situated on the opposite shore. "O My companions," He thus addressed the faithful band that surrounded Him before He embarked, "I entrust to your keeping this city of Baghdad, in the state ye now behold it, when from the eyes of friends and strangers alike, crowding its housetops, its streets and markets, tears like the rain of spring are flowing down, and I depart. With you it now rests to watch lest your deeds and conduct dim the flame of love that gloweth within the breasts of its inhabitants."

The muezzin had just raised the afternoon call to prayer when Bahá'u'lláh entered the Najíbíyyih Garden, where He tarried twelve days before His final departure from the city. There His friends and companions, arriving in successive waves, attained His presence and bade Him, with feelings of profound sorrow, their last farewell....

Small wonder that, in the face of so many evidences of deep-seated devotion, sympathy and esteem, so strikingly manifested by high and low alike, from the time Bahá'u'lláh announced His contemplated journey to the day of His departure from the Najíbíyyih Garden—small wonder that those who had so tirelessly sought to secure the order for His banishment, and had rejoiced at the success of their efforts, should now have bitterly regretted their act. "Such hath been the interposition of God," 'Abdu'l-Bahá, in a letter written by Him from that garden, with reference to these enemies, affirms, "that the joy evinced by them hath been turned to chagrin and sorrow, so much so that the Persian consul-general in Baghdad regrets exceedingly the plans and plots the schemers had devised. Námiq Páshá himself, on the day he called on Him (Bahá'u'lláh) stated: 'Formerly they insisted upon your departure. Now, however, they are even more insistent that you should remain.'"

(Shoghi Effendi, *God Passes By,* p. 147-150)

---

## Declaration of Bahá'u'lláh's Mission

The arrival of Bahá'u'lláh in the Najíbíyyih Garden, subsequently designated by His followers the Garden of Ridván, signalizes the commencement of what has come to be recognized as the holiest and most significant of all Bahá'í festivals, the festival commemorating the Declaration of His Mission to His companions. So momentous a Declaration may well be regarded both as the logical consummation of that revolutionizing process which was initiated by Himself upon His return from Sulaymáníyyih, and as a prelude to the final proclamation of that same Mission to the world and its rulers from Adrianople.

# Bahá'u'lláh: The Glory of God – References

Through that solemn act the "delay," of no less than a decade, divinely interposed between the birth of Bahá'u'lláh's Revelation in the Síyáh-Chál and its announcement to the Báb's disciples, was at long last terminated. The "set time of concealment," during which as He Himself has borne witness, the "signs and tokens of a divinely-appointed Revelation" were being showered upon Him, was fulfilled. The "myriad veils of light," within which His glory had been wrapped, were, at that historic hour, partially lifted, vouchsafing to mankind "an infinitesimal glimmer" of the effulgence of His "peerless, His most sacred and exalted Countenance." The "thousand two hundred and ninety days," fixed by Daniel in the last chapter of His Book, as the duration of the "abomination that maketh desolate" had now elapsed. The "hundred lunar years," destined to immediately precede that blissful consummation (1335 days), announced by Daniel in that same chapter, had commenced. The nineteen years, constituting the first "Váhid," preordained in the Persian Bayán by the pen of the Báb, had been completed. The Lord of the Kingdom, Jesus Christ returned in the glory of the Father, was about to ascend His throne, and assume the sceptre of a world-embracing, indestructible sovereignty. The community of the Most Great Name, the "companions of the Crimson Colored Ark," lauded in glowing terms in the Qayyúmu'l-Asmá', had visibly emerged. The Báb's own prophecy regarding the "Ridván," the scene of the unveiling of Bahá'u'lláh's transcendent glory, had been literally fulfilled.

…The festive, the soul-entrancing odes which He revealed almost every day; the Tablets, replete with hints, which streamed from His pen; the allusions which, in private converse and public discourse, He made to the approaching hour; the exaltation which in moments of joy and sadness alike flooded His soul; the ecstasy which filled His lovers, already enraptured by the multiplying evidences of His rising greatness and glory; the perceptible change noted in His demeanor; and finally, His adoption of the taj (tall felt head-dress), on the day of His departure from His Most Holy House—all proclaimed unmistakably His imminent assumption of the prophetic office and of His open leadership of the community of the Báb's followers.

…Of the exact circumstances attending that epoch-making Declaration we, alas, are but scantily informed. The words Bahá'u'lláh actually uttered on that occasion, the manner of His Declaration, the reaction it produced, its impact on Mírzá Yahyá, the identity of those who were privileged to hear Him, are shrouded in an obscurity which future historians will find it difficult to penetrate. The fragmentary description left to posterity by His chronicler Nabíl is one of the very few authentic records we possess of the memorable days He spent in that garden. "Every day," Nabíl has related, "ere the hour of dawn, the gardeners would pick the roses which lined the four avenues of the garden, and would pile them in the center of the floor of His blessed tent. So great would be the heap that when His companions gathered to drink their morning tea in His presence, they would be unable to see each other across it. All these roses Bahá'u'lláh would, with His own hands, entrust to those whom He dismissed from His presence every morning to be delivered, on His behalf, to His Arab and Persian friends in the city." "One night," he continues, "the ninth night of the waxing moon, I happened to be one of those who watched beside His blessed tent. As the hour of midnight approached, I saw Him issue from His tent, pass by the places where some of His companions were sleeping, and begin to pace up and down the moonlit, flower-bordered avenues of the garden. So loud was the singing of the nightingales on every side that only those who were near Him could hear distinctly His voice. He continued to walk until, pausing in the midst of one of these avenues,

## Bahá'u'lláh: The Glory of God – References

He observed: 'Consider these nightingales. So great is their love for these roses, that sleepless from dusk till dawn, they warble their melodies and commune with burning passion with the object of their adoration. How then can those who claim to be afire with the rose-like beauty of the Beloved choose to sleep?' For three successive nights I watched and circled round His blessed tent. Every time I passed by the couch whereon He lay, I would find Him wakeful, and every day, from morn till eventide, I would see Him ceaselessly engaged in conversing with the stream of visitors who kept flowing in from Baghdad. Not once could I discover in the words He spoke any trace of dissimulation."

As to the significance of that Declaration let Bahá'u'lláh Himself reveal to us its import. Acclaiming that historic occasion as the "Most Great Festival," the "King of Festivals," the "Festival of God," He has, in His Kitáb-i-Aqdas, characterized it as the Day whereon "all created things were immersed in the sea of purification," whilst in one of His specific Tablets, He has referred to it as the Day whereon "the breezes of forgiveness were wafted over the entire creation." "Rejoice, with exceeding gladness, O people of Bahá!", He, in another Tablet, has written, "as ye call to remembrance the Day of supreme felicity, the Day whereon the Tongue of the Ancient of Days hath spoken, as He departed from His House proceeding to the Spot from which He shed upon the whole of creation the splendors of His Name, the All-Merciful... Were We to reveal the hidden secrets of that Day, all that dwell on earth and in the heavens would swoon away and die, except such as will be preserved by God, the Almighty, the All-Knowing, the All-Wise. Such is the inebriating effect of the words of God upon the Revealer of His undoubted proofs that His pen can move no longer." And again: "The Divine Springtime is come, O Most Exalted Pen, for the Festival of the All-Merciful is fast approaching.... The Day-Star of Blissfulness shineth above the horizon of Our Name, the Blissful, inasmuch as the Kingdom of the Name of God hath been adorned with the ornament of the Name of Thy Lord, the Creator of the heavens....Take heed lest anything deter Thee from extolling the greatness of this Day—the Day whereon the Finger of Majesty and Power hath opened the seal of the Wine of Reunion, and called all who are in the heavens and all who are on earth.... This is the Day whereon the unseen world crieth out: 'Great is thy blessedness, O earth, for thou hast been made the footstool of thy God, and been chosen as the seat of His mighty throne' ...Say ...He it is Who hath laid bare before you the hidden and treasured Gem, were ye to seek it. He it is who is the One Beloved of all things, whether of the past or of the future." And yet again: "Arise, and proclaim unto the entire creation the tidings that He who is the All-Merciful hath directed His steps towards the Ridván and entered it. Guide, then, the people unto the Garden of Delight which God hath made the Throne of His Paradise... Within this Paradise, and from the heights of its loftiest chambers, the Maids of Heaven have cried out and shouted: 'Rejoice, ye dwellers of the realms above, for the fingers of Him Who is the Ancient of Days are ringing, in the name of the All-Glorious, the Most Great Bell, in the midmost heart of the heavens. The hands of bounty have borne round the cups of everlasting life. Approach, and quaff your fill.'" And finally: "Forget the world of creation, O Pen, and turn Thou towards the face of Thy Lord, the Lord of all names. Adorn, then, the world with the ornament of the favors of Thy Lord, the King of everlasting days. For We perceive the fragrance of the Day whereon He Who is the Desire of all nations hath shed upon the kingdoms of the unseen and of the seen the splendors of the light of His most excellent names, and enveloped them with the radiance of the luminaries of His most gracious favors, favors which none can reckon except Him Who is the Omnipotent Protector of the entire creation."

(Shoghi Effendi, *God Passes By*, p. 151-155)

## The Promised One

When Bahá'ís say that the various religions are one, they do not mean that the various religious creeds and organizations are the same. Rather, they believe that there is only one religion and all of the Messengers of God have progressively revealed its nature. Together, the world's great religions are expressions of a single unfolding Divine plan, "the changeless Faith of God, eternal in the past, eternal in the future."

People from all of the major religious backgrounds have found that the promises and expectations of their own beliefs are fulfilled in the Bahá'í Faith. Bahá'ís from Native American, African and other indigenous backgrounds, similarly, find in the Bahá'í teachings fulfillment of prophetic visions.

For Bahá'ís of Jewish background, Bahá'u'lláh is the appearance of the promised "Lord of Hosts" come down "with ten thousands of saints." A descendent of Abraham and a "scion from the root of Jesse," Bahá'u'lláh has come to lead the way for nations to "beat their swords into plowshares." Many features of Bahá'u'lláh's involuntary exile to the Land of Israel, along with other historical events during Bahá'u'lláh's life and since are seen as fulfilling numerous prophecies in the Bible.

For Bahá'ís of Buddhist background, Bahá'u'lláh fulfils the prophecies for the coming of "a Buddha named Maitreye, the Buddha of universal fellowship" who will, according to Buddhist traditions, bring peace and enlightenment for all humanity. They see the fulfillment of numerous prophecies, such as the fact that the Buddha Maitreye is to come from "the West," noting the fact that Iran is West of India.

For Bahá'ís of Hindu background, Bahá'u'lláh comes as the new incarnation of Krishna, the "Tenth Avatar" and the " Most Great Spirit. " He is "the birthless, the deathless" the One who, "when goodness grows weak," returns "in every age" to "establish righteousness" as promised in the Bhagavad-Gita.

For Bahá'ís of Christian background, Bahá'u'lláh fulfils the paradoxical promises of Christ's return "in the Glory of the Father" and as a "thief in the night." That the Faith was founded in 1844 relates to numerous Christian prophecies. Bahá'ís note, for example, that central Africa was finally opened to Christianity in the 1840s, and that event was widely seen as fulfilling the promise that Christ would return after "the Gospel had been preached "to all nations." In Bahá'u'lláh's teachings Bahá'ís see fulfillment of Christ's promise to bring all people together so that " there shall be one fold, and one shepherd."

For Bahá'ís of Muslim background, Bahá'u'lláh fulfils the promise of the Qur'án for the "Day of God" and the "Great Announcement," when "God" will come down "overshadowed with clouds." They see in the dramatic events of the Bábí and Bahá'í movements the fulfillment of many traditional statements of Muhammad, which have long been a puzzle.

(Excerpted from *The Bahá'ís,* a publication of the Bahá'í International Community, p. 37. Used with permission)

Bahá'u'lláh: The Glory of God – References

# LESSON #3

## Exiles and Imprisonment

*Teachers may wish to study the following references in order to gain a deeper understanding of the material presented in each lesson.*

### Exile to Constantinople

The departure of Bahá'u'lláh from the Garden of Ridván, at noon, on the 14th of Dhi'l-Qa'dih 1279 A.H. (May 3, 1863), witnessed scenes of tumultuous enthusiasm no less spectacular, and even more touching, than those which greeted Him when leaving His Most Great House in Baghdad. "The great tumult," wrote an eyewitness, "associated in our minds with the Day of Gathering, the Day of Judgment, we beheld on that occasion. Believers and unbelievers alike sobbed and lamented. The chiefs and notables who had congregated were struck with wonder. Emotions were stirred to such depths as no tongue can describe, nor could any observer escape their contagion."

Mounted on His steed, a red roan stallion of the finest breed, the best His lovers could purchase for Him, and leaving behind Him a bowing multitude of fervent admirers, He rode forth on the first stage of a journey that was to carry Him to the city of Constantinople. "Numerous were the heads," Nabíl himself a witness of that memorable scene, recounts, "which, on every side, bowed to the dust at the feet of His horse, and kissed its hoofs, and countless were those who pressed forward to embrace His stirrups." …"He (God) it was," Bahá'u'lláh Himself declares, "Who enabled Me to depart out of the city (Baghdad), clothed with such majesty as none, except the denier and the malicious, can fail to acknowledge." These marks of homage and devotion continued to surround Him until He was installed in Constantinople. Mirzá Yahyá, while hurrying on foot, by his own choice, behind Bahá'u'lláh's carriage, on the day of His arrival in that city, was overheard by Nabíl to remark to Siyyid Muhammad: "Had I not chosen to hide myself, had I revealed my identity, the honor accorded Him (Bahá'u'lláh) on this day would have been mine too."

…A caravan, consisting of fifty mules, a mounted guard of ten soldiers with their officer, and seven pairs of howdahs,* each pair surmounted by four parasols, was formed, and wended its way, by easy stages, and in the space of no less than a hundred and ten days, across the uplands, and through the defiles, the woods, valleys and pastures, comprising the picturesque scenery of eastern Anatolia, to the port of Samsun, on the Black Sea.

…"According to the unanimous testimony of those we met in the course of that journey," Nabíl has recorded in his narrative, "never before had they witnessed along this route, over which governors and mushirs continually passed back and forth between Constantinople and Baghdad, any one travel in such state, dispense such hospitality to all, and accord to each so great a share of his bounty."

(Shoghi Effendi, *God Passes By*, p. 155-157)

---------------
* A seat, usually fitted with a canopy, for riding on the back of a horse, camel or elephant.

## Tribulations

But for the tribulations that have touched Me in the path of God, life would have held no sweetness for Me, and My existence would have profited Me nothing. For them who are endued with discernment, and whose eyes are fixed upon the Sublime Vision, it is no secret that I have been, most of the days of My life, even as a slave, sitting under a sword hanging on a thread, knowing not whether it would fall soon or late upon him. And yet, notwithstanding all this We render thanks unto God, the Lord of the worlds. Mine inner tongue reciteth, in the daytime and in the night-season, this prayer: "Glory to Thee, O my God! But for the tribulations which are sustained in Thy path, how could Thy true lovers be recognized; and were it not for the trials which are borne for love of Thee, how could the station of such as yearn for Thee be revealed? Thy might beareth Me witness! The companions of all who adore Thee are the tears they shed, and the comforters of such as seek Thee are the groans they utter, and the food of them who haste to meet Thee is the fragments of their broken hearts. How sweet to my taste is the bitterness of death suffered in Thy path, and how precious in my estimation are the shafts of Thine enemies when encountered for the sake of the exaltation of Thy Word! Let me quaff in Thy Cause, O my God and my Master, whatsoever Thou didst desire, and send down upon me in Thy love all Thou didst ordain. By Thy glory! I wish only what Thou wishest, and cherish what Thou cherishest. In Thee have I, at all times, placed My whole trust and confidence. Thou art verily the All-Possessing, the Most High. Raise up, I implore Thee, O my God, as helpers to this Revelation such as shall be counted worthy of Thy Name and of Thy sovereignty, that they may remember Thee among Thy creatures, and hoist the ensigns of Thy victory in Thy land, and adorn them with Thy virtues and Thy commandments. No God is there but Thee, the Help in Peril, the Self-Subsisting."

(Bahá'u'lláh, *Epistle to the Son of the Wolf,* p. 94-95)

---

And further We have said: "As My tribulations multiplied, so did My love for God and for His Cause increase, in such wise that all that befell Me from the hosts of the wayward was powerless to deter Me from My purpose. Should they hide Me away in the depths of the earth, yet would they find Me riding aloft on the clouds, and calling out unto God, the Lord of strength and of might.

(Bahá'u'lláh, *Epistle to the Son of the Wolf,* p. 52-53)

---

The Abhá Beauty Himself—may the spirit of all existence be offered up for His loved ones—bore all manner of ordeals, and willingly accepted for Himself intense afflictions. No torment was there left that His sacred form was not subjected to, no suffering that did not descend upon Him. How many a night, when He was chained, did He go sleepless because of the weight of His iron collar; how many a day the burning pain of the stocks and fetters gave Him no moment's peace. From Níyávarán to Tihrán they made Him run—He, that embodied spirit, He Who had been accustomed to repose against cushions of ornamented silk—chained, shoeless, His head bared; and down under the earth, in the thick darkness of that narrow dungeon, they shut Him up with murderers, rebels and thieves. Ever and again they assailed Him with a new torment, and all were certain that from one moment to the next He would suffer a martyr's death. After some time they banished Him from His native land, and sent Him to countries alien and far away. During many a year in Iraq, no moment passed but the arrow of a new anguish struck His holy heart; with every breath a sword came down upon that sacred body, and He could hope for no moment of security and rest. From every side His enemies mounted their attack with unrelenting hate; and singly and alone He withstood them all. After all these tribulations, these body blows, they flung Him out of Iraq in the continent of Asia, to the continent of Europe, and in that place of bitter exile, of wretched hardships, to the wrongs that were heaped upon Him by the people of the Qur'án were now added the virulent persecutions, the powerful attacks, the plottings, the slanders, the continual hostilities, the hate and malice, of the people of the Bayán. My pen is powerless to tell it all; but ye have surely been informed of it. Then, after twenty-four years in this, the Most Great Prison, in agony and sore affliction, His days drew to a close.

('Abdu'l-Bahá, *Selections from the Writings of 'Abdu'l-Bahá,* p. 262-263)

---

The Blessed Perfection gave up a hundred lives at every breath. He bore calamities. He suffered anguish. He was imprisoned. He was chained. He was made homeless and was banished to distant lands. Finally, then, He lived out His days in the Most Great Prison.

('Abdu'l-Bahá, *Selections from the Writings of 'Abdu'l-Bahá,* p. 73)

---

To sum it up, the Ancient Beauty was ever, during His sojourn in this transitory world, either a captive bound with chains, or living under a sword, or subjected to extreme suffering and torment, or held in the Most Great Prison. Because of His physical weakness, brought on by His afflictions, His blessed body was worn away to a breath; it was light as a cobweb from long grieving. And His reason for shouldering this heavy load and enduring all this anguish, which was even as an ocean that hurleth its waves to high heaven—His reason for putting on the heavy iron chains and for becoming the very embodiment of utter resignation and meekness, was to lead every soul on earth to concord, to fellow-feeling, to oneness; to make known amongst all peoples the sign of the singleness of God...

('Abdu'l-Bahá, *Selections from the Writings of 'Abdu'l-Bahá,* p. 263)

---

## Arrival in Akká

The arrival of Bahá'u'lláh in 'Akká marks the opening of the last phase of His forty-year long ministry, the final stage, and indeed the climax, of the banishment in which the whole of that ministry was spent. A banishment that had, at first, brought Him to the immediate vicinity of the strongholds of Shí'ah orthodoxy and into contact with its outstanding exponents, and which, at a later period, had carried Him to the capital of the Ottoman empire, and led Him to address His epoch-making pronouncements to the Sultan, to his ministers and to the ecclesiastical leaders of Sunni Islam, had now been instrumental in landing Him upon the shores of the Holy Land—the Land promised by God to Abraham, sanctified by the Revelation of Moses, honored by the lives and labors of the Hebrew patriarchs, judges, kings and prophets, revered as the cradle of Christianity, and as the place where Zoroaster, according to 'Abdu'l-Bahá's testimony, had "held converse with some of the Prophets of Israel," and associated by Islam with the Apostle's night-journey, through the seven heavens, to the throne of the Almighty. Within the confines of this holy and enviable country, "the nest of all the Prophets of God," "the Vale of God's unsearchable Decree, the snow-white Spot, the Land of unfading splendor" was the Exile of Baghdad, of Constantinople and Adrianople condemned to spend no less than a third of the allotted span of His life, and over half of the total period of His Mission. "It is difficult," declares 'Abdu'l-Bahá, "to understand how Bahá'u'lláh could have been obliged to leave Persia, and to pitch His tent in this Holy Land, but for the persecution of His enemies, His banishment and exile."

Indeed such a consummation, He assures us, had been actually prophesied "through the tongue of the Prophets two or three thousand years before." God, "faithful to His promise," had, "to some of the Prophets" "revealed and given the good news that the 'Lord of Hosts should be manifested in the Holy Land.'" Isaiah had, in this connection, announced in his Book: "Get thee up into the high mountain, O Zion that bringest good tidings; lift up thy voice with strength, O Jerusalem, that bringest good tidings. Lift it up, be not afraid; say unto the cities of Judah: 'Behold your God! Behold the Lord God will come with strong hand, and His arm shall rule for Him.'" David, in his Psalms, had predicted: "Lift up your heads, O ye gates; even lift them up, ye everlasting doors; and the King of Glory shall come in. Who is this King of Glory? The Lord of Hosts, He is the King of Glory." "Out of Zion, the perfection of beauty, God hath shined. Our God shall come, and shall not keep silence." Amos had, likewise, foretold His coming: "The Lord will roar from Zion, and utter His voice from Jerusalem; and the habitations of the shepherds shall mourn, and the top of Carmel shall wither."

'Akká, itself, flanked by the "glory of Lebanon," and lying in full view of the "splendor of Carmel," at the foot of the hills which enclose the home of Jesus Christ Himself, had been described by David as "the Strong City," designated by Hosea as "a door of hope," and alluded to by Ezekiel as "the gate that looketh towards the East," whereunto "the glory of the God of Israel came from the way of the East," His voice "like a noise of many waters." To it the Arabian Prophet had referred as "a city in Syria to which God hath shown His special mercy," situated "betwixt two mountains …in the middle of a meadow," "by the shore of the sea …suspended beneath the Throne," "white, whose whiteness is pleasing unto God." "Blessed the man," He, moreover, as confirmed by Bahá'u'lláh, had declared, "that hath visited 'Akká, and blessed he that hath visited the visitor of 'Akká." Furthermore, "He that raiseth therein the call to prayer, his voice will be lifted up unto Paradise." And again: "The poor of 'Akká are the kings of Paradise and the princes thereof. A month in 'Akká is better than a thousand years elsewhere." Moreover, in a remarkable tradition, which is contained in Shaykh Ibnu'l-'Arabí's work, entitled "Futúhát-i-Makkíyyih," and which is recognized as an authentic utterance of Muhammad, and is quoted by Mírzá Abu'l-Fadl in his "Fará'id," this significant prediction has been made: "All of them (the companions of the Qá'im) shall be slain except One Who shall reach the plain of 'Akká, the Banquet-Hall of God."

Bahá'u'lláh Himself, as attested by Nabíl in his narrative, had, as far back as the first years of His banishment to Adrianople, alluded to that same city in His Lawh-i-Sáyyah, designating it as the "Vale of Nabíl," the word Nabíl being equal in numerical value to that of 'Akká. "Upon Our arrival," that Tablet had predicted, "We were welcomed with banners of light, whereupon the Voice of the Spirit cried out saying: 'Soon will all that dwell on earth be enlisted under these banners.'"

The banishment, lasting no less than twenty-four years, to which two Oriental despots had, in their implacable enmity and shortsightedness, combined to condemn Bahá'u'lláh, will go down in history as a period which witnessed a miraculous and truly revolutionizing change in the circumstances attending the life and activities of the Exile Himself, will be chiefly remembered for the widespread recrudescence of persecution, intermittent but singularly cruel, throughout His native country and the simultaneous increase in the number of His followers, and, lastly, for an enormous extension in the range and volume of His writings.

(Shoghi Effendi, *God Passes By,* p. 183-185)

## The Most Great Prison

His arrival at the penal colony of 'Akká, far from proving the end of His afflictions, was but the beginning of a major crisis, characterized by bitter suffering, severe restrictions, and intense turmoil, which, in its gravity, surpassed even the agonies of the Síyáh-Chál of Tihrán, and to which no other event, in the history of the entire century can compare, except the internal convulsion that rocked the Faith in Adrianople. "Know thou," Bahá'u'lláh, wishing to emphasize the criticalness of the first nine years of His banishment to that prison-city, has written, "that upon Our arrival at this Spot, We chose to designate it as the 'Most Great Prison.' Though previously subjected in another land (Tihrán) to chains and fetters, We yet refused to call it by that name. Say: Ponder thereon, O ye endued with understanding!"

…'Akká, the ancient Ptolemais, the St. Jean d'Acre of the Crusaders, that had successfully defied the siege of Napoleon, had sunk, under the Turks, to the level of a penal colony to which murderers, highway robbers and political agitators were consigned from all parts of the Turkish empire. It was girt about by a double system of ramparts; was inhabited by a people whom Bahá'u'lláh stigmatized as "the generation of vipers"; was devoid of any source of water within its gates; was flea-infested, damp and honey-combed with gloomy, filthy and tortuous lanes.

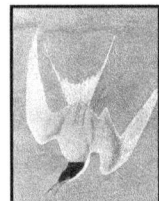
"According to what they say," the Supreme Pen has recorded in the Lawh-i-Sultán, "it is the most desolate of the cities of the world, the most unsightly of them in appearance, the most detestable in climate, and the foulest in water. It is as though it were the metropolis of the owl." So putrid was its air that, according to a proverb, a bird when flying over it would drop dead.

(Shoghi Effendi, *God Passes By,* p. 186-187)

Having, after a miserable voyage, disembarked at 'Akká, all the exiles, men, women and children, were, under the eyes of a curious and callous population that had assembled at the port to behold the "God of the Persians," conducted to the army barracks, where they were locked in, and sentinels detailed to guard them. "The first night," Bahá'u'lláh testifies in the Lawh-i-Ra'ís, "all were deprived of either food or drink... They even begged for water, and were refused." So filthy and brackish was the water in the pool of the courtyard that no one could drink it. Three loaves of black and salty bread were assigned to each, which they were later permitted to exchange, when escorted by guards to the market, for two of better quality. Subsequently they were allowed a mere pittance as substitute for the allotted dole of bread. All fell sick, except two, shortly after their arrival. Malaria, dysentery, combined with the sultry heat, added to their miseries. Three succumbed, among them two brothers, who died the same night, "locked," as testified by Bahá'u'lláh, "in each other's arms." The carpet used by Him He gave to be sold in order to provide for their winding-sheets and burial. The paltry sum obtained after it had been auctioned was delivered to the guards, who had refused to bury them without first being paid the necessary expenses. Later, it was learned that, unwashed and unshrouded, they had buried them, without coffins, in the clothes they wore, though, as affirmed by Bahá'u'lláh, they were given twice the amount required for their burial. "None," He Himself has written, "knoweth what befell Us, except God, the Almighty, the All-Knowing... From the foundation of the world until the present day a cruelty such as this hath neither been seen nor heard of."

(Shoghi Effendi, *God Passes By,* p. 186)

## The Death of Mírzá Mihdí

To the galling weight of these tribulations was now added the bitter grief of a sudden tragedy—the premature loss of the noble, the pious Mírzá Mihdí, the Purest Branch, 'Abdu'l-Bahá's twenty-two year old brother, an amanuensis of Bahá'u'lláh and a companion of His exile from the days when, as a child, he was brought from Tihrán to Baghdad to join his Father after His return from Sulaymáníyyih. He was pacing the roof of the barracks in the twilight, one evening, wrapped in his customary devotions, when he fell through the unguarded skylight onto a wooden crate, standing on the floor beneath, which pierced his ribs, and caused, twenty-two hours later, his death, on the 23rd of Rabí'u'l-Avval 1287 A.H. (June 23, 1870). His dying supplication to a grieving Father was that his life might be accepted as a ransom for those who were prevented from attaining the presence of their Beloved.

In a highly significant prayer, revealed by Bahá'u'lláh in memory of His son—a prayer that exalts his death to the rank of those great acts of atonement associated with Abraham's intended sacrifice of His son, with the crucifixion of Jesus Christ and the martyrdom of the Imám Husayn—we read the following: "I have, O my Lord, offered up that which Thou hast given Me, that Thy servants may be quickened, and all that dwell on earth be united." And, likewise, these prophetic words, addressed to His martyred son: "Thou art the Trust of God and His Treasure in this Land. Erelong will God reveal through thee that which He hath desired."

(Shoghi Effendi, *God Passes By,* p. 188)

"At this very moment," Bahá'u'lláh testifies, "My son is being washed before My face, after Our having sacrificed him in the Most Great Prison. Thereat have the dwellers of the Abhá Tabernacle wept with a great weeping, and such as have suffered imprisonment with this Youth in the path of God, the Lord of the promised Day, lamented. Under such conditions My Pen hath not been prevented from remembering its Lord, the Lord of all nations. It summoneth the people unto God, the Almighty, the All-Bountiful. This is the day whereon he that was created by the light of Bahá has suffered martyrdom, at a time when he lay imprisoned at the hands of his enemies."

"Upon thee, O Branch of God!" He solemnly and most touchingly, in that same Tablet, bestows upon him His benediction, "be the remembrance of God and His praise, and the praise of all that dwell in the Realm of Immortality, and of all the denizens of the Kingdom of Names. Happy art thou in that thou hast been faithful to the Covenant of God and His Testament, until Thou didst sacrifice thyself before the face of thy Lord, the Almighty, the Unconstrained. Thou, in truth, hast been wronged, and to this testifieth the Beauty of Him, the Self-Subsisting. Thou didst, in the first days of thy life, bear that which hath caused all things to groan, and made every pillar to tremble. Happy is the one that remembereth thee, and draweth nigh, through thee, unto God, the Creator of the Morn."

"Glorified art Thou, O Lord, my God!" He, in a prayer, astoundingly proclaims, "Thou seest me in the hands of Mine enemies, and My son bloodstained before Thy face, O Thou in Whose hands is the kingdom of all names. I have, O my Lord, offered up that which Thou hast given Me, that Thy servants may be quickened and all that dwell on earth be united."

(From Shoghi Effendi, *Messages to America,* p. 33-34)

# LESSON #4

## Clouds of Glory

*Teachers may wish to study the following references in order to gain a deeper understanding of the material presented in each lesson.*

### Denial

Should you acquaint yourself with the indignities heaped upon the Prophets of God, and apprehend the true causes of the objections voiced by their oppressors, you will surely appreciate the significance of their position. Moreover, the more closely you observe the denials of those who have opposed the Manifestations of the divine attributes, the firmer will be your faith in the Cause of God.

(Bahá'u'lláh, *The Kitáb-i-Iqán*, p. 6)

---

Reflect, what could have been the motive for such deeds? What could have prompted such behavior towards the Revealers of the beauty of the All-Glorious? Whatever in days gone by hath been the cause of the denial and opposition of those people hath now led to the perversity of the people of this age.

(Bahá'u'lláh, *Gleanings from the Writings of Bahá'u'lláh*, p. 17-18)

---

Consequently, such behaviour can be attributed to naught save the petty-mindedness of such souls as tread the valley of arrogance and pride, are lost in the wilds of remoteness, walk in the ways of their idle fancy, and follow the dictates of the leaders of their faith. Their chief concern is mere opposition; their sole desire is to ignore the truth. Unto every discerning observer it is evident and manifest that had these people in the days of each of the Manifestations of the Sun of Truth sanctified their eyes, their ears, and their hearts from whatever they had seen, heard, and felt, they surely would not have been deprived of beholding the beauty of God, nor strayed far from the habitations of glory. But having weighed the testimony of God by the standard of their own knowledge, gleaned from the teachings of the leaders of their faith, and found it at variance with their limited understanding, they arose to perpetrate such unseemly acts

(Bahá'u'lláh, *The Kitáb-i-Iqán*, p. 14-15)

---

Leaders of religion, in every age, have hindered their people from attaining the shores of eternal salvation, inasmuch as they held the reins of authority in their mighty grasp. Some for the lust of leadership, others through want of knowledge and understanding, have been the cause of the deprivation of the people. By their sanction and authority, every Prophet of God hath drunk from the chalice of sacrifice, and winged His flight unto the heights of glory.

(Bahá'u'lláh, *The Kitáb-i-Iqán*, p. 15)

## Response to Opposition

Pay ye no heed to aversion and rejection, to disdain, hostility, injustice: act ye in the opposite way. Be ye sincerely kind, not in appearance only…In this way, the light of divine guidance will shine forth, and the blessings of God will cradle all mankind…

('Abdu'l-Bahá, *Selections from the Writings of 'Abdu'l-Bahá*, p. 3)

## Proclamation to the Kings and Rulers

The years following Bahá'u'lláh's arrival in Adrianople witnessed His Revelation's attainment, in the words of Shoghi Effendi, of "its meridian glory" through the proclamation of its Founder's message to the kings and rulers of the world. During this relatively brief but turbulent period of the Faith's history, and in the early years of His subsequent exile in 1868 to the fortress town of 'Akká, He summoned the monarchs of East and West collectively, and some among them individually, to recognize the Day of God and to acknowledge the One promised in the scriptures of the religions professed by the recipients of His summons. "Never since the beginning of the world", Bahá'u'lláh declares, "hath the Message been so openly proclaimed."

(Introduction to *The Summons of the Lord of Hosts*, p. i)

When Bahá'u'lláh arrived at 'Akká, through the power of God He was able to hoist His banner. His light at first had been a star; now it became a mighty sun and the illumination of His Cause expanded from the east to the west. Inside prison walls He wrote epistles to all the kings and rulers of nations summoning them to arbitration and Universal Peace. Some of the kings received His words with disdain and contempt. One of these was the sultan of the Ottoman kingdom. Napoleon III of France did not reply. A second epistle was addressed to him. It stated: "I have written you an epistle before this, summoning you to the cause of God but you are of the heedless. You have proclaimed that you were the defender of the oppressed; now it hath become evident that you are not. Nor are you kind to your own suffering and oppressed people. Your actions are contrary to your own interests and your kingly pride must fall. Because of your arrogance God shortly will destroy your sovereignty. France will flee away from you and you will be overwhelmed by a great conquest….

Read it and consider: One prisoner, single and solitary, without assistant or defender, a foreigner and stranger imprisoned in the fortress of 'Akká writing such letters to the emperor of France and sultan of Turkey. Reflect upon this how Bahá'u'lláh upraised the standard of His Cause in prison. Refer to history. It is without parallel. No such thing has happened before that time nor since; a prisoner and an exile advancing His Cause and spreading His teachings broadcast so that eventually He became powerful enough to conquer the very king who banished Him.

('Abdu'l-Bahá, *Bahá'í World Faith*, p. 222-223)

One hundred years ago, Bahá'u'lláh, Founder of the Bahá'í Faith, proclaimed in clear and unmistakable language, to the kings and rulers of the world, to its religious leaders, and to mankind in general that the long-promised age of world peace and brotherhood had at last dawned and that He Himself was the Bearer of the new message and power from God which would transform the prevailing system of antagonism and enmity between men and create the spirit and form of the destined world order.

At that time the splendour and panoply of the monarchs reflected the vast power which they exercised, autocratically for the most part, over the greater portion of the earth. Bahá'u'lláh, an exile from His native Persia for His religious teaching, was the prisoner of the tyrannical, all-powerful Sultan of the Ottoman Empire. In such circumstances He addressed the rulers of the world. His Tablets to particular kings and to the Pope, although delivered, were either ignored or rejected, their wise counsels and dire warnings went unheeded, and in one instance the bearer was cruelly tortured and killed.

(Introduction to *The Proclamation of Bahá'u'lláh,* p. ix)

---

Let us now consider the consequences that have ensued. The reaction of these monarchs was, as already stated, varied and unmistakable and, as the march of events has gradually unfolded, disastrous in its consequences.... The recital of Bahá'u'lláh's sufferings, embodied in those Messages, failed to evoke compassion in their hearts. His appeals, the like of which neither the annals of Christianity nor even those of Islam have recorded, were disdainfully rejected. The dark warnings He uttered were haughtily scorned. The bold challenges He issued were ignored. The chastisements He predicted they derisively brushed aside.

What, then—might we not consider—has, in the face of so complete and ignominious a rejection, happened, and is still happening, in the course, and particularly in the closing years, of this, the first Bahá'í century...? Empires fallen in dust, kingdoms subverted, dynasties extinguished, royalty besmirched, kings assassinated, poisoned, driven into exile, subjugated in their own realms...

...Surely, no man, contemplating dispassionately the manifestations of this relentless revolutionizing process, within comparatively so short a time, can escape the conclusion that the last hundred years may well be regarded, in so far as the fortunes of royalty are concerned, as one of the most cataclysmic periods in the annals of mankind.

(Shoghi Effendi, *The Promised Day is Come,* p. 48-50)

---

Ye are but vassals, O Kings of the earth! He Who is the King of kings hath appeared, arrayed in His most wondrous glory, and is summoning you unto Himself, the Help in Peril, the Self-Subsisting. Take heed lest pride deter you from recognizing the Source of Revelation; lest the things of this world shut you out as by a veil from Him Who is the Creator of heaven. Arise, and serve Him Who is the Desire of all nations, Who hath created you through a word from Him, and ordained you to be, for all time, the emblems of His sovereignty.

By the righteousness of God! It is not Our wish to lay hands on your kingdoms. Our mission is to seize and possess the hearts of men.

(Bahá'u'lláh, *The Proclamation of Bahá'u'lláh*, p. 5-6)

## To Sultán 'Abdu'l-Azíz

HEARKEN, O King, to the speech of Him that speaketh the truth... Observe, O King, with thine inmost heart and with thy whole being, the precepts of God, and walk not in the paths of the oppressor.... Place not thy reliance on thy treasures. Put thy whole confidence in the grace of God, thy Lord.... Overstep not the bounds of moderation, and deal justly with them that serve thee.

(Bahá'u'lláh, *The Proclamation of Bahá'u'lláh*, p. 47-50)

## To Násiri'd-Dín Sháh

O KING! I was but a man like others, asleep upon My couch, when lo, the breezes of the All-Glorious were wafted over Me, and taught Me the knowledge of all that hath been. This thing is not from Me, but from One Who is Almighty and All-Knowing. And He bade Me lift up My voice between earth and heaven, and for this there befell Me what hath caused the tears of every man of understanding to flow. The learning current amongst men I studied not; their schools I entered not. Ask of the city wherein I dwelt, that thou mayest be well assured that I am not of them who speak falsely. This is but a leaf which the winds of the will of thy Lord, the Almighty, the All-Praised, have stirred. Can it be still when the tempestuous winds are blowing? Nay, by Him Who is the Lord of all Names and Attributes!

(Bahá'u'lláh, *The Proclamation of Bahá'u'lláh*, p. 57)

## To Napoleon III

O KING of Paris! Tell the priest to ring the bells no longer. By God, the True One! The Most Mighty Bell hath appeared... Say: He Who is the Unconditioned is come, in the clouds of light, that He may quicken all created things with the breeze of His Name, the Most Merciful, and unify the world, and gather all men around this Table which hath been sent down from heaven. Beware that ye deny not the favour of God after it hath been sent down unto you. Better is this for you than that which ye possess; for that which is yours perisheth, whilst that which is with God endureth.

(Bahá'u'lláh, *The Proclamation of Bahá'u'lláh*, p. 17)

## Second Tablet to Napoleon III

For what thou hast done, thy kingdom shall be thrown into confusion, and thine empire shall pass from thine hands, as a punishment for that which thou hast wrought. Then wilt thou know how thou hast plainly erred. Commotions shall seize all the people in that land, unless thou arisest to help this Cause, and followest Him Who is the Spirit of God (Jesus Christ) in this, the Straight Path. Hath thy pomp made thee proud? By My Life! It shall not endure; nay, it shall soon pass away, unless thou holdest fast by this firm Cord. We see abasement hastening after thee, whilst thou art of the heedless. It behoveth thee when thou hearest His Voice calling from the seat of glory to cast away all that thou possessest, and cry out: 'Here am I, O Lord of all that is in heaven and all that is on earth!'

(Bahá'u'lláh, *The Proclamation of Bahá'u'lláh*, p. 20-21)

---

## To Kaiser Wilhelm I

O KING of Berlin! Give ear unto the Voice calling from this manifest Temple: Verily, there is none other God but Me, the Everlasting, the Peerless, the Ancient of Days. Take heed lest pride debar thee from recognizing the Dayspring of Divine Revelation, lest earthly desires shut thee out, as by a veil, from the Lord of the Throne above and of the earth below.... Do thou remember the one whose power transcended thy power (Napoleon III), and whose station excelled thy station. Where is he? Whither are gone the things he possessed? Take warning, and be not of them that are fast asleep. He it was who cast the Tablet of God behind him, when We made known unto him what the hosts of tyranny had caused Us to suffer. Wherefore, disgrace assailed him from all sides, and he went down to dust in great loss. Think deeply, O King, concerning him, and concerning them who, like unto thee, have conquered cities and ruled over men. The All-Merciful brought them down from their palaces to their graves. Be warned, be of them who reflect... O banks of the Rhine! We have seen you covered with gore, inasmuch as the swords of retribution were drawn against you; and you shall have another turn. And We hear the lamentations of Berlin, though she be today in conspicuous glory.

(Bahá'u'lláh, *The Proclamation of Bahá'u'lláh*, p. 39)

---

## To Czar Alexander II

O CZAR of Russia! Incline thine ear unto the voice of God, the King... Whilst I lay chained and fettered in the prison, one of thy ministers extended Me his aid. Wherefore hath God ordained for thee a station which the knowledge of none can comprehend except His knowledge. Beware lest thou barter away this sublime station... Beware lest thy sovereignty withhold thee from Him Who is the Supreme Sovereign.

(Bahá'u'lláh, *The Proclamation of Bahá'u'lláh*, p. 27)

## To Queen Victoria

O QUEEN in London! Incline thine ear unto the voice of thy Lord, the Lord of all mankind…We have been informed that thou hast forbidden the trading in slaves, both men and women. This, verily, is what God hath enjoined in this wondrous Revelation. God hath, truly, destined a reward for thee, because of this….

We have also heard that thou hast entrusted the reins of counsel into the hands of the representatives of the people. Thou, indeed, hast done well, for thereby the foundations of the edifice of thine affairs will be strengthened, and the hearts of all that are beneath thy shadow, whether high or low, will be tranquillized. It behoveth them, however, to be trustworthy among His servants… Blessed is he that entereth the assembly for the sake of God, and judgeth between men with pure justice.

(Bahá'u'lláh, *The Proclamation of Bahá'u'lláh*, p. 33-34)

## To Emperor Francis Joseph

O EMPEROR of Austria! He who is the Dayspring of God's Light dwelt in the prison of 'Akká, at the time when thou didst set forth to visit the Aqsa Mosque (Jerusalem). Thou passed Him by, and inquired not about Him, by Whom every house is exalted, and every lofty gate unlocked. We, verily, made it (Jerusalem) a place whereunto the world should turn, that they might remember Me, and yet thou hast rejected Him Who is the Object of this remembrance, when He appeared with the Kingdom of God, thy Lord and the Lord of the worlds. We have been with thee at all times, and found thee clinging unto the Branch and heedless of the Root. Thy Lord, verily, is a witness unto what I say. We grieved to see

thee circle round Our Name, whilst unaware of Us, though We were before thy face. Open thine eyes, that thou mayest behold this glorious Vision, and recognize Him Whom thou invokest in the daytime and in the night-season, and gaze on the Light that shineth above this luminous Horizon.

(Bahá'u'lláh, *The Proclamation of Bahá'u'lláh*, p. 43)

## To the Rulers of America

HEARKEN ye, O Rulers of America and the Presidents of the Republics therein, unto that which the Dove is warbling on the Branch of Eternity: There is none other God but Me, the Ever-Abiding, the Forgiving, the All-Bountiful… The Promised One hath appeared in this glorified Station, whereat all beings, both seen and unseen, have rejoiced. Take ye advantage of the Day of God. Verily, to meet Him is better for you than all that whereon the sun shineth, could ye but know it.

O concourse of rulers! Give ear unto that which hath been raised from the Dayspring of Grandeur: Verily, there is none other God but Me, the Lord of Utterance, the All-Knowing. Bind ye the broken with the hands of justice, and crush the oppressor who flourisheth with the rod of the commandments of your Lord, the Ordainer, the All-Wise.

(Bahá'u'lláh, *The Proclamation of Bahá'u'lláh,* p. 63)

## To the World's Religious Leaders

O LEADERS of religion! Weigh not the Book of God with such standards and sciences as are current amongst you, for the Book itself is the unerring balance...

The eye of My loving-kindness weepeth sore over you, inasmuch as ye have failed to recognize the One upon Whom ye have been calling in the daytime and in the night season, at even and at morn...

O ye leaders of religion! Who is the man amongst you that can rival Me in vision or insight? Where is he to be found that dareth to claim to be My equal in utterance or wisdom? No, by My Lord, the All-Merciful! All on the earth shall pass away; and this is the face of your Lord, the Almighty, the Well-Beloved.

(Bahá'u'lláh, *The Proclamation of Bahá'u'lláh,* p. 73)

## To Pope Pius IX

O POPE! Rend the veils asunder. He Who is the Lord of Lords is come overshadowed with clouds, and the decree hath been fulfilled by God, the Almighty, the Unrestrained... He, verily, hath again come down from Heaven even as He came down from it the first time. Beware that thou dispute not with Him even as the Pharisees disputed with Him (Jesus) without a clear token or proof. On His right hand flow the living waters of grace, and on His left the choice Wine of justice, whilst before Him march the angels of Paradise, bearing the banners of His signs. Beware lest any name debar thee from God, the Creator of earth and heaven... Dwellest thou in palaces whilst He Who is the King of Revelation liveth in the most desolate of abodes? Leave them unto such as desire them, and set thy face with joy and delight towards the Kingdom... Arise in the name of thy Lord, the God of Mercy, amidst the peoples of the earth, and seize thou the Cup of Life with the hands of confidence, and first drink thou therefrom, and proffer it then to such as turn towards it amongst the peoples of all faiths...

Call thou to remembrance Him Who was the Spirit (Jesus), Who when He came, the most learned of His age pronounced judgment against Him in His own country, whilst he who was only a fisherman believed in Him. Take heed, then, ye men of understanding heart! Thou, in truth, art one of the suns of the heaven of His names. Guard thyself, lest darkness spread its veils over thee, and fold thee away from His light... Consider those who opposed the Son (Jesus), when He came unto them with sovereignty and power. How many the Pharisees who were waiting to behold Him, and were lamenting over their separation from Him! And yet, when the fragrance of His coming was wafted over them, and His beauty was unveiled, they turned aside from Him and disputed with Him... None save a very few, who were destitute of any power amongst men, turned towards His face. And yet, today, every man endowed with power and invested with sovereignty prideth himself on His Name!

(Bahá'u'lláh, *The Proclamation of Bahá'u'lláh*, p. 83-84)

# ADDITIONAL REFERENCES

## Station and Titles of Bahá'u'lláh

To Israel He was neither more nor less than the incarnation of the "Everlasting Father," the "Lord of Hosts" come down "with ten thousands of saints"; to Christendom Christ returned "in the glory of the Father," to Shí'ah Islam the return of the Imám Husayn; to Sunni Islam the descent of the "Spirit of God" (Jesus Christ); to the Zoroastrians the promised Shah-Bahram; to the Hindus the reincarnation of Krishna; to the Buddhists the fifth Buddha.

In the name He bore He combined those of the Imám Husayn, the most illustrious of the successors of the Apostle of God -- the brightest "star" shining in the "crown" mentioned in the Revelation of St. John -- and of the Imám Ali, the Commander of the Faithful, the second of the two "witnesses" extolled in that same Book. He was formally designated Bahá'u'lláh, an appellation specifically recorded in the Persian Bayán, signifying at once the glory, the light and the splendor of God, and was styled the "Lord of Lords," the "Most Great Name," the "Ancient Beauty," the "Pen of the Most High," the "Hidden Name," the "Preserved Treasure," "He Whom God will make manifest," the "Most Great Light," the "All-Highest Horizon," the "Most Great Ocean," the "Supreme Heaven," the "Pre-Existent Root," the "Self-Subsistent," the "Day-Star of the Universe," the "Great Announcement," the "Speaker on Sinai," the "Sifter of Men," the "Wronged One of the World," the "Desire of the Nations," the "Lord of the Covenant," the "Tree beyond which there is no passing." He derived His descent, on the one hand, from Abraham (the Father of the Faithful) through his wife Katurah, and on the other from Zoroaster, as well as from Yazdigird, the last king of the Sasaniyan dynasty. He was moreover a descendant of Jesse, and belonged, through His father, Mírzá 'Abbás, better known as Mírzá Buzurg -- a nobleman closely associated with the ministerial circles of the Court of Fath-'Ali Shah -- to one of the most ancient and renowned families of Mázindarán.

To Him Isaiah, the greatest of the Jewish prophets, had alluded as the "Glory of the Lord," the "Everlasting Father," the "Prince of Peace," the "Wonderful," the "Counsellor," the "Rod come forth out of the stem of Jesse" and the "Branch grown out of His roots," Who "shall be established upon the throne of David," Who "will come with strong hand," Who "shall judge among the nations," Who "shall smite the earth with the rod of His mouth, and with the breath of His lips slay the wicked," and Who "shall assemble the outcasts of Israel, and gather together the dispersed of Judah from the four corners of the earth." Of Him David had sung in his Psalms, acclaiming Him as the "Lord of Hosts" and the "King of Glory." To Him Haggai had referred as the "Desire of all nations," and Zachariah as the "Branch" Who "shall grow up out of His place," and "shall build the Temple of the Lord." Ezekiel had extolled Him as the "Lord" Who "shall be king over all the earth," while to His day Joel and Zephaniah had both referred as the "day of Jehovah," the latter describing it as "a day of wrath, a day of trouble and distress, a day of wasteness and desolation, a day of darkness and gloominess, a day of clouds and thick darkness, a day of the trumpet and alarm against the fenced cities, and against the high towers." His Day Ezekiel and Daniel had, moreover, both acclaimed as the "day of the Lord," and Malachi described as "the great and dreadful day of the Lord" when "the Sun of Righteousness" will "arise, with healing in His wings," whilst Daniel had pronounced His advent as signalizing the end of the "abomination that maketh desolate."

# Bahá'u'lláh: The Glory of God – References

To His Dispensation the sacred books of the followers of Zoroaster had referred as that in which the sun must needs be brought to a standstill for no less than one whole month. To Him Zoroaster must have alluded when, according to tradition, He foretold that a period of three thousand years of conflict and contention must needs precede the advent of the World-Savior Shah-Bahram, Who would triumph over Ahriman and usher in an era of blessedness and peace.

He alone is meant by the prophecy attributed to Gautama Buddha Himself, that "a Buddha named Maitreye, the Buddha of universal fellowship" should, in the fullness of time, arise and reveal "His boundless glory." To Him the Bhagavad-Gita of the Hindus had referred as the "Most Great Spirit," the "Tenth Avatar," the "Immaculate Manifestation of Krishna."

To Him Jesus Christ had referred as the "Prince of this world," as the "Comforter" Who will "reprove the world of sin, and of righteousness, and of judgment," as the "Spirit of Truth" Who "will guide you into all truth," Who "shall not speak of Himself, but whatsoever He shall hear, that shall He speak," as the "Lord of the Vineyard," and as the "Son of Man" Who "shall come in the glory of His Father" "in the clouds of heaven with power and great glory," with "all the holy angels" about Him, and "all nations" gathered before His throne. To Him the Author of the Apocalypse had alluded as the "Glory of God," as "Alpha and Omega," "the Beginning and the End," "the First and the Last." Identifying His Revelation with the "third woe," he, moreover, had extolled His Law as "a new heaven and a new earth," as the "Tabernacle of God," as the "Holy City," as the "New Jerusalem, coming down from God out of heaven, prepared as a bride adorned for her husband." To His Day Jesus Christ Himself had referred as "the regeneration when the Son of Man shall sit in the throne of His glory." To the hour of His advent St. Paul had alluded as the hour of the "last trump," the "trump of God," whilst St. Peter had spoken of it as the "Day of God, wherein the heavens being on fire shall be dissolved, and the elements shall melt with fervent heat." His Day he, furthermore, had described as "the times of refreshing," "the times of restitution of all things, which God hath spoken by the mouth of all His holy Prophets since the world began."

To Him Muhammad, the Apostle of God, had alluded in His Book as the "Great Announcement," and declared His Day to be the Day whereon "God" will "come down" "overshadowed with clouds," the Day whereon "thy Lord shall come and the angels rank on rank," and "The Spirit shall arise and the angels shall be ranged in order." His advent He, in that Book, in a surih said to have been termed by Him "the heart of the Qur'án," had foreshadowed as that of the "third" Messenger, sent down to "strengthen" the two who preceded Him. To His Day He, in the pages of that same Book, had paid a glowing tribute, glorifying it as the "Great Day," the "Last Day," the "Day of God," the "Day of Judgment," the "Day of Reckoning," the "Day of Mutual Deceit," the "Day of Severing," the "Day of Sighing," the "Day of Meeting," the Day "when the Decree shall be accomplished," the Day whereon the second "Trumpet blast" will be sounded, the "Day when mankind shall stand before the Lord of the world," and "all shall come to Him in humble guise," the Day when "thou shalt see the mountains, which thou thinkest so firm, pass away with the passing of a cloud," the Day "wherein account shall be taken," "the approaching Day, when men's hearts shall rise up, choking them, into their throats," the Day when "all that are in the heavens and all that are on the earth shall be terror-stricken, save him whom God pleaseth to deliver," the Day whereon "every suckling woman shall forsake her sucking babe, and every woman that hath a burden in her womb shall cast her burden," the Day "when the earth shall shine with the light of her Lord, and the Book shall be set, and the Prophets shall be brought up, and the witnesses; and judgment shall be given between them with equity; and none shall be wronged."

The plenitude of His glory the Apostle of God had, moreover, as attested by Bahá'u'lláh Himself, compared to the "full moon on its fourteenth night." His station the Imám Ali, the Commander of the Faithful, had, according to the same testimony, identified with "Him Who conversed with Moses from the Burning Bush on Sinai." To the transcendent character of His mission the Imám Husayn had, again according to Bahá'u'lláh, borne witness as a "Revelation whose Revealer will be He Who revealed" the Apostle of God Himself.

About Him Shaykh Ahmad-i-Ahsá'í, the herald of the Bábí Dispensation, who had foreshadowed the "strange happenings" that would transpire "between the years sixty and sixty-seven," and had categorically affirmed the inevitability of His Revelation had, as previously mentioned, written the following: "The Mystery of this Cause must needs be made manifest, and the Secret of this Message must needs be divulged. I can say no more, I can appoint no time. His Cause will be made known after Hin (68)" (i.e., after a while).

Siyyid Kázim-i-Rashtí, Shaykh Ahmad's disciple and successor, had likewise written: "The Qá'im must needs be put to death. After He has been slain the world will have attained the age of eighteen." In his Sharh-i-Qasídiy-i-Lámíyyih he had even alluded to the name "Bahá." Furthermore, to his disciples, as his days drew to a close, he had significantly declared: "Verily, I say, after the Qá'im the Qayyúm will be made manifest. For when the star of the former has set the sun of the beauty of Husayn will rise and illuminate the whole world. Then will be unfolded in all its glory the 'Mystery' and the 'Secret' spoken of by Shaykh Ahmad.... To have attained unto that Day of Days is to have attained unto the crowning glory of past generations, and one goodly deed performed in that age is equal to the pious worship of countless centuries."

The Báb had no less significantly extolled Him as the "Essence of Being," as the "Remnant of God," as the "Omnipotent Master," as the "Crimson, all-encompassing Light," as "Lord of the visible and invisible," as the "sole Object of all previous Revelations, including The Revelation of the Qá'im Himself." He had formally designated Him as "He Whom God shall make manifest," had alluded to Him as the "Abhá Horizon" wherein He Himself lived and dwelt, had specifically recorded His title, and eulogized His "Order" in His best-known work, the Persian Bayán, had disclosed His name through His allusion to the "Son of Ali, a true and undoubted Leader of men," had, repeatedly, orally and in writing, fixed, beyond the shadow of a doubt, the time of His Revelation, and warned His followers lest "the Bayán and all that hath been revealed therein" should "shut them out as by a veil" from Him. He had, moreover, declared that He was the "first servant to believe in Him," that He bore Him allegiance "before all things were created," that "no allusion" of His "could allude unto Him," that "the year-old germ that holdeth within itself the potentialities of the Revelation that is to come is endowed with a potency superior to the combined forces of the whole of the Bayán." He had, moreover, clearly asserted that He had "covenanted with all created things" concerning Him Whom God shall make manifest ere the covenant concerning His own mission had been established. He had readily acknowledged that He was but "a letter" of that "Most Mighty Book," "a dew-drop" from that "Limitless Ocean," that His Revelation was "only a leaf amongst the leaves of His Paradise," that "all that hath been exalted in the Bayán" was but "a ring" upon His own hand,

and He Himself "a ring upon the hand of Him Whom God shall make manifest," Who, "turneth it as He pleaseth, for whatsoever He pleaseth, and through whatsoever He pleaseth." He had unmistakably declared that He had "sacrificed" Himself "wholly" for Him, that He had "consented to be cursed" for His sake, and to have "yearned for naught but martyrdom" in the path of His love. Finally, He had unequivocally prophesied: "Today the Bayán is in the stage of seed; at the beginning of the manifestation of Him Whom God shall make manifest its ultimate perfection will become apparent." "Ere nine will have elapsed from the inception of this Cause the realities of the created things will not be made manifest. All that thou hast as yet seen is but the stage from the moist-germ until We clothed it with flesh. Be patient until thou beholdest a new creation. Say: Blessed, therefore, be God, the Most Excellent of Makers!"

(Shoghi Effendi, *God Passes By,* p. 93-98)

---

## Photographic Narrative of the Life of Bahá'u'lláh

From the Bahá'í International Community: www.bahaullah.org

# BIBLIOGRAPHY

*A Bahá'í Coloring Book.* Compiled by Evelyn Musacchia with drawings by Dorrine Sadilek. National Child Education Committee of the National Spiritual Assembly of the Bahá'ís of the Hawaiian Islands: Hawaii, 1975.

*Bahá'í Education: A Compilation.* Compiled by the Research Department of The Universal House of Justice. Bahá'í Publishing Trust: Wilmette, Illinois, 1978.

*Bahá'í Prayers.* A Selection of Prayers Revealed by Bahá'u'lláh, The Báb and 'Abdu'l-Bahá. Bahá'í Publishing Trust: Wilmette, Illinois, 1954, 1991 edition.

*Bahá'í World Faith.* A Selection of Writings from Bahá'u'lláh and 'Abdu'l-Bahá. Bahá'í Publishing Trust: Wilmette, Illinois, 1943, 1976.

*The Bahá'ís: A Profile of the Bahá'í Faith and its Worldwide Community.* Office of Public Information, Bahá'í International Community: New York, 1992.

*Bahá'u'lláh: The King of Glory.* H.M. Balyuzi. George Ronald, Publisher: Oxford, England, 1980.

*Brilliant Star, Special Edition for Summer Schools.* National Spiritual Assembly of the Bahá'ís of the United States: Wilmette, Illinois, 1991.

*Building Bridges: A Bahá'í Songbook.* Compiled and prepared by Peggy Caton and Dale Nomura under the direction of the Bahá'í National Education Committee. Kalimát Press: Los Angeles, 1984.

*Core Curriculum Learning Activities, Central Figures Strand: Bahá'u'lláh.* National Bahá'í Education Task Force. National Spiritual Assembly of the Bahá'ís of the United States: Wilmette, Illinois, 1995.

*Core Curriculum Lesson Planning Guide: The Central Figures: Bahá'u'lláh.* National Bahá'í Education Task Force. National Spiritual Assembly of the Bahá'ís of the United States: Wilmette, Illinois, 2002.

*The Dawn-Breakers: Nabíl's Narrative of the Early Days of the Bahá'í Revelation.* Translated and edited by Shoghi Effendi. Bahá'í Publishing Trust: Wilmette, Illinois, 1932, 1996 reprint.

*Epistle to the Son of the Wolf.* Bahá'u'lláh. Translated by Shoghi Effendi. Bahá'í Publishing Trust: Wilmette, Illinois, 1941, 1988 edition.

*The Hidden Words.* Bahá'u'lláh. Translated by Shoghi Effendi with the assistance of some English friends. Bahá'í Publishing Trust: Wilmette, Illinois, 1954.

*Kitáb-i-Íqán (The Book of Certitude)*. Bahá'u'lláh. Translated by Shoghi Effendi.
Bahá'í Publishing Trust: Wilmette, Illinois, 1931, 1983 edition.

*Letter to the Continental Boards of Counsellors*. International Teaching Centre.
Bahá'í World Centre: Haifa, Israel, 5 December 1988.

*The Proclamation of Bahá'u'lláh*. Bahá'u'lláh. Bahá'í World Centre: Haifa, Israel, 1967.

*The Promised Day Is Come*. Shoghi Effendi. Bahá'í Publishing Trust: Wilmette, Illinois, 1967.

*The Promulgation of Universal Peace*. Talks by 'Abdu'l-Bahá during His visit to the U.S. and Canada in 1912. Bahá'í Publishing Trust: Wilmette, Illinois, 1982 edition.

*The Revelation of Bahá'u'lláh: Book 1*. Adib Taherzadeh. George Ronald, Publisher: Oxford, England, 1974.

*The Revelation of Bahá'u'lláh: Book 2*. Adib Taherzadeh. George Ronald, Publisher: Oxford, England, 1977.

*Ridván 2000 Message to the Bahá'ís of the World*. Universal House of Justice.
Bahá'í World Centre: Haifa, Israel, 2000.

*The Twin Manifestations: Ruhi Institute Book 4*. Ruhi Institute Foundation.
Palabra Publications: West Palm Beach, Florida, 2002.

*Selections from the Writings of 'Abdu'l-Bahá*. Translated by a Committee at the Bahá'í World Centre and Marzieh Gail. Bahá'í World Centre: Haifa, Israel, 1978, 1982 printing.

*The Summons of the Lord of Hosts: Tablets of Bahá'u'lláh*. Bahá'í World Centre: Haifa, Israel, 2002.

*Tablets of Bahá'u'lláh Revealed After the Kitáb-i-Aqdas*. Translated by Habíb Taherzadeh with the assistance of a Committee at the Bahá'í World Centre. Bahá'í World Centre: Haifa, Israel, 1978.

*The World Order of Bahá'u'lláh*. Selected Letters by Shoghi Effendi.
Bahá'í Publishing Trust: Wilmette, Illinois, 1938, 1974 rev. ed., 1982 reprint.

# WORKS BY THE SAME AUTHOR

# www.UnityWorksStore.com

Some books also available from: www.BahaiBookStore.com, (800) 999-9019
and Special Ideas: www.bahairesources.com, (800) 326-1197

Check our website for high-quality, low-cost, easy-to-use Bahá'í resources. Download PowerPoint firesides, Five Year Plan study guides, children's class materials, Bahá'í mini ads, and much more!

## Activity Books for Bahá'í Children's Classes

This series of easy-to-use teacher's guides is filled with fun, hands-on, kid-tested learning activities designed for ages 8-12. A useful resource for Bahá'í summer and winter schools, Holy Day programs, academic classes and weekend retreats. The activities were developed and tested in the field, in response to the needs of teachers and children, and have been used successfully in multiple settings over many years. Each book includes detailed lessons, copy-ready student handouts, song sheets, craft instructions and more!

*"Your curriculum is the best I've seen to teach kids about the Faith. I love it!! They aren't being taught principles, they are investigating, exploring, and owning the principles."*
– **Sue Walker, PhD**

## Bahá'í Children's Retreats (A Complete Planning Guide)

Want to plan an unforgettable Bahá'í activity for children ages 8-12, but don't know where to begin? This retreat planning guide covers the following topics:

- Sponsorship, Schedules, Forms
- Teachers, Facility, Finances, Publicity
- Registration, Materials, Menus
- Orientation, Children's Performance
- Outdoor Activities and more!

Also included are medical release forms, recipes, a planning checklist and a graduation certificate—everything you need to organize a successful children's retreat. This planning guide is the perfect companion to the activity books on each theme.

*"This retreat was life changing. You feel a renewal of passion for educating children!"*
– **Lynn Haug, parent**

## Bahá'í Public Speaking (Teacher's Guide with Nine Workshops)

This practical, easy-to-use teacher's guide contains nine hands-on workshops on Bahá'í public speaking. It is designed to equip youth, adults and children with the skills and confidence needed to become more effective teachers of the Faith. Participants will learn to speak with clarity and conviction—from the kitchen table to the conference hall. Be prepared for home visits, devotional meetings, fireside talks, direct teaching campaigns and public discourse. Great for junior youth groups, youth workshops and campus clubs!

This training manual can be used in conjunction with Ruhi Book 6.
It comes complete with copy-ready student handouts. Each lesson includes:

- Warm-up activities
- Speaking tips
- Practice exercises
- Homework assignment

*"Fabulous! I'm very glad that you're publishing this, and I hope it is widely circulated!"*
— **Erica Toussaint**


## Once to Every Man and Nation (Stories About Becoming a Bahá'í)

A great gift for seekers, this book brings together 37 heartwarming stories of how people became Bahá'ís. The contributors to *Once to Every Man and Nation* come from all over North America and represent a wide variety of cultural, racial, social and ethnic backgrounds. Young and old, black and white, each with a different experience of life, their very diversity demonstrates the universal appeal of the Bahá'í teachings.

*"Will be enjoyed by many believers...thoroughly recommend it."*
— **Bahá'í Reviewing Panel of the United Kingdom**


## Bahá'í Mini Ads

Thirty small print ads for use with local media campaigns. The series is designed to complement our Bahá'í teaching efforts by creating greater awareness and positive interest in the Faith. It includes basic Bahá'í beliefs and principles, short quotations from the Bahá'í Writings, offers of free literature, an invitation to the core activities, and an invitation to join the Bahá'í community. The file is in Microsoft Word format so it is easy to insert local contact information.

*"These will surely boost teaching efforts in all communities that use them!"*
— **Dale Eng**

# PowerPoint Firesides on the Bahá'í Faith

  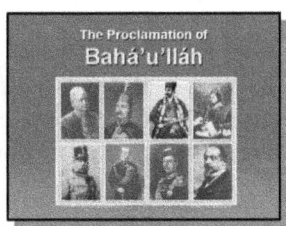 

(1)
**The Bahá'í Faith:
An Introduction***

(2)
**Central Figures
of the Bahá'í Faith**

(3)
**The Proclamation
of Bahá'u'lláh**

(4)
**The Power
of Unity**

These colorful slide shows are designed to introduce the Bahá'í Faith. They offer an overview of the Faith: its Central Figures, purpose, core beliefs and teachings, photographs of its World Center, Houses of Worship, and scenes from Bahá'í community life. The programs have been used to effectively share the Bahá'í teachings in churches, classrooms, public libraries and community firesides.

- Perfect for high school and university students
- Ideal for projecting in large group settings
- Can also be used with a laptop one-on-one

\* Also available in French and Spanish

## What People Are Saying

*"I don't know if the presentation could have gone any better!...This was one of the most amazing teaching experiences I've ever had!"* — **Charisse Johnson, student**

*"... a wonderful conclusion to our study of world faiths...it makes for a great end of semester presentation."* — **Steve Deligan, high school religion teacher**

*"...a fantastic presentation...very understandable...excellent to use for youth."*
— **Seth Walker, youth**

*"A wonderful trilogy for humans everywhere to learn from."* — **Beth Shevin, seeker**

*"...a great success tonight in Australia...the Baha'is were very pleased with their professional quality."* — **Nancy Watters, traveling teacher**

*"...straight-forward...high-quality...a wonderful introduction to the Teachings"*
— **Shannon Javid, Regional Bahá'í Council member**

*"Very respectful and professional. Job well done!"* — **Warren Odess-Gillett**

 **Download from: www.UnityWorksStore.com**

## Starting a Bahá'í-Inspired Academic School

This booklet presents basic guidelines and suggestions for those considering the establishment of a Bahá'í-inspired academic school. It provides a useful framework for organizing critical tasks and decisions, utilizing a detailed checklist with hundreds of practical tips.

## Escuela de las Naciones (School of the Nations)

Description with color photographs of a Bahá'í-inspired K-6 elementary school established in Puerto Rico in 1991. This monograph provides an overview of the establishment and functioning of the private, non-profit, competency-based school, including the students, facilities, classroom design, curriculum, instructional methods and materials, system of evaluation, schedule, integration of the arts, and service.

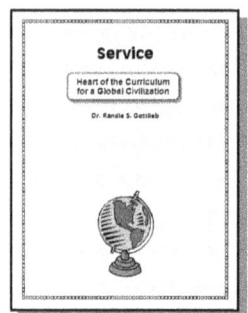

## Service: Heart of the Curriculum for a Global Civilization

This monograph considers the significance of service to mankind as a central organizing principle for our educational endeavors, and recommends practical strategies for systematically integrating service into the daily life and culture of our schools.

## Principles into Practice

Workshop and compilation of Bahá'í Writings on education. This resource is offered as a tool for educators who wish to put Bahá'í principles into practice in their classrooms. Detailed step-by-step instructions for conducting the workshop are presented, and copy-ready student handouts are included. The workshop complements Ruhi Book 3 training and is appropriate for Bahá'ís and friends of the Faith.

## Needs Assessment Survey to Determine the Training Requirements of International Bahá'í Traveling Teachers

This doctoral thesis details the training needs of personnel on international service projects. The survey of 200 returned volunteers and Bahá'í Institutions in the 81 countries they visited, was done under the auspices of the U.S. Bahá'í International Goals Committee. The study focuses on cross-cultural communication, critical incidents, training and materials design.

Bahá'u'lláh: The Glory of God

# List of Activities by Chapter

**Opening Activities**   **Page**
1. Registration crafts (see theme book #1 on *God and the Universe* for details) ........ 13
2. Unity Bingo (ice-breaker) ................................................................. 14-15
3. What Am I? (ice-breaker) ................................................................. 16-17
4. Just for Fun (ice-breaker jokes) ........................................................ 18-20
5. Group singing (instructions, song sheets and musical scores) ... 13, 127-28, 149-166

**Lesson 1: His Birth, Early Life and Station**
1. Shine Your Light (song) .................................................................... 22
2. Introduction to Bahá'u'lláh (reading and pictures) ........................... 22, 27-31
3. Stories from the Life of Bahá'u'lláh (groups read and report back) ...... 22-24, 32
4. Peer Questions (students ask and answer questions) ............................. 24
5. Black Pit Experience (simulation) ................................................... 24-26

**Lesson 2: The Declaration of Bahá'u'lláh**
1. Bahá'u'lláh (song) .......................................................................... 36
2. The Promised One (felt lesson and blank chart) ............................ 36, 56-75
3. Verily I say (memory quote) ........................................................... 36
4. The Declaration of Bahá'u'lláh (reading with questions) ...................... 37
5. Can't You See the New Day (song) .................................................. 38
6. Craft Activities ........................................................................... 38-55
   A. Drawings, poems, letters (creative writing and art) ........................ 39
   B. Ridván Greeting Cards (cut, paste, draw) .................................... 39
   C. The Prison at Akká (coloring page) ........................................... 40
   D. The Shrine of Bahá'u'lláh (coloring page) ................................... 41
   E. Hidden Message (decoding) ...................................................... 42
   F. Timeline of Bahá'u'lláh's Life (cut, color, glue) ........................... 43-44
   G. God's Treasure (gluing gemstones) ......................................... 45-47
   H. A Dream of Many Fish (mobile) ............................................... 48-53
   I. Ridván Roses (paper folding) .................................................. 54-55

**Lesson 3: Exiles and Imprisonment**
1. Remember My days (introductory quote) ........................................... 78
2. The Most Great Prison (story with questions) ................................... 78
3. Exiles of Bahá'u'lláh (map activity) ................................... 79, 85-86, 90
4. Quiz on the Life of Bahá'u'lláh (quiz) .......................................... 79, 84
5. Hardships and Suffering (review) ................................................... 80
6. Sacrifice (group discussion) ................................................... 80, 87-88
7. The Ancient Beauty hath consented to be bound (memory quote) ........ 80, 87
8. Walk to Baghdad (simulation hike) ............................................. 80-83

Bahá'u'lláh: The Glory of God

## List of Activities by Chapter (continued)

### Lesson 4: Clouds of Glory
1. Can't You See the New Day (song) .................................................................. 92
2. Sun and Cloud (demonstration) ............................................................... 92, 95-96
3. Proclamation to the Kings (story with questions) ................................. 92-93, 97-104
4. Ye are but vassals (memory quote) ..................................................................... 93
5. Clouds of Glory (group discussion) ................................................................ 94, 105
6. Nine Important Facts (brainstorming review) ....................................................... 94
7. Who Is Bahá'u'lláh? (practice answering) ............................................................ 94
8. King of Kings (song) ........................................................................................ 94
9. Salt Dough Sun (craft) ............................................................................... 94, 106
10. Spiritual Light Switch (craft) ..................................................................... 94, 107

### Children's Performance
1. Various songs, demonstrations, stories and memory quotes ............ 109-124, 127-30
2. Stories from the Life of Bahá'u'lláh (stories) ............................................ 113, 131-146
3. The Heavy Chain (demo) ................................................................................. 114
4. The Promised One (felt lesson) ................................................................... 114, 116
5. Presentation of arts and crafts ........................................................................ 114
6. Exiles of Bahá'u'lláh (map demo) ..................................................................... 119
7. The Life of Bahá'u'lláh (quiz show) ........................................... 113, 117-118, 147
8. The Promise (dramatic play) ..................................................................... 114, 120-22

### Music
1. Instructions for group singing ................................................................... 149-151
2. Song sheet ........................................................................................ 127-28, 152-53
3. Musical scores ............................................................................................ 154-166
   A. Bahá'u'lláh ............................................................................................... 155
   B. Can't You See the New Day ........................................................................ 156
   C. God Is Sufficient Unto Me ........................................................................... 157
   D. I Have Found Bahá'u'lláh ............................................................................ 158
   E. King of Kings and Lord of Lords .................................................................. 159
   F. The Nightingale ......................................................................................... 160
   G. Prince of Peace ......................................................................................... 161
   H. El Rey de los Reyes ................................................................................... 162
   I. Shine Your Light ........................................................................................ 163
   J. Song of the Prophets .................................................................................. 164
   K. Soon Will All That Dwell on Earth ............................................................... 165
   L. We Are the People of Bahá ........................................................................ 166

### Closing and Follow-up Activities .................................................................. 167-69

Bahá'u'lláh: The Glory of God

# Index of Activities by Category

(Note: Some items are listed in more than one category.)

### Arts and Crafts — Page
- A Dream of Many Fish (mobile) .................................................. 48-53
- Children's Performance (project presentations) .......................... 114
- Exiles of Bahá'u'lláh (map activity) .................................. 79, 85-86, 90
- Folder decorations (draw, cut-and-paste) ..................................... 13
- Freehand drawing (markers, pencils, crayons) ............................. 39
- God's Treasure (glue, glitter, gemstones) ................................. 45-47
- Ridván Greeting Cards (markers, stickers, stamps) ...................... 39
- Ridván Roses (tissue paper, pipe cleaners) ............................... 54-55
- Salt Dough Sun (dough sculpting) ........................................ 94, 106
- Spiritual Light Switch (clay modeling) .................................. 94, 107
- The Shrine of Bahá'u'lláh (coloring page) .................................. 41
- The Prison at Akká (coloring page) ......................................... 40
- Timeline of Bahá'u'lláh's Life (color, cut-and-paste) ................. 43-44

### Audio-Visual
- Exiles of Bahá'u'lláh (map) ............................................ 79, 85-86, 90
- Images of Iran and Iraq (drawings and photographs) ........ 22, 28-31, 33-34
- Kings and rulers (photographs) ..................................... 92-93, 97-104

### Creative Writing
- Letter to Bahá'u'lláh .......................................................... 39
- Student poems ................................................................ 39

### Demonstrations and Felt Lessons
- Children's Performance (presentations to an audience) ............. 109-124
- Exiles of Bahá'u'lláh (map activity) .................................. 79, 85-86, 90
- Sun and Clouds (demonstration) ........................................ 92, 95-96
- The Heavy Chain (demonstration) ........................................... 114
- The Promised One (felt lesson) ........................... 36, 56-75, 114, 116

### Games and Puzzles
- Hidden Message (decoding) .................................................. 42
- Just for Fun (jokes) ........................................................ 18-20
- Unity Bingo (ice-breaker) ................................................ 14-15
- What Am I? (ice-breaker) ................................................. 16-17

Bahá'u'lláh: The Glory of God

## Group Discussion, Questions and Answers

Clouds of Glory (small group discussion) .................................................. 94, 105
Exiles of Bahá'u'lláh (map activity) ................................................ 79, 85-86, 90
Peer Questions (student questions) ............................................................... 24
Quiz on the Life of Bahá'u'lláh (quiz) .............................. 79, 84, 113, 117-118, 147
Sacrifice (small group discussion) ................................................... 80, 87-88
Stories from the Life of Bahá'u'lláh (readings) ..... 22-24, 32, 37, 92-93, 97-104, 113, 131-46
The Promised One (felt lesson) ................................................. 36, 56-75, 114, 116
Who Is Bahá'u'lláh? (practice answering) ............................................... 94

## Memory Quotes and Prayers

All quotations .................................................................................. 129-130
Children's Performance ................................................................... 112, 114
O God! Educate these children ............................................................. 115
Remember My days during thy days ......................................................... 78
The Ancient Beauty hath consented to be bound with chains ....................... 80, 87
Verily I say, this is the Day ..................................................................... 36
Ye are but vassals, O kings of the earth! ................................................. 93

## Music

Children's Performance ........................................................................ 112
Instructions for group singing ........................................................ 149-151
List of songs ....................................................................................... 154
Musical scores ............................................................................... 155-166
Song sheet ................................................................... 127-28, 152-53
Bahá'u'lláh ................................................................................. 36, 120, 155
Can't You See the New Day ........................................................ 38, 92, 156
God Is Sufficient Unto Me .................................................................. 157
I Have Found Bahá'u'lláh .................................................................... 158
King of Kings ............................................................................... 94, 159
The Nightingale ................................................................................. 160
Prince of Peace ................................................................................. 161
Rey de los Reyes ............................................................................... 162
Shine Your Light ......................................................................... 22, 163
Song of the Prophets ......................................................................... 164
Soon Will All That Dwell on Earth ..................................................... 165
We Are the People of Bahá ................................................................ 166

# Bahá'u'lláh: The Glory of God

### Readings and Stories
| | |
|---|---|
| Children's Performance | 112-13 |
| Stories from the Life of Bahá'u'lláh | 22-24, 32, 131-46 |
| Introduction to Bahá'u'lláh | 22, 27-31, 133 |
| The Baby Who Never Cried | 134 |
| A Dream of Many Fish | 135 |
| The Puppet Show | 136 |
| Father of the Poor | 137 |
| The Black Pit | 138 |
| Banished to Baghdad | 139 |
| The Hermit in the Mountains | 140 |
| The Writing Lesson | 141 |
| The Declaration of Bahá'u'lláh | 37, 142-143 |
| The Most Great Prison | 78, 144-45 |
| Proclamation to the Kings | 92-93, 146 |

### Review
| | |
|---|---|
| Exiles of Bahá'u'lláh (map activity) | 79, 85-86, 90, 119 |
| Hardships and Suffering | 80 |
| Nine Important Facts | 94 |
| Peer Questions | 24 |
| Quiz on the Life of Bahá'u'lláh | 79, 84, 113, 117-118, 147 |
| Who Is Bahá'u'lláh? (practice answering) | 94 |

### Simulations
| | |
|---|---|
| The Black Pit Experience (in the Síyáh-Chál) | 24-26 |
| The Most Great Prison (story with bread and water) | 78 |
| Walk to Baghdad (outdoor hike) | 80-83 |

### Skits and Role Plays
| | |
|---|---|
| The Promise (dramatic play) | 114, 120-22 |